# Learning Nature
# by a Country Road

Tom Anderson

Voyageur Press

Thanks
—to the *Chisago County Press* for use of selected "Reading Sign" columns.

—to *Minnesota Sportsman* magazine for permission to reprint "Prize of the Autumn Bog."

—to A. B. Guthrie, Jr., for permission to use an excerpt from the novel *Big Sky*.

Library of Congress Cataloging-in-Publication Data

Anderson, Tom.
    Learning nature by a country road.

    1. Nature.   2. Seasons.   I. Title.
QH81.A574 1989      508      89-5543
ISBN 0-89658-085-7

Published by Voyageur Press, Inc.
123 North Second Street
Stillwater, MN 55082 U.S.A.
1-800-888-9653

Voyageur Press books are also available at discounts in bulk quantities for premium or sales-promotion use. For details contact the Marketing Manager.

Please write or call for our free catalog of natural history and wildlife publications.

# Dedication

To the memory of my father, who carefully set the roots for my love
of the natural world
To my mother, who tolerated and nurtured their fruition
To my wife, Susan, who now puts up with my ways and wanderings
And to my daughters, Britta and Maren, with whom I share the fruit

# CONTENTS

# PREFACE

For most of my life I have lived along a country road. In fact, I have never pursued a career that wasn't on the edge of such a road. Together, the familiar roads and I have aged and been altered. The greater change, however, has come to me. For the sake of my children and following generations, I hope that some of these roads will remain relatively unchanged long after I have become a memory.

The various country roads served in more ways than an artery from home to the rest of the world. They served me best in that they provided a rural setting rich in natural "signs."

Some of the signs are easy to read, others more difficult, and many will always remain a mystery. Deciphering the roadside activities is one of the reasons I am a naturalist by profession.

Undoubtedly, the most famous of puzzle solvers was Sir Arthur Conan Doyle's creation, Sherlock Holmes. In one particular mystery, Holmes states, ". . . it is my business to know things. Perhaps I have trained myself to see what others overlook." These are stout words for all naturalists or would-be naturalists to live by. And everyone who has considered the "whys" in nature is in varying degrees a naturalist.

Early native Americans and the following immigrant settlers lived in a wilderness that played by one rule—survival of the fittest. Such an environment demanded skills in "reading sign." Subtle signs or clues of a passing track, a bent grass, the alarm call of a bird, or smells of beaver-scented mud all had a special story to tell. The very lives of these peoples depended on their skills in interpreting the natural world.

We live in a time where luxury reigns. People seem more concerned with accumulating the most and the best. However, it seems we have forgotten the freshness of a gentle rainfall in an early spring woods. How often do we ponder the determination of screen-hitting June bugs on a warm night? Or how often do we stoop to consider the many moods and hues of a blue jay feather?

Increasing one's awareness of the natural world is one way everyone can more fully enjoy outdoor experiences. Outdoor adventures happen every day as we take a walk, go for a drive, weed the garden, go fishing or hunting, or take part in any other activity that brings us in contact with open places.

A hidden benefit of increasing our outdoor knowledge is that it will make us more aware and appreciative of our respective environments.

Throughout this book, I have gleaned much from the work of other biologists and naturalists before me. Though I did not give them due credit, I would hope that they would think favorably of my presenting it.

A goodly part of these writings are recollections of my meanderings through youth. It is hard for me to let go of those times for they are fond memories, and I often feel my current status in life is simply an extension of boyhood. There remains a continual thirst.

*     *     *

A special thanks is due to John Silver, publisher of the *Chisago County* Press and the rest of the newspaper staff for their continual support and encouragement. John's cooperation in releasing past "Reading Sign" columns is sincerely appreciated.

Perhaps none of this would have been possible had it not been for Bernie Fashingbauer, director of the Lee and Rose Warner Nature Center, near Marine on St. Croix, Minnesota, who hired me as a naturalist in the spring of 1977. As with most jobs, this one has its moments of tedium. However, the questions that come from the broad range of nature center visitors have spurred me on in ferreting out answers. Because of them, I continue to better my skills at reading sign.

For several years, I have been chided, poked, chewed out, and coddled by my good friend and fellow employee Charlie Johnston. He is most responsible for refusing to let the boy in me get too old for his own good. Charlie, more than anyone else, has encouraged me to gather an assemblage of columns together and get them published in book form. I know that it was his connection with Voyageur Press that made this book a reality. For his help, friendship, and inspiration, I will always be in his debt.

It seemed only logical that Charlie should share his art skills by illustrating this book. His sensitivity and skills are well portrayed in the fine pencil drawings and cover that grace this book. They truly are the salt and pepper.

This book has been a family effort, and though my mother, Bev Anderson, may not have been one to share a marsh or campsite with, she has always been supportive. She is far more skilled in typing than I, and she generously offered her help in typing the manuscript. A thank you here seems so inadequate, for my gratitude goes beyond words.

Family outings, story readings, and togetherness suffer when taking on an additional load besides the normal workday. I must thank my wife, Susan, daughters Britta and Maren, and other family members who put up with my selfishness. Though I wasn't always available, they were always there when I needed them, and for this I thank them and love them all the more.

I regret that I am unable to hand a copy of this book to my father. I think he would have enjoyed it. Perhaps his influence is best illustrated in a column I wrote in April, 1982:

> People often ask me how I became a naturalist. My reply has usually been simple and brief. I have always loved the outdoors, and after completion of classwork in the field of wildlife biology in college, I was very fortunate to find work that broadened my experience, until I arrived where I am now employed.
>
> But it really isn't so simple as that, because somewhere along the road there had to be a catalyst that nurtured my love for the natural world. There had to

be an introduction. Unquestionably, my catalyst has been my father.

As far back as my memory allows, my father was an avid hunter and fisherman. One of my early recollections was sitting out behind the garage watching him clean the ducks he had bagged that morning. My sister, brother, and I were a source of questions, and he tried his best to answer.

We particularly liked the iridescent blue in the mallard's wings, and Dad would always cut open the huge, hard gizzard to show us the mixture of sand, gravel, and wild rice grains. We learned that the gizzard and the sand were the duck's "teeth."

Occasionally, Dad would take us kids along on a duck hunt out to one of the lakes at grandpa's farm. There he would find a spot for us in the tall grass at the wood's edge, well back from his blind. Our orders were to sit very still. So special was it to join him on one of these outings that we would stay as statuesque as possible, which was not easy for an eight- or ten-year-old.

It was from these grassy hideouts that I first learned what ducks and wild rice stands had in common. Not only did I learn to distinguish various ducks in flight, but Dad started my education, not only as a hunter but, more importantly, as a hunter who respected wildlife, other hunters, and landowners.

There were a couple of years when literally thousands of mallards would magically appear and funnel into the lake at sunset to feed in the thick beds of wild rice. Those mallards were wise to hunting schedules and would appear just as the sun settled in the west, signaling the end of a day's shoot.

For some hunters on the lake, the flocks of ducks proved too great a temptation, and they would continue to shoot after the legal shooting hours. Dad would become very upset, and it was only at such times that I ever heard him angrily yell across the waters, telling the late shooters that it was time to quit shooting. He explained to me that the birds needed a period to feed and rest without being harassed.

We often stood on the shoreline well after the sun had set just to watch the swarming spectacle of ducks. Even as it got dark and viewing became difficult, I'll never forget the mingled sounds of wings, quacks, and feet settling onto the water. Even in the darkness, Dad knew the way through the woods, and we would follow his dim form along an unseen trail back to the car.

In the spring, when the sunfish were hitting on nearly anything that came near their scoured nests, Dad would rent a rowboat for a dollar at Lofboom's on Fish Lake. He would row us to favorite sandy shallows out near Squirrel Point, where we had many splendid evenings catching panfish on colored, floating poppers.

Green frogs would be calling, and sometimes we got close to a peculiar-sounding bird, which according to bird guides was an American bittern but according to Dad was a "sloughpumper."

Whenever I hear a squeaky oarlock, my memory takes me back to Dad rowing us in the cool darkness back to the car with a bucket of still-flopping sunnies.

Boy Scouts was another area in which more outdoor experience was added. Dad was scoutmaster for several years, and although his desire for camping was hardly fervent, he was with us on my first winter camp-out.

We used an old canvas wall tent that had no floor. Luckily, someone had struggled with hauling a bale of straw out to the campsite, which we spread thickly inside the tent. It got cold that night, several degrees below zero. But with six of us crowded into the tent and myself sandwiched next to Dad, who took an outside wall position, I actually slept rather well.

Apparently not everyone slept so well, because the next morning Dad declared that he had heard forty-two trains pass by in the distance.

With Dad being a certified gun safety instructor, I had to be especially conscious of my gun handling when I was old enough to join him in hunting. I could expect a stern reprimand for any slipups in properly handling a loaded or unloaded gun—for every gun was to be treated as if it were loaded.

Much of my outdoor learning took place in hunting experiences.

I don't know who was more thrilled that opening day when I bagged my first duck, a hen ringbill. I won't forget my first deer hunt, when Dad led me through the predawn darkness to a windfall that he had located a few days before the season. It seemed like I sat perched in that tree for hours. Amazingly, it was less than two hours before my freezing feet forced me down to the ground.

Without any care of being quiet or not, I shuffled back to the car. I was sitting in the back seat rubbing my now bootless toes when Dad came walking up wearing a broad grin. He was not only amused by my predicament but by the fact that he had just bagged a fine buck—the first ever for him. And I got to be there to share in the excitement.

As I grew older, I could count on receiving a book from Dad on Christmas. Invariably, its pages dealt with hunting, canoeing, north country wilderness, or some other woods lore topic. And my first pair of binoculars started a time when observation of birds and other wildlife would stretch beyond the hunting and fishing seasons.

So you can see it was very difficult for me when Dad was buried last week because of what he has meant to me as a father and as a person who, more than anyone else, has most influenced my career choice.

I can only hope that I may be such a father someday—one that recognizes his children's interests and then nurtures those interests.

Seven months after his sudden death, I became a father. Now as a father of two, I have someone to grasp my finger as we slowly stroll the ruts and thick sand of a country road.

# JANUARY

# Riders of an Unseasonable Wind

Winter for the most part is a silent affair. Frigid temperatures have a way of stilling and quieting the world. It is a season when we are without frog, insect, and bird choruses. Summer's trembling popple leaves and their constant chatter are gone, buried under winter's stuffing.

What few sounds there are, however, carry farther in cold air. Even wearing a stocking hat, I hear more distant dogs on a black winter night than I do in the summer. Those bold or questioning barks of winter have no barriers of lush, green walls or forested countryside to impede their invisible waves of sound.

Snowflakes, especially in flight, have a way of absorbing noises. Normally, I can hear traffic passing on the blacktop a quarter mile to the east of our place, but when there is a measurable snowfall in progress, I am unaware of both passing traffic and the neighbors.

There is nothing like a snowstorm to isolate oneself from the rest of the world. I suspect that may be the very reason we feel snug in our homes during such a riot of flakes. We find ourselves marooned, with schedules impossible to keep and a realization that we are truly alone. Oddly enough, there is a certain comfort and a sense of pioneerism when sentenced to such isolation.

No month better typifies the mettle of winter than January. The other night, I lay in our upstairs bedroom listening to the unseasonal dull roar of a powerful wind. Several times during the long night, I awoke to the constant din of maddened winds. This wind carried no snowflakes; it was empty and unrelentless in its hunger.

The winds of winter sweep down out of the northwest, flowing over a sparse landscape, picking up the chill of the snow and ice. It is a wind that shimmies up our legs or steals under our overcoats to touch our backs, giving rise to an awful shudder. Is it any wonder that even from the comfort of our homes we shiver on hearing the howl of arctic-borne winds?

Summer's breezes, on the other hand, seem more evident among the racing clouds and in the treetops where the leaves catch the gusts. July's winds moving through the grasses and leaves are not so lonely and distinct as those of January. With the countryside now bare, the winds have more freedom to pick up speed. Hence they blow louder and more furiously.

During several sleepless interruptions throughout the night, I was reminded of past campsites where we had lain in our tent that had perhaps been staked too close to a nearby rapids or waterfalls. Such water noises can be calming or they can keep one awake. Usually sleep comes quickly along such water routes because we had earned in physical exertion the right to hear such a tumultuous lullabye.

When I arose the following morning, the wind had not lessened. As I stoked the basement stove, I could hear the wind hungrily suck up the heat of the fire. At the breakfast table, I watched several intrepid chickadees make their way to our bird feeder. Rather than drop in directly from the surrounding trees, the small birds made their way against the wind to the offering of sunflower seeds using a hopscotch approach. They seemed almost to be sneaking in as they made their way low to the ground, moving from hazel stem to hazel stem. A last burst carried them desperately to the feeder for a quick seed before they were blown back toward their starting point.

This was an unseasonal wind that might have felled many trees in the summer. But now, for the most part, the tree canopies are bare and permit the winds to slip freely through the limbs. Other than a scattering of blown-down twigs and branches, the only tree blown over was the discarded Christmas tree that had been propped in the snow near the bird feeder for the likes of chickadees and such.

To the north of our place is a cornfield, which like so many area cornfields this winter remains unpicked. Thanksgiving snowstorms have a way of fouling up harvest plans. Though farming operations have grown substantially in recent years, the amount of time to get crops in has not increased. Consequently, it's no surprise to find a standing cornfield in midwinter. The only ones not complaining are the squirrels, pheasants, and deer that wander into the fields in search of sustenance.

On this day of a strong westerly blow, the corn was most noisy in its clattering and rattling. Out of the field and over the snow raced pale, dried leaves of corn. And bursting from the corn were occasional faded, yellow streamers of leaf that twisted and twirled high into the sky.

Sharing the skies with the corn fragments was a single crow. It seemed intent in its twisting and tumbling flight to be headed in the only direction that anything could go—downwind.

The woods downwind from the cornfield is now fenced with a windrow of dried corn leaves that have become tangled in the underbrush. If we hadn't had the warm weather prior to the wind, the snow covering would have been swept away to form sculptured drifts elsewhere. Instead, the flakes had bonded together in the thaw and on refreezing gave the landscape a look of glazed frosting.

There was also a sense of autumn to the irregular winter scene. Racing even faster than the corn streamers were the smaller dried leaves of red oaks. There is hardly a footprint or hollow in the snow where a pile of brown oak leaves hasn't settled.

Some trees, particularly red oaks, are stubborn about shedding their leaves in the customary months of October and November. It is not at all unusual to find these trees still holding the bulk of their dried foliage throughout a winter. This trait is not true to all members of the species, for some red oaks are as naked as a December tamarack. Most often, it is the red oaks that border an opening that retain their leaves. Does the better exposure to the sun make these trees more resistant to leaf fall?

Several years ago, after searching unsuccessfully for references to help answer the question, I called on a past professor of plant ecology. "Why," I asked him, "do some dead leaves cling to their summer places all winter?" His reply was simply, "That's a good question."

I wasn't disappointed in his answer. In fact, I found it challenging and refreshing. We live in a world where news of organ transplants, space shuttles, and genetic manipulation give rise to little more than yawns. It is wonderfully humbling to know that there are still an infinite number of questions afloat that we can only answer with a succinct, "Just because."

The chickadee that struggled to my feeder is perfectly content in not knowing why leaves fall or not. The bird's interest in the dried hanging oak leaves is that they provide a shelter from hungry day-time shrikes and evening heat-robbing winds.

As daylight turned to darkness, the wind finally spent itself, leaving behind a tattered cornfield, a leaf-littered landscape, some tired chickadees, and a disheveled crow.

Under starry skies, the temperatures dropped into their more seasonable range and the world, for the time being was quiet.

For the most part, winter is a silent affair.

# Sumac's Winter Offering

The cold dark shadows created by the westerly sinking moon were about to be erased by the graying of dawn.

I looked out the window and shivered when I saw the ghostly shadow of billowing smoke that streamed steadily from the chimney.

It wasn't the thought of spirits that caused the chill, it was the realization of how cold it must be to see such a vivid dancing shadow. A loud crack sounded from the wall of the house—almost as if to confirm any doubts I had about the frigid temperatures outside.

My eye caught a dark movement out beyond the streaming shadow. It moved again and then stood up on its hind legs and stretched as high as it could to grasp the branch of a sumac.

I knew then that I was looking at a cottontail, perhaps the same one that had boldly pruned my dwarf spirea at the back door stoop. Now its attention was on girdling the bark from the sumac's stem.

Though the sumac is not a preferred winter food item, cottontails must sometimes lower their standards, especially when February, the "Hunger Moon," is staring them in the face.

Across the road from where I grew up was a lush thicket of sumac that had quickly established itself in a clearing at the edge of the woods. Like milkweed or mullein, sumac thrives in sandy soils, neglected pastures, or openings in the woods. During the summer, we used to roam freely beneath its canopy of green.

Once this shrub establishes itself, it outgrows its competition, leaving the ground beneath it clear and easy to move through.

In the winter, long after we had watched the green thicket change to autumn hues of oranges and scarlets, cottontails would course through the naked stems, creating runways from shrub to shrub. During severe winters, these stems shone white above the snow where the rabbits had stripped the bark for the promise of a winter meal.

I must admit, I would rather feast on the color of the sumac's autumn fire than I would on the clumps of velvety red berries that are left after the leaflets drop.

I have drunk sumac "lemonade" made from their berries and have found that "lemonade" can be created from nearly anything if you simply add enough sugar.

Sumac pie is interesting and a novelty but a far cry from the tartness of a fresh apple pie. So it comes as no surprise that most wildlife don't find the sumac a preferred food choice.

The sumac that I share my property with belongs to the genus *Rhus*, which some references claim is derived from a Greek word meaning to run. This description fits the plant well, as it ranks up there with cattails and woodbine as being stubbornly persistent in spreading its roots in all directions through the soil to thrust new stems upward.

I was continually frustrated by the renewed life of the sumac after I had cleared some of the shrubs from the long-abandoned pasture that my house now sits on. Armed with a grub hoe and Swedish stubbornness, I have won most encounters with sumac stubs.

However, the victory is often short-lived. If there is even a small section of its long creeping root still buried, this tenacious shrub will refuse to quit its climb to the sky.

It seems, though, that the bite of the backhoe that was used to clear the copse of the sumac I shared with the cottontails so many years ago did a thorough job of pulling the roots. Instead of sumac, there is a house, a yard landscaped with hybrid shrubs, and a carpet of Kentucky blue grass.

Gone are the engulfing jungles of our youth and the maze of rabbit runways that twisted underneath. Now one is lucky to see the occasional rabbit boldly venture into the yard at dusk for a nibble of clover or a taste of tender June cabbage.

Several days after I had watched the cottontail, I startled a small flock of evening grosbeaks that were feeding on the berries atop the candelabra branches of the sumac. Not only was I reminded that I had better replenish my bird feeders, but again I had witnessed the call of the sumac.

As the sun disappeared that evening, Sue spotted a great horned owl perched at the tip of a burr oak that grows next to our house. It, too, is fond of sumac. Instead of plucking the berries or stripping the bark, it prefers its sumac converted into cottontail.

It's been over a week now since we watched the still owl, and the soft hopping tracks of the rabbit have been absent from under the sumac and the snow below the spirea is untouched.

# Reading the Fine Print

To many folks, winter seems a harsh and barren season. Numbing winds rushing from the arctic and a landscape swallowed in snow and ice would seem to make it impossible for life to exist. But exist it must, and the story of survival is never more evident than after a snowfall.

Across the clean-swept surface of snow are the "signatures" of those creatures that make survival their full-time occupation during the short days of winter.

A track is not just an impression left in the snow—it is a free education. The track maker's travels, activities, and secrets are laid out for us to decipher if we take the time to do so. Those mammals and birds that are not hibernating or dormant must be out and about seeking food and cover. In their daily doings, they are leaving a record or chapter of their lives. Only in winter can we expect such an easy reading of their life story.

On finding a track, our questions should go beyond "Who dun it?" The real challenge is to analyze why the tracks pause for a moment, turn abruptly, scratch deeper into the snow, or change their pace.

I've often been asked which field guide to tracks is best. I never hesitate to reply that there is no best guide that stands above the others. No book will ever be able to portray something so changeable as a track in the snow.

Daily weather conditions such as wind, melting snow, and newly fallen snow can alter a set of tracks so that they appear quite different from one day to the next. Another problem is that the animal's behavior gives rise to a great variety of prints. Unfortunately, field guides are limited to a minimum of track illustrations.

In my opinion, there is no better way to learn tracks than to get out and practice. The best of all situations is to witness the track maker and then study its spoor. One mustn't limit the scrutinizing to a single print; instead, one should follow it some distance for a more complete picture.

Some of my best memories of learning the meanderings of tracks took place quite a few winters ago. Before I had a license to drive, one of my parents would drive me several miles from our house to a large area of grasslands and willow thickets, known locally as "the meadows."

Here, they would drop me off with my single-shot .22 rifle and a lunch carried on my back in a worn army pack still bearing the faded U.S. letters.

After being dropped off, I would start walking back home, cutting cross-country, going the long way. My intentions were to find a fox track, one fresh enough for me to follow.

Although I occasionally spotted a distant, speeding fox, I never shot one during those Saturday or Christmas vacation hikes. But the trails I crossed and followed taught me much. As a result, I feel a special affinity for the red fox and especially for its wandering tracks.

The beauty of following and learning the skills of tracking is that there is no need to go off into a secluded area to better one's skills. Our own backyard provides ample opportunities.

I recall an outing in recent years in which friend Nels and I were out in the woods at dawn, just after a light snow had fallen the evening before. Typical of January fashion, nearby trees were popping up in the cold stillness as we briskly snowshoed away from the truck.

The first tracks we encountered were the bounding prints left by a weasel as it zigzagged through a willow thicket. The fist-sized prints are made by the two pairs of feet landing nearly on top of one another as the animal lopes along. The tracks made their way to an old abandoned car, circled it, and then disappeared inside only to come out and move on. I suspect the derelict auto is occasionally a haven for mice, but not on this hunting foray.

We crossed the dainty trails of deer mice. The paths of mice and other small mammals such as voles and shrews are brief in their message—the short stories of a winter woods. Their scamperings in the open world are brief and usually hurried. The tiny imprints emerge from a small burrowed opening in the snow and hop for a brief distance before disappearing. Concealment and insulation are the snow's gift to the small mammals.

All that remains of the deer mice antics are the tiny leapfrog footprints. Oftentimes, their long, trailing tail leaves a thin furrow between each series of prints. However, if the mouse is in a hurry, the tail is held high and the distance between each impression becomes greater as it lengthens its leaps.

Sometimes there would be several mouse trails adjacent to one another, as if a small "herd" had traveled back and forth together. More likely is the possibility that a single rodent was responsible for all the tracks. Perhaps the numerous trips were made to a hidden food cache of seeds.

As curious as I was about the food stash or whiskered little beast under the snow, it seemed unforgiveable to disrupt the beauty of the fragile tracks, not to mention the mouse's pantry. Some questions are best left unanswered.

Along the edge of an alder swamp, we found the runways of snowshoe hares. Scattered on the hare's trail were pellet-shaped droppings. Further up the slope, away from the swamp, we found the smaller, hopping tracks of a single cottontail that had lingered under a toppled red oak.

Moving across a hayfield, we encountered the distinct path of a fox. These slender animals are built for speed. Similar to other narrow-chested mammals, they leave a narrower trail than a heavier-chested beast.

The single-file series of tracks led from one clump of grass to the next, hoping perhaps to flush a mouse or vole. One clump of dried grass was sprinkled with the yellow stain of urine.

At this time of year, fox tracks are often found in pairs, as January is the advent of their breeding season. Males periodically pause in their travels, raise a leg, and urinate on a tuft of grass, a boulder, or a fallen log to advertise their presence or affirm territorial boundaries. This marking habit makes it easier to determine the sex of the fox.

An additional aid in interpreting tracks is the discovery of droppings. Biologists usually refer to such clues as scat.

Once while following a fox track, I came upon some fresh, not yet frozen, scat. Underneath the droppings was the stain of urine, leading me to believe that the track maker was a female, as she, like my dog, prefers to squat to void her urine.

Carefully, I dissected the scat with the aid of sticks for probes. There is no need to question my sanity—I just wanted to see what undigestible food remnants might be found.

After finding intertwined, matted gray hairs tipped with white, it was evident that this particular vixen had recently dined on a gray squirrel. There were also the scalelike remains of a ruffed grouse foot, complete with the wintertime fringes found on grouse's toes. Perhaps the fox had surprised the grouse while the bird had roosted under the fluffy blanket of snow.

As Nels and I snowshoed into a growth of young popple and birch, we came across the fox's spoor once again. We followed the tracks toward a beaver pond. Crossing the pond, the tracks led us up a slope of mixed hazel and popple. The tracks disappeared into a recently renovated den. Only a few feet from where the fox vanished was a second opening into the earth. It is likely that at one time a woodchuck had excavated the den. Foxes, it seems are partial to this rodent's handiwork.

We peered at the frost-rimmed entrance of the den and could barely make out a whisper of vapor as it eased into daylight. After a

11

few seconds, a second touch of vapor followed the first. The pungent odor of fox told us that we had found the end of the fox's trail.

Tracking any animal carries a sense of anticipation because you know that somewhere up ahead of you there is very likely a living creature. Given time and luck, there is a good chance of seeing the track maker. However, the usual scenario is a string of tracks that seem tireless or the disappearance of the trail as the animal takes to the air or the treetops.

So as we pondered the rhythmic rise of fox vapor, we felt privileged to know that the animal lay at our very feet, separated from us by a thin layer of soil, roots, and snow.

One doesn't ponder things too long on such frigid days, so we moved back down the slope out onto the pond. The nervous fox was left alone. We had concluded this chapter of the ways of a fox knowing full well that next time we take its trail there will be another chapter to read.

# The Bragging Bird

The game of one-upmanship seems most evident when it comes to such activities as fishing, exclaiming over babies, and advertising. But I fear it has also become deep-rooted in bird feeding.

Just so much as mention the feathered activity at your bird feeder and a bystander will jump in and with an air of sober-faced smugness tell of a particular bird that is attracted to his or her feeder on a regular basis. Chickadees, sparrows, juncos, and goldfinches visiting a feeder will hardly raise an eyebrow. However, should something more out of the ordinary, like a flock of pine grosbeaks, Bohemian waxwings, or a tufted titmouse appear, they become worthy of gloats and boasts.

Perhaps the bird that inspires the most consistent bragging is the crimson-feathered cardinal. I am convinced that those folks who harbor such cardinal-rich feeders know that I cannot attract a single one. Not only do they enjoy telling of their scarlet visitors, but they tell of everyday visits of a half a dozen or more cardinals, all feasting on sunflower seeds at the same time.

The last cardinal I attracted to a feeder was about nine years ago, during the closing days of winter. That lone male seemed bent on self-destruction. Everyday, at the same time, during the golden moments just before sunset, we would hear a banging against the living room window. Quietly peeking into the living room, we would find the solitary male perched just outside the window on the feeder. With his brilliant crest flaring erect, he stared at the window. With jerking movements and nervous flaps of the wings, he appeared upset over something. Then, all of a sudden, he launched himself at the window, beating it with wings and buffeting it with his breast. This time a tiny down feather was loosened from his breast and it slowly drifted to the ground. Again, the bird glared at the window for a moment before repeating the window bashing.

Though he appeared to be peering at us, he was in fact viewing his own reflection in the glass. Being unable to reason, as most humans can, he was convinced that the duplicate image was another male. Since it was approaching spring, his hormones had started readying him for the upcoming breeding season. Part of his annual rite was to establish a breeding territory, which he would jealously guard from other wandering male cardinals. This bird had become enraged at the presence of the "ghost" intruder.

The mirror image was not paying the least bit of attention to the visual messages such as the raised crest on the head. In fact, it seemed that the trespasser was giving the same threatening display. This was too much for the cardinal to take, so he lashed out. Repeatedly, he flew at and bounced off the window, but his nemesis never retreated.

We have moved north, some twenty miles, since then, leaving the confused cardinal and its window feeder behind. At our current homestead, the only cardinals I can show my daughters are those found in picture books. These birds are seemingly nonexistent around our yard. It seems that every feeder blessed with the raiments of cardinals has a nearby growth of evergreens for them to retreat into. It also helps if there is a tangle of grapevines, wild cucumber, bittersweet, or other growth of vines. A forgotten plum thicket or hedge is also desirable for attracting a cardinal or two.

These oversize, colorful finches are not birds of the deep forest.

Instead, they prefer the edges and secondary growth that we find nearly impenetrable.

Before the turn of the century, the cardinal was strictly a southern gentleman or belle. By 1932, when Dr. Thomas S. Roberts wrote his two volume classic, *The Birds of Minnesota,* the cardinal had pushed northward through the southeastern corner of the state up to the Minneapolis-St. Paul region. Rarely was the bird observed north of the Twin Cities.

Since the depression years, the cardinal has slowly established itself northward and westward. In the past twenty years, there have been very few records of the bird nesting in the northern reaches of the state. Apparently, a few cardinals find themselves in the coniferous range of the state after the fall and spring shuffle. However, these are more likely visitors, and most of the pausing cardinals move back to southerly thickets in search of more favorable habitat and better breeding numbers.

The cardinal is such a rarity in the northern counties that recently a sighting along the North Shore in the Lutsen area, some 60 miles from the Canadian border, made the local newspaper. Cardinals are capable of producing that kind of "news."

For the past eleven years, local bird counters in east central Minnesota have tallied cardinals during the Christmas Bird Count. Every December, the intrepid counters patrol the same 177-square-mile area looking and listening for birds. For the first five years of the count, 34 cardinals were observed. However, the past six years have shown a dramatic increase, with 198 cardinals sighted.

Why the exploratory surge to the north?

We can only speculate, but perhaps the increase has come as a result of a changing landscape. In the past eighty years, there have been millions of forested acres cleared. Some of those openings became farmland, others have slowly grown back to shrubby hedges and thickets or have given rise to miles of overgrown edges—ideal cardinal cover.

Perhaps more of a factor has been the surge of interest in feeding birds. With scattered food stations loaded with oil-rich sunflower or safflower seeds, the cardinals are able to fuel themselves against a harsh winter.

14

The cardinal is a stay-put sort of bird. It prefers to spend the four seasons in the same general region. An adult pair of cardinals will spend the year near their breeding and nesting grounds.

Since cardinals do not make an energy-demanding flight to a distant wintering grounds, they do not accumulate the great fat reserves that many other migrant birds do. Some shorebirds that eventually end their fall flight somewhere along the South American coastline are wrapped in a sheath of fat prior to their epic journey.

Starting in the late fall, the cardinal begins to accumulate fat under its skin. Should bad weather set in, the cardinal has enough fat reserves to carry it through about three days. After four or five days, the bird will begin to starve without a source of food.

The cardinal's appeal lies largely in its color. But its song, sometimes heard on a mild winter day, oftentimes brings us to a stop. A winter bird song is a welcome note, for it carries a dream of spring.

Upon glimpsing the blood-red plumage of the male cardinal, even the person who is only casually interested in birds will pause to admire. These birds are the show stoppers at the bird feeders.

In 1245, a formal decree made by Innocent IV in Rome established that the clergy in the Pope's Council—the Cardinals—were to wear red hats as part of their official vestments. These brilliant, showy hats were to become the inspiration for the feathered cardinal's name.

I suspect there are those folks who tend feeders that are unaware of the cardinal's visits. This bird has a timid nature and is most often viewed shortly after the break of day and again as the sun settles into evening.

Unlike the usual flocks of feeder visitors such as nuthatches, chickadees, finches, and woodpeckers, cardinals prefer to mingle with their own kind rather than integrate. They can hardly be considered snooty, because they would rather pick their share of seed from the ground rather than the seed-filled platform. For that reason, it is a good idea to sprinkle some seed on the ground, even if it does attract the ever-hungry squirrel.

It is not unusual to see a flock of cardinals from early to midwinter. However, by late February, this feeling of togetherness breaks down. The males become less tolerant of each other. Hence the reason for the window banging.

When the pussy willows first show their softness, we can expect to hear the cardinal's song. The song is a bit of an oddity because the female will often duet with the male. Generally in the bird world, the song is a male trait. Though the female cardinal's song has a softer quality, it sounds similar to the whistling notes of the male. Such dueting is important in strengthening their pair bond.

Someday, my bittersweet and nearby wild grape vines will have climbed high in their twisting journey to the sun. Out near the driveway and garden is a youthful windbreak of white spruce and red pine. There will be a day when these trees will stand tall and full in their skirts of green. With these ingredients and a well-stocked feeder, I expect to share this piece of property with cardinals.

And I will sit patiently, waiting for an evening grosbeak with its splash of yellow, a jay to add a stroke of blue, and finally a cardinal for the long-awaited finishing touch of red. Such a summit meeting may be next to impossible, considering the brassy nature of the jay, the unreliability of the grosbeak, and the shyness of the cardinal. But if I can coax the three of them to my feeder at the same moment, then it will be my turn to brag.

**UPDATE:** Less than a year has passed since I wrote this piece, and I am happy to report that a lone male cardinal paused for a moment on a late fall morning at our feeder. Actually, my oldest daughter spotted it while she was eating breakfast. No one else saw it, but she described the bird as being very red and having black on its face. I questioned her further about the size and so on, but she wasn't sure because the bird had stayed for only a few seconds.

Later in the morning, I was out by the woodshed busying myself when I heard the unmistakable weak whistle of a nervous cardinal. I turned and trotted a few steps to give me a view of the feeder, and there was Britta's red bird—a cardinal. In the same instant that I spied the bird, it flashed off into the nearby woods.

Since that day, the cardinal has been far too erratic in its appearances. It has, however, acquired an identity. The kids pondered over a name for awhile, but without any argument settled on "Cherry."

Now if anyone wants to talk cardinals, let's sit down.

# A Change of Script

Those of us who follow the course of a year in the Upper Midwest know that the four "acts" we call seasons are somewhat predictable in their appearance and manner.

We look forward to the passing of each season because every one is unique and worthy of notice. Each "act" blends harmoniously with the next; there is no sameness in the year.

With the passing of summer, the air becomes fresh again, and as autumn gains the upper hand, the freshness gives way to a chill—a chill that incites a riot of colors. In time, autumn's blaze is snuffed out in the shortening of days and the drop of temperatures. Flakes of snow, telling of winter, become props for the next act.

And just when we begin to wonder if there really is another scene in this drama of seasons, we hear the gentle sounds of meltwater and smell the alarm of a winter-weary skunk. Finally the longest "act" loses its battle to the climbing sun. Spring is finally won.

The most subtle of transitions, however, is from spring to summer. In appearance, both seasons are similar when they meet. However, summer's energy level is not nearly as intense as spring's.

Perhaps the difference between these joining seasons is best seen in watching the greens as they change from the soft, spring colors that only a new leaf can show to the more rich and deeper tones of summer green.

Each season has its highlights, and each has its inconveniences. Perhaps inconvenience is a poor choice of words, because what may seem an inconvenience to you or me is a "necessary" for something else.

Summer's inconveniences, in my mind, are few. But for my comfort, I find the annoyance of certain insects and the sweltering humidity to be barely tolerable at times.

On the other hand, the little brown bat that loops through the summer evening skies would be noticeably absent if there were no small, pesky insects. The heat that melts my ambition and patience gives my tomatoes and green peppers their fullness and color.

For its bad moments, some consider spring's slush and accompanying mud to be the worst.

Autumn, on the other hand, seems to be without any bad habits, but then I admit a strong bias for the latter third of the year. Some would consider autumn rains to be the most chilling and penetrating, fully capable of messing up ripened fields of corn and beans. However, these same rains inspire both autumn's ducks and fungi.

But it is winter that seems to top the list in carrying the greatest of inconveniences. For me, January is the most trying of the months—short of day and long of cold and dark.

Lore has it that this is the month when a flickering match will freeze in eternal light or at least until a mid-winter thaw. It is the month when the evening woods are most often at war with the cold. Loud riflelike shots crack in the darkness as the moisture trapped in the heart of the tree freezes and expands, splitting the internal tree fibers and the skin of bark.

Yet, this year the script of winter has changed. January has actually shown us a tender face. Like stocking hats, icicles have come and gone. The snow has settled, and on some slopes it has vanished entirely. Recent days have had a flavor of March rather than January.

Warm breezes borne from the Pacific have given us a reprieve from the numbing cold that gripped us a few days ago. Some people may have decided to delay their winter trip to the "sun," others have rejoiced by sitting out on the lake, using the excuse that they are fishing. Some folks break their dormancy by taking an extended hike.

Rather than squeaking, the snow now sloshes underfoot. My wood stove, which demanded constant gorging during the bitter days, is now enjoying a postholiday diet, much to my relief.

To break away from the cold-induced bondage, I went in search of winter relief. On snowshoes, I meandered through a tree-covered coulee that sports a dark ribbon of a stream. I enjoy coming here in the winter to watch the water move and listen to its noises as it runs through and over the midstream rocks. Even though it is January and most waters are locked in ice and incapable of emitting the summery tune of a splash, this stream is a tireless songster. Night and day, through the parade of months, the hypnotic tumble of water accompanies the beat of the seasons.

I'm not sure which I prefer, the streams ramblings or the sighting of a midwinter trout as it knifes through the shallows seeking security from a bundled form trudging along the snowy bank. A winter brook trout holding in its midstream lie, helps ease the bite of January. For a moment, it seems like May or June.

Reinforcing the dream of spring was an illusion of insects bobbing just over the water's surface. But was it really an illusion? As I got closer, the insects did not fade as a mirage. Instead, they took on an identity. The swarm of stoic, winter adventurers became tiny midges.

Without question, the greatest contradiction to January is the bold appearance of insects. My walk along the stream gave rise to two different forms of insects—midges and stoneflies. Midges are equipped with only one pair of functional wings, which distinguishes them as Diptera—the two-winged flies. Stoneflies have two pair.

Midges and especially stoneflies resemble mosquitoes. Indeed, stoneflies are often referred to as "winter skeeters." However, neither midges nor stoneflies are capable of stinging, for they are without the blood-sucking proboscis.

After going through the egg, larval, and pupal stages in a water environment, stoneflies and midges emerge as adult air breathers. Given the right temperatures, their emergence can be a winter happening.

Due to their diminutive nature, much of the midge's life history remains a mystery. However, it is known that they will complete their aquatic metamorphosis and emerge from sun-warmed shallows on a mild winter day. Perhaps the dark-colored pupae and adult gain some advantage in absorbing the winter sun's feeble thrust of heat.

Upon emergence, the adult midge rests on the water's surface for a brief moment before taking to the air. Once in flight, the adult males form swarms, using teamwork to attract the females. The midge's objective during its brief adult life is to produce future generations. Usually, the slow rise and fall flight of the churning swarm takes place over a landmark such as a stump or rock.

When a female is ready to mate, she locates a highly visible swarm of advertising males and boldly flies into it. Momentarily, all teamwork is forgotten, as only one male will probably mate with her. After the mating, the gravid female will delicately lay her eggs on the surface of the stream. Slowly, the microscopic eggs settle to the bottom, where they begin their transformation towards full-fledged midges.

Of the many midge species in our region, only a handful emerge as adults during a winter thaw.

Stoneflies are remnants of the Ice Age some 12,000 years ago. They thrived during the march of the glaciers, and as the climate slowly warmed, melting the ice sheets, the stoneflies took refuge in the chilly waters of spring-born streams.

Adult stoneflies hold their two pairs of wings flat over the body, and they extend a bit past the tip of the abdomen. Both pairs of wings are nearly the same size, which makes for awkward flight. Their aerial travels cannot be compared to the graceful swoops of a butterfly or the stationary hovering of a dragonfly.

Stoneflies have two antennae, which are quite long. In fact, if it were not for their wings, they would look very similar to a roach, to which they are closely related.

The name stonefly is derived from the fact that their larvae are often found hiding among the stones on the stream's bottom. The crawling larvae are often seen on the underside of an overturned rock. The adults sometimes fly great distances from the stream from which they emerge.

From November through March, many stoneflies transform into adults. After mating, the females return to the cold water nurseries to lay their eggs. Winter-active stoneflies must feed on algae or dead plant material.

The trout thrives in this rocky stream because of an energetic flow of untainted, cold water that carries oxygen, midges, and stoneflies. Such insects are an important trout fodder.

I'll never forget my first trout caught on an artificial fly. It was a rainbow trout, glistening in its silver color, that was tempted from the riffles of a dancing stream by my imitation stonefly nymph. These flies, commonly known as nymphs, work especially well in early spring fishing when the waters are full and cold. The first recorded artificial fly was tried in Great Britain over four centuries ago to simulate a stonefly nymph.

I fear that this surprise performance by the midges and stoneflies will be short-lived. Nonetheless, their appearance is a timely ad lib. It adds a nice element of change from the routine.

However, I'm confident that winter's "act" will once again slip into its predictable script, and the midges will be dropped from the cast until late winter. But so far, the performance has been sterling and most deserving of a stand-up "Bravo."

# FEBRUARY

# Box Elder Spoor

There were snowflakes in the air—a white gift from dirty gray skies. However, these flakes were not the gently floating variety. Instead, they were driven more horizontally than vertically by winds spawned in the northeast.

My destination was the far corner of the lake, exactly in the direction from which the needlelike flakes were being driven. Crossing in comfort was not easy, as tears were being coaxed from my eyes by the biting blow. My face felt locked in a permanent mask of frigidity.

Walking backwards offered some relief. But I opted for the faster, head-on approach to be done with the misery. Even walking fast, the sheltering shoreline seemed distant. With my head down and eyes fixed on the monotonous white floor ahead of me, I blinked away the tears and forged on.

Suddenly, against the snow, like a smear on the canvas of white, lay a single, winged "helicopter seed," a remnant from a box elder tree. The seed offered not only a break for my eyes but the message that the shoreline goal was getting closer. Soon I would be out of the full force of the wind.

Then a second seed met my downward gaze, and soon a third, fourth, and fifth clustered close to one another were left behind. I followed the trail of seeds to the shelter of the shoreline and found the frozen lake surface littered with grounded seeds that had twirled and fluttered their last.

I worked my way up the brushy, drifted slope, following the path of seeds. I was intent on finding their source.

Two hundred yards from the lake was a grove of box elder trees surrounding and growing within an old foundation of quarried sandstone blocks.

Nearby was an old sunken cellar partially covered by rotten, fallen walls of gray. Box elders likewise encircled this remnant of the past.

The box elder is actually a member of the maple tribe and is known to some as the "ash-leaf maple" because its leaves are more ashlike than maple. But true to form among the maples, the box elder has paired, winged fruits.

The two winged seeds, each about two inches long, develop, ripen, and mature, resembling an inverted V. Clusters of these Vs are now without the protection of summer leaves. After they autumn-ripen, they are subject to the raking winds of winter. Some clusters will persist and hang on until spring. To children, these airborne seeds are fondly known as "helicopters." Botanists label the same seeds as samara.

It was not unusual to find the thick grove of box elders around the remains of this long-forgotten farmstead. The box elder, more than any other tree, is often the companion tree to vacant or old farms. At one time, the box elder was much planted for its quick growth and youthful beauty. Some folks were convinced that the box elder's shade was cooler than other trees.

Box elders were extensively planted in the Midwest as wind-breaks during the turn of the century. The trees easily naturalized and readily spread on their own. Like the ubiquitous dandelion, this lowly maple does especially well in those areas where the ground has been disturbed, such as a once-active farm or fallow field.

Hardy against drought and freezing, the box elders required no demanding care. No green thumb was needed in nurturing this amiable tree. In fact, this is a tree that often thrives where other tree species refuse to grow.

Funny how such trees are often labeled "weed trees." It is the tenaciousness and hardiness of weeds that allow them to flourish under adverse conditions. Are such traits worthy of scorn and condemnation?

Consider the gaudily colored evening grosbeaks or the wine-colored purple finches that occasionally find their way southward from their coniferous summer haunts in pursuit of winter food and survival. During such bird-rich winters, we often find the naked limbs of box elders hosting the bright colors of grosbeaks and finches. These birds effortlessly crack the tough seed hulls with their powerful mandibles.

However, these birds do not dally in one spot too long, and sometimes the only clue of their presence are the shredded parchments of the clipped seed "wings" covering the snow.

Some of the seeds that go untouched by the birds will float down only to be gathered by chipmunks, squirrels, and mice. These rodents will strip off the seed's wing and hull, saving the seed meat for a future meal.

Even when seeds from box elders and other trees are scarce, some of these same rodents will girdle the bark of box elder trees to ease them through the pain of winter.

I know of a forty-acre piece of property that had long ago been cleared of its oak and maple. For years it was plowed, planted, cultivated, and harvested of its crop. For over ten years now, it has been forgotten and is slowly reverting back to the forest.

At the northwest end of the field is an old farm that has a ragged, gnarled old windbreak of box elders. Every winter these trees have released thousands of seeds. Riding the predominant northwest winter winds, the helicoptering seeds have traveled across the graveled county road to the now-fallow field.

Some of the seeds have fulfilled their destiny, and now there is a lush growth of young purple-stemmed box elder saplings. Gradually, the stand of young trees is working its way east, determined to claim the grassy field.

Every July, I can count on finding at least one summer-yellow goldfinch courting from several of the fast-growing saplings in the forgotten field. The goldfinch, it seems, finds the branches of the young trees perfect for holding its nest.

Years from now, the trees will continue to shrink the old field's girth, and the thistles that the finch so keenly desires for food and nesting material will be shaded out. Then I may have to go elsewhere to seek the nest of the "wild canary."

Here on the slope above the frozen lake, I was protected from the wind. I felt the numbness slowly leave my cheeks and nose. Over head, the faint rattling in the box elder limbs showed that the wind was still relentless.

Sparse clusters of box elders seeds shivered in the wind. Occasionally, one or more of the seeds would flutter off, joining the driven flakes on a ride down the slope to the lake's bleak surface. The future of those seeds is equally bleak when ice-out comes in the months to come.

An involuntary shudder raced across my shoulders, signaling that it was time to put the wind at my back and follow the seed spoor back to the warmth of a furnace.

# Goldenrod's Winter Treat

For the sake of fattening wallets, some call fallow fields unproductive. However, I hold the same opinion as the meadow vole and the pheasant. Such an ignored field is home and dinner to these two beasts. As for me, such a field is more pleasurable to stroll in than a monotonous stretch of corn or beans.

A nearby field has been forgotten for some time now. At one time, it gave rise to corn and little else. Now all vestiges of a cornfield are gone. Instead, a mosaic patchwork of grasses, weeds, shrubs, and a steadily advancing wall of popple are taking advantage of the lack of overshadowing competition from other trees.

Above the feeble cover of snow project the various hues of dead-grass browns. The old field seems lifeless. Other than the occasional flock of tree sparrows that skitters along the tangled edges or the redpolls that hop under the bowing grasses and weed for a taste of seed, few birds find such a February field inviting.

Recently, however, I watched a small distant bird break from the woods and bob in its characteristic up-and-down flight to a patch of brown that stood higher than the matted carpet of grasses. The moment the bird landed, I could see that it was a woodpecker—not your usual meadow bird.

By the time I made my way to the patch, the now recognizable downy woodpecker had grown uneasy with my approach and returned quickly to the woods.

It was a dry, brittle collection of goldenrod stems that had summoned the woodpecker. Many of the stems in this patch had slender stems that were swollen into a pregnant knob slightly more than half-way up the stalk. The obese growth, known as a gall, is a nursery for a tiny fly that will emerge in the spring. However, many of these galls will be excavated by this or other downy woodpeckers, thus cutting short the developing larvae's metamorphosis.

I examined about a dozen of the galls in the patch of dried goldenrod stems and found that most had been already chiseled open by a prying beak. Cutting them open with my jackknife verified that the woodpecker had found nourishment. I did, however, find a couple of galls that had not been tampered with. I cut one open and found an oblong, eighth-inch-long white grub. Like the woodpecker, I had condemned this larva in exposing it to the cold air. Unlike the woodpecker, I would not gain the necessary calories from eating it.

Some fishermen who are patient, and usually retired, will gather these round galls during the early winter months. The gathered galls will be carefully dissected and the grub gently removed. Tipped on a tiny ice-fly, these larvae make an enticing bait for panfish.

As youngsters, we used to pick the whole stem from a knobbed goldenrod. The stem above the gall was snapped off, leaving a wand topped with a hard gall. The plucked stem resembled a Zulu warrior's knobkerrie, a wooden club with a hard knob at the striking end. With our smaller version of this weapon, we would rap our playmate foes on the head. The half-inch to one-inch knob was never a life-threatening weapon, but it could smart if a direct hit was made. Little did we realize that there was life within that tiny club head.

In June, as spring gives way to summer, the adult female gall fly seeks out the new growth of goldenrod. No other plant will do. The fly lays an egg on the stem, and soon after hatching, the microscopic larva bores into the new stalk. Inside the plant's tissue, the larva's presence causes the surrounding goldenrod tissue to swell, forming a gall. Through the summer and autumn months, the larva grows, eating the same plant material that enshrouds it.

By the time the goldenrods are butter-yellow in August and

September, the swollen galls have completed their growth. Some of the plants have two or even three galls on the same stem. Though the plant may be girdled with galls, the blossoming of the plant is not affected.

After the flowers have gone to seed and drifted for destinations unknown, winter sets in and the fly larva snugly waits out the cold months.

It is during the lean winter months that a downy woodpecker might probe the gall for needed fuel. How the woodpecker ever discovered that a meal of insect might be found in a treeless meadow on patches of dried goldenrod stems is an interesting and baffling question. Is the behavior learned, or is the woodpecker simply an intrepid explorer who leaves no stones unturned?

If the gall should escape the ravages of the woodpecker, the fisherman, and winter, the larva will chew an exit tunnel through the corky tissue to the outermost skin of the gall. Before it cuts an opening to the sunlit world, it retreats to the winter chamber and completes its metamorphosis to the pupa. Shortly after it pupates, the insect will transform to the adult fly.

Crawling out the previously made tunnel, the adult fly works its way through the last barrier, the outer skin. A successful escape is betrayed by a clean, neat little round hole found usually on the upper half of the gall.

Soon after mating, the new generation of flies seek out a new crop of goldenrod on which to deposit their eggs.

And so the forgotten cornfield has become much more than a quiltwork of goldenrod, milkweed, canary grass, bramble, and popples. It is a complicated interchange of give and take, which is just fine for a winter-hungry woodpecker who boldly ventures away from the trees.

# Life under the Tracks

Though the woods are quiet, they are bustling with tracks. There is hardly a sweep of snow that hasn't been ruffled with an imprint.

Some are bold, while others are mere wisps. Some move purposefully, and others are erratic in their explorations. As I write these words, plump masses of flakes are falling, and like an eraser, they will temporarily wipe the cluttered slate clean.

Tracks are but sentences of a particular beast's life. The better we interpret or "read" the telltale footprints, the greater our knowledge and understanding of the track maker. Though the chapters repeat themselves every year—spring, summer, fall, and winter—their content is everchanging.

Obviously, there is no easier season to "read" than winter, when the antics and wanderings of wildlife are not so secretive. We seldom see the creatures, yet their comings and goings are clearly left recorded in the snow.

Inhabitants such as squirrels leave a portion of their story in the treetops, where I am unable to follow. Yet they, like all other creatures, are tied to the earth and must sooner or later return. When the urge for a buried acorn becomes great, which is quite often in the season of snow, their story is resumed after descending the tree.

Those creatures that take to the wing leave no trail for me to follow. But every so often they punctuate the clean surface with their mark as they scratch through the snow's crust for a seed or abruptly end the dainty "sentence" of a mouse with an encompassing wing print, which can best be described as an exclamation point rather than a period.

The collection of mouse essays are brief, especially for those rodents that explore the stark surface of snow. On the other hand, those mice and small creatures that roam the world under the snow usually have longer lives than their bolder counterparts.

Voles and shrews prefer a ceiling of snow and rarely leave a string of tracks for us to ponder. Instead, they lead a subnivean existence—a life under the snow.

Through eons of trial and error, shrews and voles have learned that not only is a deep snow-covered countryside a haven from searching predatory eyes, but it may prevent them from freezing.

In times when synthetics rule the world of fashion, I am still not convinced that there is a warmer garment than one that is a sandwich of fabrics filled with dry down feathers. It is not the down feathers that are so warm, it is their superior ability to hold air. The mixture of trapped air and feather slows down heat loss and we, in turn, remain comfortable.

A blanket of snow works on the same principle. The fluffier the cover of snow, the greater its insulating ability.

We tend to think of snow as a unique collection of ice crystals. Ice can only be described as cold, and therefore snow follows that rule. As countless, six-sided snowflakes drift earthward from winter's skies, they settle noiselessly and gently on the ground. The blanket of flakes is, by volume, more air than crystal. That's why I prefer shoveling snow over shoveling sand—the former is usually much lighter than the latter.

If the snowflakes have been wind-driven, they may collide among themselves. Soon their crystalline spires are tumbled off, leaving an altered flake that is rounded, more akin to a grain of sand. The resultant snow cover is denser and less fluffy.

Among the smallest of mammals, the shrews are constantly battling the dilemma of heat loss. Their ratio between body weight and surface area is not favorable for any long-term heat retention.

To counter the problem of rapid heat loss, shrews must generate more heat than they lose. This is accomplished by conserving their heat by living in the quiet world under the snow and by increasing their activity level. Moving muscles translate to work, and work creates heat. Work, however, demands a source of fuel.

The shrew's quest for fuel seems an insurmountable task. During the winter, these little insectivores consume over three times their body weight in a single day. Such an incredible feat may bring on uncomfortable thoughts of indigestion to you and I, though I admit we persist in trying to duplicate the shrew during the gluttonous Christmas holidays.

Shrews feed primarily on insect life found under the leaves and grasses. Sometimes, if the opportunity presents itself, they will prey on other shrews or mice.

Winter makes for lean hunting, since most of the insect world is dormant. At such times, the wee shrews will enhance their diet with autumn's gift of tiny seeds.

In the Upper Midwest, the tiniest of mammals honor goes to one of two species. Both the rare pygmy shrew *(Microsorex hoyi)*, and the more common masked shrew *(Sorex cinereus)*, are nearly identical in size and appearance. Individuals of either species would be considered heavy if they outweighed a dime. Both of these secretive, taper-snouted mammals are dingy gray. The secret in distinguishing their identities lies in mundane tooth differences, which are too small to easily scrutinize.

When under stress, from either a quick escape or the prolonged touch of frigid air, these tiny shrews may harbor a heart that pulses over a thousand beats per minute. Such stress only adds to the already heavy demand for a constant supply of fuel.

I once caught a short-tailed shrew, which I housed in a leaf-littered aquarium for observation. This dark, velvet-furred shrew is mouselike in length and girth, making it the largest of local shrews.

My captive shrew had an incredible appetite, with a real love for hamburger, though I fed it mostly chicken necks. On weekends, its diet was supplemented with sunflower seeds.

After a month of captivity, the shrew died. Perhaps the stress was too much for it, or maybe the temperature or humidity were not optimum for its survival. I suppose it could have died of old age. A shrew is lucky if it experiences one winter; two winters is nothing short of a miracle.

Though these beasts are interesting to watch, I can't say they make great pets. I prefer something that wags its tail and shoves its cold wet nose into my hand.

The shrew's passion for seeds is greater in winter, when insect leavings are lean. It's not uncommon to find their small exit holes perforating the packed snow under bird feeders, where they venture out for spilled seed.

Several years ago, a barred owl made a daily appearance near the nature center feeder. On ghostly wings, the owl quietly made its way through the trees just before dusk to perch in an oak over the feeder. Motionless except for its swiveling head, the owl patiently peered at the feeder. By this time, the last of the chickadees had fed before going to roost, and the owl was probably waiting for a different sort of "bird food."

The flakes have quit falling for the time being and it won't be long

33

before there will be new messages scrawled across the landscape. Yet the shrew cannot afford to pause. Through blizzard or cold, they persistently continue to write their story between the pages of snow.

# Emptying of the Crow Roosts

Folks up in the northeastern corner of the state are used to seeing the antics of ravens throughout the winter. But when a crow is sighted in February or early March, their hopes rise. The crow does to them what the horned lark does to me, it carries the first banner of a coming spring.

Yet it seems that in farming country, the crow is too often considered a loud, brassy pest, an outcast that eats nothing but forgotten standing corn or flattened, road-killed squirrels and rabbits. Instead of seeing this bird as a master opportunist and survivor, the crow is usually considered one of the bad guys dressed in black.

Though some crows prefer to migrate south where winters are less severe, there are many that tough out the harshest of seasons. During the winter, crows are most social, and they gather in large flocks. At dusk, the scattered daytime flocks all rally back at the favorite nighttime roost. Secure roosts are highly prized and used year after year as long as they are not disturbed.

The sand country, where I live, is home to vigorous patches of sand burrs, mining pocket gophers, and lush stands of red pine, scotch pine, and lesser plantings of spruce.

During the 1950s and 1960s, it seemed that everyone was putting in thousands of evergreens either to raise as Christmas trees or to create shelterbelts. Now many of those seedlings have created stands that support a tall regiment of trees growing so close together that a midday hike under such a grove seems more like an evening encounter. The liberal sprinklings of yellow and orange Amanitas and the gregarious, bronzed slippery jack mushrooms that push up through the duff of shed pine needles in late August grow best in a world of shade and pine-driven acidity.

When winter's wrath covers the sand country, mushrooms are

forgotten and Christmas trees are hauled home from more youthful plantings. It is during winter that the crows will reap the benefits of the thick cover of the overgrown pines.

There are several advantages in sharing a roosting site. Crows are especially wary and nervous, yet they find added security in large flocks. There are twice as many eyes in the flock than there are crows. This makes it especially difficult for a predator to catch the crows off guard.

Another advantage of the communal flock is that it gives the young birds-of-the-year a chance to learn from the older, experienced crows the choice feeding areas and best-protected roosting sites to cope with the likes of winter.

As a teen, I remember an overgrown red pine plantation that lay a little better than a mile north of our place. Though the barren fields surrounding the pine plantation were entrenched in winter, the world underneath the pines portrayed only a dusting of snow. Much of the snow flocked the pines until a stiff wind shook them clean.

I could walk from a blazing countryside of reflected sunlight into the twilight world underneath the ranks of pines. And if I lingered and waited patiently for the rest of the world to darken as the sun set, I could count on seeing flock after flock of crows quietly pass over the pines. Some of the birds would settle in the branches above me and in turn would serve to decoy others. It always seemed so eerie to hear the rustling wings and the occasional squawk in the dark limbs overhead as the crows settled into the roost for the night.

Eventually, I would have to leave. As soon as I moved under the birds, there was a great rush of wings—no caws, only flapping wings as the disturbed birds leapfrogged to a quieter section of the plantation.

Crows best show their suspicious nature during the daylight hours while on the prowl.

Like many of my boyhood chums, I trapped pocket gophers from nearby fields for some extra pocket change. The gopher's long-clawed front feet assured me of two dimes, which meant four packets of baseball cards or two comic books.

As I had no use for the rest of the gophers, I would place them, almost like an offering, out along the windbreak behind our house.

35

By the next morning, the carcasses appeared as if they had been turned inside out by the scavenging crows.

I had read about a particularly wily old crow that seemed smarter than any human in Ernest Thompson Seton's book *Wild Animals I Have Known.* So to me all crows were like that rascal of a crow named Silverspot. At that time, crows were not protected under federal law, so every morning I would take my single-shot .22 rifle and try sneaking up to the pile of dead gophers with the hope of sniping a crow.

Many mornings I crawled through the dew-covered grasses with my knees and elbows picking up their share of "stickers." Slowly, I would inch my way along the windbreak toward the fussing crows. Oh, I got close a couple of times, but somehow they always discovered me and loudly departed for safer hunting grounds. I never did pick off one of those well-fed crows.

I pass a couple favorite crow-roosting pine plantations on my way to work each morning. Some mornings the crows are just leaving as I pass by. At dawn, the large flock seems full of the dickens and ready to take on the world as they scatter over the countryside. The only thing more arrogant than a morning crow is the proud dog strutting home with a newfound ham bone.

On my return home in the late afternoon, the crows are gathering again into their large flock. Though they are still loud, their calls seem less frequent. They even seem slower, appearing tired in flight. Their daily flights may take them miles from the roost in search of food. If food is found, the source is shared.

As March merges into April, the crows will be in smaller bands and sometimes in pairs. Aerial acrobatics and skirmishes with other crows will be more frequent. Soon the birds will be paired off as mates, searching for a nesting site.

When spring starts tearing loose, at about the same time when the redwings are loudly claiming their rights from every cattail slough in the area, the crows will be silent and secretive in their actions. They will have nests and eggs to tend to.

Then the roosts in the pine groves will be fairly empty of crows—a quiet celebration of spring.

# The Special Place

Everyone has a "special place." Sometimes we have several. These are the places we can walk alone and converse with ourselves. Special places can be shared, but they are really meant to visit alone. There is a motherlike quality in a special place, they bring an enfolding comfort.

In my early teens, I found such a spot. It seems that during those fast, confusing years, when the pull of independence is most strong, one needs a special place. My retreat was a tamarack swamp about three-quarters of a mile from our place, just below the pastured woods of my great-grandparents' farm.

Most of the time I had a purpose when I ventured into the swamp.

In early May, I would step lightly along the tiny creek that wound its way east through the swamp. One had to tread carefully over the wet seeps, the gnarled tamarack roots, and the frequent holes where ice-cold water flowed slowly over the peat and under the roots to join the stream. One couldn't be too quiet when there were timid but richly colored brook trout to catch.

There was one memorable spot where the water flowed through a little chute created by an old log lying lengthwise in the middle of the creek. It was a dependable trout lair, where I could float a lively worm down under the mossy log and bank of yellow cowslips. The trout along that log were never big, but they were consistent. Small or not, the brookie's brilliance will forever inspire the artist's eye and sculpt smiles of awe.

In the fall, I spent much of my time racing under the oaks in the nearby pastured woods trying to outrun a fleeing, treetop gray or fox squirrel. If I could get ahead of the bushy-tailed acrobats without stepping into a woodchuck hole, the squirrel would often stop and freeze among the upper limbs. It wasn't the safest way to hunt, but it did produce squirrels for the pan.

I did a lot of running. Consequently, some days I had quite a thirst. A short hike east along the worn cattle trail took me down into the tamarack swamp, where I could drink my fill of the clear, earthborne water. Refreshed, I would move back upland to chase more squirrels.

Whether I was fishing, hunting, or just hiking, there were always a few hefty tamaracks one could sit down and rest against while watching the slow flow of moving water. Water in motion, whether it is inspired by the gradual pull seaward or by the rhythmic wash against a lakeshore, has a hypnotic effect—not unlike the magic of a dancing campfire.

Some days I would hike up to my great-grandparents' farm for a visit. I'll never forget one day when Grandpa Schmidt asked me what I would do if I were down in the swamp tromping around and should happen upon a man's skeleton hanging by its neck from a tree.

Now Grandpa was known for his ability to tell stories, so naturally I continued to listen with a half-believing ear. He proceeded to tell me that many years ago, before he and Grandma had settled here in 1916, three outlaws had taken to the swamp. In pursuit was a posse and the county sheriff. It seems that the ruffians had murdered someone during a holdup. After they were caught, according to Grandpa, "One of 'em was hung on the spot."

I don't remember my reply to his question about finding a skeleton, but it was years later before I learned that the story is based on a true incident having taken place in 1896. One man was shot and killed in the swamp; the leader was tried and hung later, though not in the swamp.

The tamarack swamp held other mysterious qualities. One night nearly twenty-five years ago, on the eve of the trout opener, some buddies and I were camped up in the pastured "squirrel woods."

We had decided to take an evening stroll before hitting the sack. At thirteen or fourteen years of age, a fellow can't expect to crawl into the sleeping bag too early in the evening. It was a dark night. The only place that looked blacker was the tamarack swamp, and we kept our distance from it.

All of a sudden, from within the blackness of the swamp, we heard a shrill, womanlike scream. We stopped in our tracks, not uttering a word. Finally one of the guys whispered that maybe we should think about getting back to the tent to get some sleep.

The rest of us agreed that this was a good idea. Boys need to rest to handle those six- to eight-inch brookies.

Perhaps the shriek had come from a rabbit in the clutches of a predator, or maybe it was one of the many utterances of a barred owl. That night, however, we were convinced that the noisemaker was a bobcat, as they had been known to wander through the area.

Perhaps it was the mysterious ways of the swamp that made it so special to me. At any rate, I recently found myself heading back to the swamp to visit the creek and trees that I hadn't seen in over a dozen years.

As I drove by the farm that my great-grandparents used to live in, I couldn't help but notice that there was now only one apple tree on the hillside above the driveway. At one time there used to be a half-dozen. The old spring house is gone, and the house is sorely in need of a coat of paint.

Had it really been that many years since I passed by here?

I didn't feel right when I parked the car next to a recently cut water ditch. The gash, with its clean-cut vertical sides, was channeling water out of the tamarack swamp. I knew my special place had been violated, yet I had to see what damage had been done.

As I walked under the birch, tamarack, and now-dead elms, I crossed the trails of fox, weasel, squirrel, and even a raccoon who must have found the February thaw irresistible. I passed over the seeps that flowed, inklike, under the mossy tamarack roots en route to the creek.

I stopped momentarily when I heard a great horned owl calling in the distance. Sunset would come in an hour. But over the hoots of the owl were the closer noises of kids playing.

Through the trees, up along my old "squirrel woods," I could make out three houses. And further in, I knew there were more homes.

From where I stood listening, I could see an impressive, three-story tree house ahead of me, next to the creek. How could anyone have the audacity to build such a monstrosity at my special place? To make matters worse, the construction was less than ten feet from the old log that still lay in midstream. The log, a bit less in stature from what it once was, supported a crude bridge made from ax-felled tamaracks.

The largest of the old trees, one that had served as a backrest while I had waited for trout, was still standing. Its trunk was deeply scarred by the steel bites of a hatchet or ax.

The castle of a tree house was solid and well built. Stout tamarack poles were nailed and lashed to trees for the framework. Plywood pieces and scrap lumber and an old canvas tent made up the floors and walls. On the ground were partial rolls of heavy steel mesh, discarded tent poles, and a few pop and beer cans.

I used to pick up the occasional empty can that I found while I wandered through the swamp along the creek. But these few cans seemed insignificant compared to the fort, so I left them.

My first reaction was to tear the structure apart to try and return the setting to the state that I had remembered and cherished. But after a few moments of taking it all in, I realized that this spot is still a special place. Only its charm is now for those youngsters who venture into the swamp—even if they do build castles in the trees. Can I deny the tree-fort builders the joy of watching a stream from up high or the pleasure of watching approaching thunderheads?

With my mind in a turmoil, I moved on. I didn't see the wake of a single trout in the shallow water. In the past, there were always a few trout fleeing for the undercut banks as I patrolled the stream.

Less than 200 yards downstream, I came to the terminus of the small creek. From this point, it had been recently gouged with a dragline in a perfectly straight, sterile line continuing east with another lateral ditch flowing perpendicular due north towards my parked car.

I had seen enough. Even the calling of the barred owl from deeper in the swamp was tarnished by the giant black furrow and the equally black clouds swirling in my mind. Though I was carrying a camera and tripod, I didn't shoot a single shot. The pictures I had wanted are still in my mind and are nearly twenty years old.

I had planned on staying in the swamp until sunset, but I left early, following the swath and ditch cut through the bulldozed piece of swamp back to the car. Though some of the tamaracks and birch still stand, I know those on this forty will be removed so that the underlying peat land can be put into sod. After all, a tamarack swamp does little to increase the local tax base. With the ever-increasing demand for instant grassed yards and turf-covered roadsides, this and other tamarack swamps are in jeopardy.

We can create a sod field, but can we take that sod field and create a lowly tamarack swamp with a clear, cold creek from which comes the green of February watercress, the lively colors of a brook trout, a place where bobcats prowl, boys dream, and the ghost of a hanged man haunts?

I drove home more slowly than I had come. Selfish or not, I had lost part of my soul—a part that cannot be regained. Knowing that hurt. But worst of all is knowing that I will not return.

# MARCH

# Into March Like a Coon

Every year at about this time, certain events forecast the end of winter. The icicles start singing their swan song and snow fleas journey up through the blanket of ice crystals to shadow the snow blanket like specks of dirt. Now the sun feels wonderfully hot as its light is reflected off the snow onto my pale face.

Accompanying the typical winter array of deer, squirrel, mouse, and rabbit tracks are the more recent meanderings of raccoon. It seems more apt in our region to say that March comes in like a raccoon instead of the foreign "king of the beasts." The arrival of raccoon tracks on the scene is nearly as reliable as the upcoming equinox, which promises to erase all winter signs.

Most February fox tracks are in pairs, breeding pairs. On the other hand, it seems that the raccoon trails I now follow are mainly solo animals. Male raccoons tend to spend the winter alone, while adult females and young are gregarious denners.

The loping coon tracks fall into pairs. Typical of tree dwellers, like squirrels, the coon's front feet fall next to each other, rather than stagger.

The trail that weaves aimlessly and alone through the woods most likely belongs to an adult male. As the days are growing longer and warmer, his passion is likewise warming. What appears to be a haphazard trail is an intent male in search of a receptive female. The males, or boars, have been on the move, and in the past two weeks, I have stopped to look over two large road-killed raccoons. Both were males. This time of the year the amorous boars may roam up to five miles in seeking mates.

Even though March is known for its final grasps at winter in the

45

form of blizzards, the raccoon's breeding season becomes foremost. Even a snowstorm cannot cool the roaming desires of a boar raccoon.

I remember after one particularly heavy late winter snowfall when I found a fresh raccoon track. In snowshoes I was able to move through the snow with greater ease than the shorter-legged raccoon. The animal I followed had forged a troughlike track. The plowed trail ended at the base of a large white oak. My eyes followed the trunk upward to an old, healed-over injury on the tree. Now a dark hollow was left, and it betrayed the coon's hideout. Since that winter, I have found similar trails under that same tree.

One fine March day, when the snow was more slush than crystalline, I followed another trail that led up to a solid red oak. I circled the tree looking for a hollow; there was none. My gaze followed each large branch from the trunk to its tip. All I could see was an old, bulky squirrel nest.

A breeze stirred, and from the nest I saw a slight flicker of movement. A wisp of brown fur quivered. I backed up to get a better angle on the tree, and only then did I spy a large raccoon curled up in the old nest basking in the sun, a picture of contentment. I can well imagine that winter could get real long curled inside of a hollow tree.

Sixty-three days after the business of breeding and late winter roaming is finished, there will be new litters of raccoons scattered in hollow trees across the countryside.

It was such a hollow red oak that I climbed many Mays ago as a kid. I was in a hurry, looking for a hiding spot because I knew the chum on the ground counted entirely too fast when he was the searcher in a round of hide-and-seek.

As I climbed higher into the tree, I noticed that the upper third of the tree's main trunk had been sheared long ago, leaving a hollow "crow's nest" sort of hiding place.

Excited at my find, I started to scurry into the hollowed trunk when I heard a growl under me. Somehow dark holes and unseen growls from within have a distinct way of halting any further exploring. I peered over the edge of the opening, and when my eyes finally adjusted to the dim light, I could make out the she-raccoon and her four little ones.

Hide-and-seek was quickly forgotten, and I relinquished my

prize hiding spot as I led the rest of the gang over to the tree for a peek. Right away, we started making plans on how to catch one of the little coons.

We were all pretty excited about the prospect of a pet raccoon. I wanted to live the experience found in reading Sterling North's fine book *Rascal,* a tale of a growing boy and a faster growing raccoon.

We waited two weeks or so for the little ones to grow larger. Then one day I found myself straddling a limb as I worked out toward one of the little ones. The mother wasn't around, and the other litter mates were in the security of the hollow.

I had a long-handled rake that was to be used as a prod to push the coon out of the tree. Down below, directly under my coon, my cohorts grasped the four corners of a blanket to catch the falling raccoon.

I learned that day that the coon's five toes on each foot are not only extremely sensitive in searching out a hidden crayfish or frog, but they can cling tighter than a tick. We left the tree and the four young boarders. Within days they were all gone. There would be no Rascal II nor would there be a secret hiding place.

I find these last weeks of winter pleasant. Thoughts of spring become more real, the breezes warmer, and the sun shines longer each day. Though I may find these days far easier to bear than January's short cold days, they are the toughest for the raccoon.

Layers of autumn-acquired fat may be burned off, or nearly so, and breeding activity only hastens the fuel loss. With little food available, raccoons become more bold in their scavenging. Ill-fitting garbage can covers, bird feeders, or the dog's food dish are considered open invitations for much-needed nourishment.

For some 30 million years, these black-masked marauders of the night have successfully passed the months of winter. They seem to thrive all the better around people, as they are nearly as adaptable to change as we are.

This is one animal that I am confident will be around for a long time. I know I can depend on finding the late winter tracks of raccoon in future years when my children are old enough to use snowshoes. On such hikes, I hope that they learn to appreciate the falling away of winter and the ways of the raccoon.

And who knows, with luck my kids might find a secret hiding spot in an old oak that will be a secret for only a brief moment.

# Roadside Entertainment

Like most folks, my day begins with routine. After waking up and shuffling downstairs, I build a fire in the kitchen stove to take off the chill and then take about 10 minutes to down a glass of juice, a piece of toast, and a bowl of hot or cold cereal. Then it is on to the bathroom to remove stubble and plaque before heading out to the car.

Even my daily trek over township, county, and state roads, taking me to the routine of earning my "bread and butter," can become monotonous. To make the drive less tedious, I watch at familiar locations for the predictable, the routine.

For example, not far from my home, as I round a curve and head into the awakening sun, I can count on seeing a haphazard flock of crows rising from their evening roost in a long-forgotten stand of red pines.

Their flight is strong and fresh. They appear to have far more vigor and enthusiasm in starting out for their daily tasks than I do. But then I would venture to say that I, too, might display more spunk early in the morning if I had the morning view of a sassy crow. Straight ribbons of asphalt and gravel can be tiring routes of travel.

Further down the road, I pass an unpicked cornfield, with its ranks of dried cornstalks appearing tattered and worn after battling with winter's winds and snows. On a regular basis, there are crows around this particular field. For what has been the farmer's bad luck in getting in his crop has been the crow's good fortune.

Along the fence line of this cornfield is a lone, leafless burr oak. If the crows are breakfasting on the corn, there are always one or two crows on the alert, scouting from the very top of the tree. More often than not, one of the crows is leaning forward and bobbing up and down as it throws its whole body into its racous morning message. There is nothing discreet or subtle about a new-day crow.

It is only later, on my return trip home in late afternoon, that the cornfield is empty. Scattered here and there across the sky are the seemingly slower flying crows returning to their roosts.

Near the crow's cornfield is a strip of oak woods on either side of the road. At this time of the year, when spring is overcoming winter, I have to pay close attention when approaching the bisected woods, for it is a favorite crossing for squirrels. This is the time of the year when squirrels are chasing each other, caught up in the frenzy of finding a mate and keeping out the competition, who share similar interests.

One stretch of my daily commute crosses a seemingly barren area with open snow-covered fields flanking both sides of the road. All winter, the county plows, with some help from northwest winds, have kept the higher road and its shoulders free of snow.

A few weeks ago, I noticed the first of the horned larks along this stretch of road. These small, bold birds advance northward well before winter melts. I can count on seeing larks along this same stretch every year in mid-February.

Horned larks are especially fond of the open places where the winds keep the roadsides free of snow, exposing the promise of last year's grass and weed seeds. Already, some of the ridges and knobs in fields and pastures have bare tops melted under the heat of a March sun, and my predictable larks are becoming unpredictable as they find these new treasures of seeds.

For nearly two weeks, my passing car has been disturbing a flock of redpolls as they likewise seek the nourishment of tiny roadside seeds. I see the flock of 100 or so birds every morning along the same section of road. As I approach them, they rise, splitting into two groups that flurry away to either side of the road. For a moment, as I pass the birds, I feel like the "returning hero" in my own parade, with the sky full of twisting and turning redpolls instead of confetti.

I may as well enjoy my make-believe parade, for soon the redpolls will be burning the fuel they acquired along the county road as they follow winter in its retreat northward. Only when the tiny finches reach the subarctic country of dwarfed trees and tundra will they settle down to the business of producing more redpolls.

Earlier this winter, I used to pass a young woman every day who drove well under the speed limit. It was just as well that she dawdled, for she was intent on putting on her fresh face for the day.

Leaning to her right with her face pressed close to the rearview mirror, she was always doing eye artwork with a mascara pencil or brushing something onto her eyelids. Every time I saw her, she wore a crown of rollers, but I never passed her when she was working on her hair—apparently that came later. Needless to say, I tried to pass her as quickly as possible to put some distance between us. I never saw a dent in her car either.

Then there was the man I used to meet who was often taking off his face. At least that is what would happen to me if I tried shaving while driving.

Once I saw the same fellow lathering up his teeth with a toothbrush. I suppose one advantage of taking care of your hygiene in the car is that one doesn't have to contend with morning battles for time in the bathroom.

I'll admit that I have a reputation for roaming eyes as I'm driving, and yes, I did go in the ditch once to take on some popples—the third one stopped me. But I will not get dressed or cleaned up while driving.

Things quiet down when I pull off the busy county road and drive the last mile and a half to the nature center on a gravel road.

There used to be a German shepherd who would hide under a mailbox and streak out after my car as I passed him. We became like friends, and I would try different tricks—like slowing down or speeding up to confuse him. Such tactics only seemed to excite him all the more.

Unfortunately, the owner of the mailbox moved, and the dog went with him. Now that stretch is pretty blasé, far too routine.

One could write reams about our patterned lives and how certain events come and go like clockwork. But at the moment, my eyes feel heavy, and I think I'll forget the ten o'clock news.

I've got to get my rest, for I have to be all smiles when I parade through the whirling and swirling flocks of redpolls in the morning as I drive to work.

# The Otter Lesson

The newly fallen snow had given March a fresh face, and once again the wanderings of deer and fox were betrayed by their tracks through woods and field. It seemed the snowfall had especially inspired the mink and raccoon, for their tracks were everywhere.

Though the predictions of meteorologists have been far from springlike, I know when I discover raccoon tracks leading to and from a hollowed antique oak that spring is close at hand.

But it was another track that caught my eye recently. The track, twice the size of a fox track, loped up a wooded hill, and on reaching the top, it "tobogganed" in a gentle curve down the back side.

There was no mistaking the track maker being anything other than an otter.

It's not unusual for another member of the weasel family, the mink, to occasionally slide on its belly, but the slide mark is much narrower than the broad ribbon left by the otter.

Even on level ground the otter prefers to slide every so often as it lopes along. Such a means of travel seems more play than work. Perhaps the real value is that gliding over the snow is more fuel efficient. Such a trail is easy to identify in its distinct Morse code messages of dot-dash-dot.

With the firm crust under the thin layer of fresh snow, it is easier for this otter to slide more often than lope. As it slid along, it would periodically give itself a scooterlike push with one of its webbed hind feet.

Only once before had I seen otter tracks in these woods. It seemed a bit unusual to find them so far from a river or creek without the promise of open water and fish. By late winter, the otter is feeling the urge to find a mate. At this time the male sometimes travels far overland in search of a receptive female.

Though the winter signature of the otter is among the most eloquent, it is in the water that the animal is pure grace. This pursuer of fish can swim along the water's surface, then slip silently underwater in a serpentine manner that seems more porpoise than quadruped.

I recall sitting with my wife, Susan, among some shoreline

boulders along a small lake in the northern canoe country. The magic of twilight was just spreading over the forest and water. The only disturbances over the mirrorlike water were the erratic paths of tiny aquatic insects. Other than the insect's zigs and zags, the moment was frozen.

Suddenly they were there. Materializing directly in front of us was a pair of otters. It was as if they had just risen from the lake's depths. Quietly, the animals swam along the shoreline, giving rise to two spreading, V-shaped wakes. Unaware of us, they dove and surfaced in near perfect unison. Their movements and timing were so fluid that it was truly poetry in motion.

As they surfaced, we could hear the light blow of their exhalations. Louder was the noise of eating a crunchy catch. In the fading light, I glimpsed the jointed leg and pincer of a crayfish. The crunching was the hard exoskeleton of the crayfish giving way to the powerful jaws of the otter.

The pair of otters worked on down the shoreline in tandem silence as we silently exited in the opposite direction for our camp before darkness set in.

Perhaps no animal appears more playful than the otter. Their sliding mode of travel makes it easy for us to assume that their life is a merry one. It is difficult not to label these animals as playful. Yet does a wild animal truly play?

There are those biologists who scoff at such ideas, claiming that any such thoughts are too "Disneyish." Play is a human quality, and in the eyes of a rigid scientist, attributing human actions to wild animals is taboo.

If play is the opposite of work, we need to determine what an otter considers work. Work is when the need for food is great. Caring for young and searching for a mate followed by the intensity of courtship are all aspects of work. Work is continually being alert for the unknown moment when a predator might appear. Indeed recreation is a liberty that we humans take for granted.

I suspect the hardest days of an animal's work might be in winter, when the burning of calories is greatest. A season of ice, fewer fishing holes, and deep snow can make it a season of work. Later, when the spring sun melts the ice and hunting waters are more accessible, maybe then the otter has a moment to frolic.

Perhaps otter play has value. After all, don't the fox pup or bobcat kitten better develop their reflexes, muscle tone, and stalking skills by playing with their littermates? Beaver kits often play a game of tag in their swimming antics. Play, among these animals, is an easygoing preparation and practice for survival.

In the days of the great buffalo herds, plains Indian boys were encouraged to play games of shooting their small bows and arrows. To increase their speed, quickness, and stamina, the boys would chase butterflies on the wing. Such playing was necessary to pass the trials of manhood.

Perhaps the otter is also in constant need of perfecting its skills by partaking in a moment of play. Perhaps what we perceive as play is actually work.

An otter taught me a lesson one day years ago. I was in college at the time, and like most students, I found it necessary to do some occasional serious studying. On a warm, late April day, I had decided to take my dog, Nibs, for a day of studying down along the river bottoms where Goose Creek empties into the St. Croix River. I also knew that I could find great patches of trilliums and dog's-tooth violets near my study site.

I had settled down with my back against an oak and my head buried in a book. Nibs, being more restless, began her own studying. Her subject matter was far more interesting than mine. She was investigating the pages at the river's edge for anything that might crawl, swim, or jump.

I had barely started when Nibs began making a commotion down by the water. I looked up to find the object of her distress—an otter treading water, peering most curiously at us.

We were close enough to easily view the long, stiff whiskers growing out from its stubby snout. It is believed that the sensitive whiskers help the otter locate prey such as bottom-dwelling crayfish in dark or murky waters. The stubby snout is also used for dislodging rocks in the search for a hiding crayfish.

The head seemed merely an extension of the thick neck. Back and forth, the otter swam in front of us. Occasionally, it would give a little bark or a chirring call.

53

The dog and I followed the otter along the grassy bank of the river. It was hard to say who was the more amused, the otter or the young man and his dog.

There is a time when book learnin' falls short. So the texts and paperwork were set aside under the leafing oak on that fine April day. Like I say, there is value in the motions of play.

# The Winds of March

March is an in-between month.

Winter begrudgingly gives way to the warmth of spring. In these parts, it is generally a wet, sloppy, dirty-snow month—a time of puddle jumping and wet shoes.

On approaching a slushy puddle, you size it up, rock back and forth a couple times, and spring across, only to come up a few inches short of a dry landing. A subtle reminder that not only are cold puddles the norm, but that another year has passed and our egos are perhaps greater than our puddle-jumping abilities.

On a recent sunny day, I was reminded of another March signal— strong winds. After all, isn't a high-flying kite synonymous with March?

We learned in January that strong winds can disrupt daily activities, yet we usually pay less attention to forecasts foretelling winds than those warning of rain or snow. To complicate matters, successful forecasting of winds is difficult.

Early folklore suggested a means of foretelling windy weather: "When hogs are restless, make loud noises, move their heads in spasmodic ways, it is a sign of high winds."

After a long winter, cattlemen like to report that their herd "has wintered well." After the onslaught of winter feasts and the months of inactive long nights, I likewise have wintered well. As the days lengthen and temperatures climb, a restless feeling and a tinge of guilt come over me. It is time to maintain a more Spartan running schedule to dislodge the fruits of winter and to ready myself for the pace of summer.

On this particularly windy day, I had halfheartedly ventured out for my four-mile run, feeling it was my duty. As I turned out of the driveway, I fairly flew down the muddy road, with the wind at my heels. It seemed effortless. Just keep lifting the legs and let the wind carry me along.

I contemplated going further on this day, since it seemed so effortless. But then I turned the corner and my boost was finished. Now the wind tried its best to push me into the ditch.

At first it didn't seem so bad, but after a roaring gust almost tripped me, I realized that I had to run with a pronounced sideways lean to offset the wind. I kept going in this awkward manner, convincing myself that the discomfort was worth the effort.

Up ahead of me two boys were playing on a shrinking snow pile. They scrambled up to the top and spread their arms to embrace the wind. Fully exposed to the wind's blast, they stood precariously perched atop the peak for only a moment before they were blown off balance and sent tumbling down the snowpile.

For youngsters, the wind is fun and gay—just another energetic playmate. Kites, soapy bubbles, helium-filled balloons, and soaring gliders would be far less exciting without the wind.

Only as we grow older and lose some of our imagination and satisfaction with the simple things does the wind become a more ominous force to deal with. Perhaps if I owned a sailboat I could greater appreciate this quiet power.

Winds would not exist without the sun. They are born as a result of the uneven heating of the earth's surface. And without a rotating earth, our winds would all flow from the equator northward to the Arctic and then the cooled air would flow back southward in a circular manner. Winds would be entirely too predictable. A global sort of tug of war, north against the south.

As a result of the earth spinning on its axis, the winds in the northern hemisphere generally move west to east.

Winds change directions as they move from an area of high pressure to an area of low pressure. If there are obstacles such as trees, mountains, or buildings in the wind's path, a turbulence is created.

On I ran. Then I felt the slight sting of a tiny grain of sand against my cheek. The first sting was followed by several more, and I was reminded of the cutting, tearing power of wind.

Every year approximately 48 million tons of Minnesota topsoil is carried away by the wind. Topsoil is the rich layer of dirt that is responsible for a region's fertility and productivity. It doesn't take a mathematical genius to figure out that the wind is winning the battle when one considers that it takes about 1,000 years to build one inch of topsoil.

In some regions, modern farming practices have been an accomplice in this thievery. Windbreaks, once planted to protect croplands from soil losses, are now an obstacle to those farmers who irrigate their fields with sweeping irrigation systems.

Other farmers find that the shelterbelt of trees is a nuisance when driving their huge rigs with their eight-bottom plows. To make maneuvering easier and to put more land into production, the answer is simple: remove the trees. Ironically, the gain may be a long-term loss when one considers the loss of topsoil.

Those regions that are snow-free during the winter are losing their topsoil faster than those fields in the upper midwest where snow lingers to help hold down the soil.

Not all the windbreaks are gone, in fact Minnesota still plants more than most states.

It is such a windbreak, one of red pines, that runs parallel to the road where I ran. For a couple of minutes, a little better than a quarter of a mile, my cheek is spared the peppering sands. Rather than run a circular route, I turned around and headed back the same way I had just come. Only now I had to lean into the wind with my other side. My left cheek felt the stings of airborne sand grains.

As I ran, I noticed a slight movement on the exposed road shoulder. When I drew closer, several horned larks reluctantly flew up into the teeth of the wind. The early spring migrants struggled as they rode up against the wind before suddenly dipping low to the ground and rising again to slowly circle back to the patch of grass I had shagged them from.

My respect for the stamina and determination of all migrating birds was greatly reinforced as I moved steadily on. Another surging gust disrupted my pace and caused me to stagger in my stride.

As I rounded the last corner for the final leg of my run, my forward progress was nearly brought to a standstill. I gritted my teeth, lowered my head, and leaned forward into the blast. It took more effort to cover the last quarter mile than the rest of the run.

I wondered if I would ever reach our mailbox. Finally, I finished. As I walked towards the house to get out of the wind, I thought I heard a different noise carried in on the wind. I paused, yes, there it was again—the sound of squealing hogs coming from the neighbors to the west.

# Two Notes of Spring

The snow has been most reluctant to leave this year, and on the eve before the celebrated celestial event we know as the vernal equinox, it appears more winter than spring. With the days becoming more tempered, approaching the phenomenon we call spring, there are, regardless of the snow cover, those indicators that forecast winter's doom.

Last Sunday afternoon, we had intended to walk to some neighbors who live about a mile and a half from our house. Three-year-old daughter, Britta, was proud of the two-mile hike she had taken the day before with her mother, and she now assured me that she could make the round trip on this day.

However, I had forgotten how slow one walks when their legs are barely sixteen inches long. Then there were the rocks that she found on the shoulder of the road. There were smooth ones, rough ones, white ones, and speckled ones, but most were the nondescript rock-gray type. At any rate, none could be tossed aside, they were handed to me for safekeeping in my pockets.

An hour passed and we were still snailing along the road, barely halfway to our destination. It was obvious that we would have to visit our neighbors on another day when we had more time or carried a picnic lunch and maybe a sleeping bag.

Though the sun was shining, the breeze was persistent and chilly. As we passed a low area of popple, dogwood, and willow, we kept our eyes tuned in for pussy willows. These slender stems, adorned with fuzzy, silver willow flowers, were needed to make an Easter tree from which to hang recently dyed and blown-out eggs.

It hardly seemed possible that we are approaching the celebrated paschal event of Easter when snow still covers the fields and woods.

We had given up our goal and were well on our way back. We found no pussy willows, though my pockets were heavy with small stone treasures. By this time, the mystique of the rocks was wearing thin, and it was apparent that a pair of sixteen-inch legs were getting weary.

Then I heard it. From high overhead came a drawn-out call of two high-pitched notes. I snapped my head upward and searched the skies for a fast-flying, slender bird that had in a single call assured me that pussy willows or not, winter is nearly done in. Hearing the first *kill -deee* of the season is a pronouncement of spring.

We paused for a moment but never heard this bold shorebird, the killdeer, again. The call had been a long trailing call, moving north, where snows lay deeper than they do around our place.

There is no fooling a killdeer. Testimony to that fact can best be witnessed when approaching a May killdeer. Ever alert, this handsome bird, wearing its two, broad black bands across its white breast, is nearly invisible if it remains still on its obscure ground nest. Early biologists postulated that the twin bands help to break the bird's outline and pattern, making it less obvious.

However, the bird is probably best known for its dramatics if you or a potential predator approaches too close to the nest. The bird stoops low to the ground, hurries away from the nest, then stops, stands erect, and gives a call. If you continue to move closer to the nest, the bird may run back toward you, drop its wing, and spread and drop its tail feathers in a flash of sudden ochre as if to exclaim a frantic, "Here I am, come and get this poor crippled bird instead of a few little eggs."

The bird's intentions are to lead the intruder a safe distance from the nest before springing haughtily into the air.

And now, after hearing the lone call of the killdeer, I was hoping there would be no fooling this one and that its voice was truly forecasting a coming spring.

We finally made it back to our driveway. Even our slower moving pacer, Britta, found new life as she started chattering about the promise of a pizza. As for me, I felt a renewed energy as well, given in a single killdeer call.

With that we moved up the driveway, and I discreetly emptied my pockets, dropping the load into newborn potholes.

APRIL

# Passing of Winter's Dream

It hardly seems fair that we have to wait so long for something we want and then when it finally comes, its gone. Such is the way of spring's first calling.

Winter has a way of holding us down and restraining our roaming spirits—it gives us time to reflect and dream of past and future days afield. One of those dreams is most pleasant—for lack of a better title, I'll call it spring.

According to the calendar, spring begins with the vernal equinox, just after mid-March, and ends with the summer solstice in June. Those dates are fine for those who like to keep schedules, but I for one find schedules hard to keep, so I often disregard them.

Spring is a phenomenon that is not as predictable as an hour and a date. Some folks realize spring's certainty when the creeks and rivers run swollen with winter's tears. Others look for signs of spring's return in the form of a solitary red-winged blackbird perched on a pussy willow at the frozen marsh's edge. Or maybe the caller is a robin, exploring, as robins do, a patch of exposed yard.

Spring speaks in many ways—some loud and others nearly silent. It is a declaration. Spring peepers, a drumming grouse, a winnowing snipe, and the gabble of geese speak the same urgent language, and all are indifferent to calendars. The soft notes of the bluebird that sits on my mailbox have the same meaning as the brown thrasher's, who repeats his every note from atop the oak at the opposite end of the driveway.

Spring is an essence that can be found floating in the air. Some, however, may argue that the thawed manure spread on April's fields and gardens is anything but fragrant. I'm not at all ashamed to admit that I enjoy drawing in a full breath of the heady aroma. As those fields are turned over, there is a smell of fresh earth, and we dream of what will be born from it.

Even the smells of a surprised skunk can be pleasant after a long winter when smells, like the rest of the countryside, are frozen. But if I could bottle spring and splash it on my face, it would be the sweetness of wild plum, with a hint of lilac.

Spring is fishing on a sunny day and not really caring if you catch anything. One doesn't even need bait to make the outing a success.

Spring is people out walking with nowhere in particular to go and no deadline to get there.

It's not easy pinpointing a single element that makes spring what it is, but if I were pressed, I would say that color best carries the message of the new season. Winter, in its colors of black, white, and the deep blue of cold shadows, has its own unique beauty, but when a plant's leaf buds burst open and that first pale or golden green emerges, we know the dream of renewal has returned. Admittedly, I pause to look at the butter yellow blossoms of the creekside cowslips, the robin's-egg blues of the hepatica, and the snow-white petals of trilliums and bloodroot. But none draw me to spring as well as the pastel greens.

It seems ludicrous to try and paint the many soft shades of green in these very words. Artists, likewise, have and always will in their frustrations try to capture the hues of April and May. Words and paints are not among natures props.

Spring's vision is short, however. Soon the greens of the oaks, birch, popple, and others will become more heavily bodied. Like a summer tan, plant's dominant pigment, chlorophyll, becomes more intense and dark in a leaf. Summer's long days and heat bring a sameness to the foliage. Green is green, and there are few variations. Soon the grass line will hardly be distinguishable from the thickets, saplings, and trees.

The summer woods will close up in a screen of green, and its secrets will be known only to those who venture through the lush wall and past the guardian mosquitoes.

With May only days away, I fear the end of my spring is near. Dreams in sleep, they say, take place in seconds or fractions thereof.

So it is with winter's dream—spring.

# So It Goes with Trees and People

"I hated to cut it down . . . it was a real landmark."

In his lilting, Scandinavian brogue, those words were spoken with both reverence and a hint of sadness by Karl Johnson, as he looked over the downed, giant elm. At nearly 67 years, Karl remembers that even as a youngster, the tree was a grand specimen.

When Karl's father, Elof, first settled and built on the north shore of Coleen Lake, just south of Shafer, the tree was larger than most others in the area.

Describing the tree as large isn't enough, it was gigantic. Three grown men, holding hands, had to stretch to reach around the tree's circumference. I walked alongside the massive, leveled trunk and fifteen feet above the cut, even when stretched on my tiptoes, I could not see over the wall of elm.

Stilled on the ground, its length of approximately 80 feet would no longer be subject to the harassment of future storms and blows.

Like so many elms in the region, this one started producing yellow leaves during midsummer. Yellow is usually reserved for the painting of an autumn elm. A summer-yellow elm leaf is a sign of stress—a stress often brought on by Dutch elm disease.

The dreaded elm disease was not a threat for most of this old tree's life. It was not until the early 1930s that the first fungus-caused disease defected to North America. The fungus had been accidently introduced from Europe and has since been slowly claiming the elms. Elm bark beetles have innocently carried the disease across the landscape from elm to elm.

On peeling back some of the elm's bark, we could see the delicately carved galleries where the bark beetle larvae prospered. Their erratic tunneling resembled spokes radiating out from an elongated hub. In another year, great sheets of elm bark would have peeled away and a host of other insects would have made their way into the wood.

It is in such elms in the area that the pileated woodpeckers have

65

been busy boring and sculpting in their search for a meal. What has been a downfall for the elms has become a windfall for the pileated and others of its kind.

Thousands of elms have died or are in the process of dying in this part of the country. But the big tree at the Johnson place was different because it could be classified as a landmark. To reach landmark status, the object must catch the eye. High-steepled churches, mountain peaks, water towers, grain elevators, and trees are often considered such prominent and obvious features.

The elm on the Johnson farm grew alone out at the tip of a narrow, steep-sided point that slopes out into small Coleen Lake. Competition for sunlight from neighboring trees is certainly limited on such a spit of land. The heavy clay soil anchored the roots firmly. Even during the dry dry years of the 1930s, its roots were able to draw up needed moisture from the deep lake to maintain growth.

The elm had to be strong to withstand many years of wrenching storms that attempted to strip it of its limbs and pull it from the exposed point of land. Yet it never lost a major limb, even after its high-reaching branches attracted the power of a lightening bolt.

Not only was the tree a survivor, it was a shelter. Even now the weathered oriole nest is still obvious among the naked, drooping branchlets. How many previous generations of orioles had woven their pouchlike nests from the reaching limbs overlooking the quiet lake?

Through the years, the tall tree had provided a fine vantage point for many hawks. At night, one could often stand out in the farmyard at dusk and spot the silhouette of a horned owl perched high in the tree as it scanned the shoreline for an inquisitive mouse or a careless muskrat.

When Karl's father farmed the area, cattle pastured under the tree. From its shade, they could drink from the lake's water or lie contentedly chewing their cuds on the hottest of summer days.

Karl remembers that he and his eleven brothers and sisters all learned to swim under the old elm. He smiled as he recalled standing out of sight behind the wide tree trunk with some of his brothers as they quickly stripped off their clothes and went into the lake. His folks, he remembers were not happy about such "indecent swimming."

Later in life, Karl learned that even some of the neighbors used to come down through the pasture and use the same screening tree trunk for their swim. Indeed, the tree had often known the fun and energy of youth under its canopy.

For years now, the few cattle that Karl tends have not been allowed to graze under the tree. Karl doesn't want them messing up this favorite picnicking and swimming spot. The Johnson grand-children and great-grandchild have also come to know the shade and joy of the lake point.

It had taken Karl only fifteen minutes to drop the tree with his chain saw. He had equipped his saw with a new three-foot bar and sharp chain to tackle the monarch. Karl admitted his relief that he didn't have to pull on a crosscut saw to drop the giant tree. He had done enough of that years ago.

Karl's calloused hand brushed off the sawdust from the stump tabletop to better read the tree's past. Our eyes scanned the broad surface of growth rings before pausing at the center—the first years of the tree's life. Here, the layers of sapwood were broad between the annual rings—evidence that the first years had been vigorous ones of rapid growth. As we passed over the years, moving from the tree's center to the outer layer of bark, the rings eventually closed in tighter and tighter to one another. Even trees are not immune to the inevitable aging process.

We tried counting the rings and finally agreed that the tree had first leafed out around the period when our forefathers were draw-ing up a controversial Declaration of Independence for a new nation some 200 years ago.

I questioned our counting, not thinking it was possible that an elm could live so long. Several weeks later, I consulted with a profes-sional forester, well-versed in dendrology—the study of trees. He said that certainly such an elm would be a rare plant but that they have the potential to flourish for a couple of centuries.

I wondered to myself how the elm had come to know this point of land. Perhaps it had come from an elm growing across the narrow lake. During late spring, the thin flat elm seeds ripen and are taken by a gust of wind and spread across the countryside. The point on the small lake became a nursery for one such seed.

Cutting the tree was not easy for Karl. It had become a symbol of past memories. It was in a very real sense a part of the family. We stood at the edge of the thawing shoreline, and looking east over the downed tree, Karl quietly remarked to no one in particular, "The sun rises and the sun sets . . . and so it goes with trees and people."

Moments later, Karl was wondering if he should plant a maple or ash to replace the cut elm. There are picnics and days of swimming still to be had by future generations of Johnsons.

But the fallen elm will yet be enjoyed by Karl, for he is intending to cut what he can into firewood to mix with his oak supply to heat his house. Next winter, the elm-fueled fire will draw well on the first cold days of winter.

As the smoke from the giant elm billows from the chimney, it may be carried by winter winds sweeping down from the northwest. Swept across the yard, the smoke will carry over the barn and frozen, lumpy barnyard before making its way down the snow-covered slope along the narrow point out over a solitary broad stump.

Perhaps the wisps of smoke will mingle among the branches of a maple or ash sapling that is trying its best to become a landmark.

**UPDATE:** It was a bitter cold February evening when I last talked with Karl. We talked about the cold winds and the virtues of wood heat. At seventy-one years now, Karl still takes pride in the fact that he puts up his own wood for heating his home. Without hesitation, he will be the first to tell you that "you get a more even heat in burning wood."

I asked him about his downed elm. His reply was to the point, "Burnt on it for two winters, finished it up last winter."

We talked of that elm and he told me about the chore it was to cut the trunk into stove wood. In order to split the base section that measured six feet across, he had to take his saw and cut the chunk into pie-shaped pieces before splitting.

In recalling the splitting job, Karl spoke with a proud sense of accomplishment, "I got seventy-two pieces of stove wood from that one chunk—not kindlin' wood either, but wood for the furnace. I counted every one of 'em."

When asked about the old stump, Karl told me that the middle of the stump had some rot, so he dug out the loose, punky wood until he had an opening of about two feet across. "Then," he said, "I planted a little hard maple right in the middle of the stump."

Maples aren't known for their tall stature. Instead, their round fullness becomes an autumn beacon of fiery orange. I suspect someday Coleen Lake, just north of Shafer, will have its own lighthouse of sorts, when that tree glows every October.

And you wait and see, people will talk about it and remember it, making it worthy of a landmark.

# Ice-Out

It's like waiting for expected company. They are a little late, and for once you are ready. You find yourself regularly looking out either the living room, bedroom, or bathroom window—the window that gives you the best view of the road to forewarn you of the late caller.

Or maybe it's watching for the mailman every day to deliver a long awaited package that is already several days overdue.

For some people, an April waiting means daily checking a special patch of soggy earth for the perennial explosion of tartness that comes bursting from the rhubarb patch.

We all make at least a mental note when we spot a long-absent flash of red that signals the first robin of spring. Or maybe the note is made when we hear the first trills of the frogs. Both of these signs have been traditional harbingers of spring.

In these parts, April brings another rite of spring that will be worthy of mentioning or noting on a daily basis. It comes in a brief question: "Is the ice off yet?" Whether or not there are robins, frogs, or rhubarb, it seems that spring really isn't spring until the last vestiges of winter disappear.

When the smudge of dirty gray or blackened ice is finally gone from the lake, folks become more serious in their talk of summer. Winter's epitaph can be found written in fresh rows of planted peas, radishes, and spuds, in patches of white-petaled trilliums, or at the end of a fishing pole on a day when dandelions wear their butter well.

For those who view lakes only as playgrounds, whose waters are meant to be planed over in the summer or driven on in the winter, now is a quiet time. The lakes are seemingly empty and silent.

The rotting, graying surface of the lakes belongs to the crows now. Singly, in pairs, or in small scattered groups, these black scavengers walk slowly over the ice in hopes of finding a dead fish or minnow that was left by a winter fisherman or a fish that was unable to find a sufficient breath in late winter's stagnant waters.

Occasionally, a bald eagle will pause during migration and stroll among the crows on the rotting ice. Such a regal bird seems out of place among scavengers, yet the raptor is more akin to scavenging than hunting.

As the lake surface darkens under the spring sun, one can find a ribbon of open water surrounding the lake. Water is slow to heat, a fact most can attest to when watching a kettle full of water placed over a burner. The land mass that encircles the lake does a far better job in retaining the April sun's heat.

Eventually, the warmer shoreline starts melting the lake's edge, leaving an ice-free moat. Only the most ardent of ice fishermen will don hip boots or waders to ford the moat to the lake's ice pack. Eventually, the channel will become too wide and the lake ice too rotted, even for the geared fisherman. And for a period each spring, the ring of water effectively prevents the invasion of those of us who enjoy the lake's company.

Those who live within sight of a lake or pond will find themselves pausing each morning to see how much of the lake is unveiled. Occasionally, there is a step back into winter, when a night wind pushes the floating raft of ice over what was open water the day before. On such days, one can listen to the lake's musical tinkle as spring's breezes put the slender pencils of ice into motion and they jostle against each other. This is winter's swan song on the lake, and usually within a few days, the wash of waves can be heard.

Not waiting for winter's last throes are the flocks of ducks or the pair of geese that swim along the lakeshore. This is the time of year when we can easily view the likes of bluebills, goldeneyes, and buffleheads. Normally, these birds prefer the deeper waters found far from shore.

However, there is an urge for most of these birds to continue northward. So closely do they follow on winter's heels that they must settle for pausing to feed and rest on the ice-free moats of lakes or risk the strong spring currents of swollen rivers.

There is no better time to view these waterfowl, for they are in their snappiest of plumages and never more handsome. From a distance, the whiter-than-ice backs of common mergansers resemble small bergs on the lake's steel gray surface. Nearby, yet off in their own group, is a tight flotilla of low-riding bluebills. Look closely and you may find a number of the black and white males crowding around the drab brown females, giving her their undivided attention as they feel the breeding urge.

It seems that the smaller, yet more handsome, pair of buffleheads prefer to stay off to the side and not mingle with the likes of bluebills and mergansers. Take your eyes off the isolated pair for a moment, and all that may be visible are two sets of growing rings on the water. These birds dive for their nourishment, and they need to refuel here. Their search for summer ends after following a northerly trail of loosening lakes to a destination where nesting occurs.

So we wait and watch. As these ducks leave us behind, so does the ice, and once again calendars will be marked with a simple, penciled-in note, "ice-out." And then the waiting will be done.

# Riding a Spring River

It is in the spring that creeks and rivers grow boisterous. Even small brooks and freshets are fat with winter's snowmelt and April's rains. Some of these flowages will be short-lived, and by midsummer only the scar of running water will remain.

But for now, the countryside is laced with traveling water. Moving quietly and sometimes noisily, the water is determined, in its tireless manner, to someday mingle with the salt of the sea.

Not only are spring's creeks and rivers frisky, but I find my

71

mind wandering in a journey down those very currents to see just what really does lie beyond the next bend . . . and the next bend . . . and the next.

I pass over six flowages as I drive to and from work. One of these is a county ditch that is entirely too straight to inspire exploration. Another is a subtle current where the water flows slowly out of a lake and travels about a quarter mile to another lake. However, both the ditch and lake's outflow have current, and if there is current, there are ripples or slight eddy currents creating tiny, swirling whirlpools. The very movement of water gives it a sense of life.

As long as there is current, I can toss a bit of a twig into the water and watch it twist, spin, falter, and then accelerate on its journey to nowhere. I'll watch the make-believe "boat" until it is out of sight, and then I will wonder where it will finally rest. Running water promotes a lot of wondering.

Recently, as I was driving home, I passed over a swollen creek that had risen well beyond its banks and into the flanking brush. This sinuous piece of water is known as the south branch. Later it joins forces with the north and west branches, creating a blend of flowing water collectively known as the Sunrise River.

According to state hydrologists, the Sunrise River usually experiences an April flow that is over four times greater than the low water month of August.

The tributaries and eventual river meander for nearly seventy miles before they add their flow to a growing St. Croix River.

The tributary I pass over to and from work makes several meandering near-loops. Each spring it seems that the bulging, cutting current undermines the anchoring roots of a creekside tree, causing it to fall into the water.

Known as sweepers, these trees can be formidable obstacles to contend with for those folks who care to navigate such streams. More than once I have seen the battle between spring's lusty current and a canoe end with the canoe upended by the tree's reaching limbs.

One learns quickly to make your move well above the sweeper. Should you casually wait until you're nearly upon the downed tree before making your move, the current only seems to mock you as you frantically flail the water with your paddle to avoid the imminent collision.

On this particular day, as I passed the cresting creek, I saw two boys, both about 12 years old, in a rubber raft out in the swiftly flowing channel of the stream. I slowed down and came to a stop as I watched them. I was concerned about the two crowded paddlers because they seemed to be barely in control of the craft. Filling with water or, worse yet, tipping over in such cold water could be risky. The two boys slid along the branches of one sweeper and spun in a circle as they moved downstream with their feeble paddles digging at the water.

For a moment I was tempted to get out of the car and yell for them to be careful or get to shore. But when the raft spun towards me, I could see the boy's faces and there was no concern, only smiles and laughter.

At that moment I remembered a raft built from some discarded lumber and three red, empty fifty-five gallon drums. It had been built and christened over twenty-five years ago by my grandpa, my step-uncle, and me. I also remember the good times—the laughing and smiling that came from the deck of that unsound barge as we floated with no control other than a long pole. From that raft we explored unknown reaches of a pond, a pond that could just as well have been in the depths of South America on the Amazon River.

I watched the boys in their rubber raft, and as they moved around a bend I quietly wished them a safe but highly adventurous float. Then, feeling a sense of envy, I drove on home.

We all observe rites of spring. Some rites, like the cleaning of windows and yards, are chores. Others, like the splash of sun on cowslips, are a confirmation of life's renewal. And then there are those rites that bring pleasure, like the fishing or baseball opener.

One particular spring event I have attended for about a dozen years is a gathering of canoes and friends on a spunky Wisconsin river known as the Wolf. The weekend of paddling is somewhat of a reunion of friends, new and old, from Minnesota, Wisconsin, Michigan, and one year even Ohio.

I've missed several years, but this spring I will again shove off in a canoe on a spring-full river littered with boulders and drops giving rise to familiar rapids with such names as Eagle Run, Sherry Rapids,

Little and Big Sloughgundy, and H.H. Taylor Rapids. I would venture to guess that above the noises of the churning river will be heard the laughs and whoops of a group of men who, for a weekend, are boys, riding the celebration of a spring river.

# Birthday in the Pond

Within the past couple of weeks, the "itch" of wearing winter's landscape has been relieved by the softness of spring—indeed a time for celebration. My daughter of nearly two and a half years was pressing her mother one day recently for a birthday cake, as she is especially fond of birthday parties. Though there was no birthday to celebrate, she wanted a cake.

After supper that evening, a layered poppy-seed cake topped with burning candles was brought forth to the darkened room. Britta's pleasure over her mother's creation was evident in the reflection of the flickering candles that shone from each of her shining eyes.

Since we were lacking a birthday celebrant, I suggested that we sing "Happy Birthday" to the frogs, who only recently had ventured out from the dormancy of winter. Britta liked the idea, and after we sang, she took it upon herself, as we lacked the company of an amphibian, to blow out each candle one at a time.

A few nights later, we were returning home from a real birthday party at a cousin's house in the cities. Britta had not slept on the way home as we had hoped she would. She was getting a bit grouchy until I suggested that we stop and listen to the frogs in a quiet spring-born pond lying in the dip of a hayfield. We stopped under a ceiling of bright stars and rolled down the window.

Britta was entranced at the singing frogs. She stared out her window into darkness, wondering, I suspect, where the noisemakers hid. I found it almost as satisfying to watch Britta as I did to listen to the frog music.

I also find myself searching for where the frogs hide. April's ponds are in constant turmoil, as the croaks, whistles, and trills seem to rise directly out of the water itself. From the confines of an awakening and thawing earth, there is a noisy release of a phantom spring.

The spring calls are not songs of joy celebrating the prospect of warmer days ahead. Instead, these are the males calling or, in a sense, advertising for a mate. The females will leave their upland hibernating quarters and make their way to the pond a week or so later than the males. A single calling frog may be difficult to hear, but the combined voices of many frogs will carry a great distance, making it easier for the females to hear their pleas.

The males are equipped with inflatable air sacs located on the floor of their mouths or in their throats. The air sacs act as resonators, making it easier to magnify the volume.

Another advantage in a large concentration of frogs is that there are more eyes to spot any potential danger, such as a heron or maybe a mink.

As I slipped into my patched chest waders the other day, I wondered, as I do every spring, if the rubber patches would hold back the pond's chill. Armed with an aquatic net, I cautiously walked into a small pond in the still-gray woods. My goal was to catch some frogs or perhaps find the fruit of their singing efforts and following orgy, the clusters of jellylike eggs.

The moment I first stepped into the water, the pond became deathly silent. I was intruding on a very sacrosanct setting for the frogs, and they were not about to advertise their location to a potential predator.

Three gaudily colored male wood ducks jumped up from behind a screen of dead grasses and quietly flew off through the naked tree limbs. Now I stood alone, pondering whether my waders would leak as the water rose over the patches. Luckily, I was to know another dry spring.

To pursue the frogs of April, one must have the patience of a heron and use similar stalking methods.

What moments before had been a noisy caldron of amorous frogs was now a seemingly barren pond. I stood still waiting for an impatient male frog to once again take up his call for the opposite sex. Once one frog begins calling, the other males quickly join in so that their respective messages can be heard and appreciated.

As I waited I peered into the clear water and watched several fairy shrimp with their undulating rows of legs swim slowly past my submerged knees. Near the water's surface, hanging upside down, where hundreds of mosquito larvae wriggling like excited black commas.

In their jerky rowing motion, backswimmers scooted in and out of the water-soaked leaves on the bottom of the pond. Fuzzy gray catkins from the popples surrounding the pond floated quietly on the water, seeming more like caterpillars than flowers. A pair of delicate duck feathers floated high on the water in testimony to the popularity of this pond.

Finally, after several minutes, from the far side of the water, a bold wood frog gave a halfhearted call. The solo notes were enough to touch off a rousing chorus.

Near a windfallen tree in the water was a "quacking" group of wood frogs. They are most anxious to get on with spring and consequently lay their eggs before the other frogs do. This year, there was a wet sheet of snow still in the woods when the wood frogs pronounced winter's end.

Closer to me, from the clumps of dead grass and the new green grass spears just now climbing out of the water, were the whistlelike notes of spring peepers and the staccato calls of the chorus frogs. It's still a bit early to hear the slow, snoring phrases of the familiar leopard frogs, but I should think they will begin any day.

Bending over to lessen my profile, I ever so slowly worked towards the sound of a nearby frog. It took a while to figure out where the calls were coming from. It seems as if these songsters can cast their voices in all directions.

Finally I spotted a tiny frog with its throat inflated like a bubble. I eased within a few feet of the fellow, and then with a rush I scooped the net over the frog. It's always humbling to miss the first frog and downright embarrassing to miss the first three attempts.

As I crept up on the next potential candidate, I heard a rush of wings overhead; without looking skyward, I watched the image of the three returning wood ducks in the reflection of the pond. Wood ducks, like frogs, are drawn to quiet woodland ponds. I had violated their solitude, and now they moved on to find another pool.

This time I caught the inch-long peeper with its characteristic

X marking over its back. Ten minutes later I caught my second and last frog for the day. It was time to leave, so I loudly splashed out of the water, and in doing so, I once again was responsible for silencing the pond.

I paused in the woods while getting my gear together. In my ears I could still hear frogs, though none were calling. Then from back on the north side of the pond came the cautious short trill of a restless peeper. In seconds, the pond was again a loud symphony of assorted trills, whistles, and croaks. No one is going to break up the frog's party for very long.

Tonight, I promised Britta an outing to listen to the frog's rendition of "Happy Birthday." Like I say, she likes birthday parties.

# MAY

# The Elusive Crow

Some creatures rush headlong and noisily into the first full month of spring. Consider the unseen frogs. They make every small woodland or field pond a setting for a tireless concert.

Scattered here and there, perched atop dried cattail stalks or a fuzzy-budded willow, are male red-winged blackbirds noisily establishing territories. At dawn's first light the robins are singing their similar message from nearly every yard. I often wonder when they sleep, for I can be assured of hearing the same song as the sun drops below the horizon.

However, there is one bird who becomes quiet and unmistakably sneaky in its April manner, and that is the crow. For much of the year, crows are known for their aggressive, brassy, and heckling personalities.

During autumn, they gather into large, noisy flocks. Though some of these crows migrate south, most, in these parts, stay in the same area year around, where they can fend for themselves. Huge winter flocks of crows give a seemingly bleak landscape a bold touch of life.

When thinking about crows, one does not usually think of one or two individuals, but a large roiling flock. Crows are typically very gregarious. But there is one time of the year, shortly after the spring equinox, when there is a predictable production of sexual hormones that have a way of changing typical behavior. I might add that this altered behavior is not unique to crows.

From my house, I have, for several days, been watching a pair of crows fly erratically through the treetops out in the woods behind our house. Always silent, they fly, then pause in a tree for a moment before flying a short distance to another tree. I strongly suspect that they are searching for that perfect crotch in the tree that will support their nest framework of branches and twigs.

When I was a teenager, there was a small ridge of white pines that grew in the wilds of the St. Croix River bottoms within a shout of the river itself. It was a favorite spot of mine—especially in the pre-mosquito days of early May when the forest floor there was carpeted with wildflowers.

Hepaticas shaded in cool pastels, Dutchman's-breeches, bloodroot, and trilliums in their clean white colors and the soft yellow blossoms of dog's-tooth violets all made up for a colorful understory beneath the white pines. Alone, I would often go down along the river to poke around or just sit. It wasn't easy for a teenaged male to admit that he sometimes enjoyed the company of wildflowers.

It was about that time that I entertained thoughts of having a pet crow. I often watched them frequent the white pine ridge. I had heard stories of these birds making interesting, clever pets. After all, no family of birds has evolved with such a high degree of intelligence as the crow family. Tales of teaching these birds how to talk, to perform tricks, and to count were all factors that added to my desire for a crow.

So one spring, well after leaf-out had started and trillium blossoms had withered from white to pink, friend Nels and I headed down to the river bottoms in search of a nest. Crows have a frustrating habit of occasionally building a number of flimsier preliminary nests before they put their efforts into the final nursery.

Unfortunately, their nests are never low, so one must climb, if possible, up into the tree for a close inspection. Adult crows, unlike many birds, do not create a ruckus when you approach a nest. Red-winged blackbirds, terns, and even the tiny hummingbird will buzz you if they feel their nests are threatened. Crows, on the other hand, are very shy and secretive about giving away the presence of a nest.

Finally, about twenty feet up in one of the white pines, I found a nest with four greenish eggs splotched with spots of brown and gray. We noted the location and decided to return in a few weeks to snatch one of the young.

It was about three weeks later that we returned to a lusher forest, now guarded by untold numbers of aggressive mosquitos. The parent crows had fled quietly and unseen from the nest well before we reached the nest tree. It was hotter work climbing the pine this trip and not made any easier by pesky mosquitos.

I cautiously peered over the edge of the nest and found four ugly, scantily feathered crow chicks all huddled in the nest, not moving or blinking an eye. We had misjudged their development, and they were too young to take from the nest. So down I came, and with our arms swinging about our heads in perpetual motion, we hurried through the woods back to the car.

That was the last time we saw that nest. Somehow our enthusiasm was drained, along with a fair amount of our blood, by the omnipresent mosquitos.

My dream of having a pet crow was never fulfilled, and then in March of 1972, it was put out of reach for good. That spring the Migratory Bird Treaty, first ratified in 1916 to protect birds that migrated between the United States and Canada, was amended. The treaty was extended to Mexico and gave extra protection to another thirty-two families of birds, which included not only all birds of prey, such as hawks, eagles, and owls, but also crows.

My days of hunting crows out near the town dump, a favorite scavenging spot for them, were over. Gone also were my hopes of robbing a crow from a nest. Since those earlier times, my desire to hunt crows has lessened, though I still own a burlap bag full of crow decoys, and somewhere I have an old crow call with a chewed-up mouthpiece.

But I still would like to have a pet crow. So the other day, I made a phone call to the enforcement division of the United States Fish and Wildlife Service. It appears that my dream must remain just that—a dream. To legally obtain and raise any protected bird such as a crow, I would need a special federal permit. And the permit can only be issued if I am using the bird for "scientific or educational" purposes.

And wouldn't you know it, just a few days ago, I saw a pair of neighborhood crows fly overhead, and one of them carried a clump of rootlike fibers—undoubtedly the finishing touches for the nest lining.

So while the frogs sing from the flooded canary grass pond behind the neighbor's house and the robins tirelessly sing, I'm going to track down the silent crows and see if I can find the nest to show my oldest daughter. And if she is willing to listen, I'll tell her stories of past crow encounters.

# A Fond Opener

From my bed, I can look out the upstairs window at the limbs of a nearby burr oak and gauge what kinds of winds are blowing. Saturday morning, the new leaves were fluttering in a lively manner, indicating a good breeze—just what is needed to put a little chop on the lakes.

The backdrop behind the leaves was a deep blue sky, and the oak's spring green was awash with the light of a welcome sunrise. The day certainly had all the markings of a made-to-order fishing opener.

But here I was still in bed instead of taking part in the ritual that has become tradition, a sort of Christmas in May. As I lay there, I searched through the morning cobwebs still bound up in my mind to the last fishing opener that I had missed. I couldn't remember the last opener where I hadn't sought the tug of line and the satisfaction of a netted lake trout, walleye, or pike.

There would be no fish on this day. Today I was going to build a treehouse with my daughter Britta. For a three-and-a-half-year-old, this is an exciting proposition. Tugging fish lines are nothing compared to a castle in the branches where one can play with the likes of ever-smiling dolls named Barbie, Ken, Lucy, and Bevy.

Actually, up until a few days before this magical Saturday, I had been planning on joining my in-law menfolk on a trip into a lake where lake trout often seem eager to cooperate. However, a busy work schedule and the fact that we had been running a lot recently, made us reconsider. Besides, I expect there will be plenty of future fishing openers, but how many first tree houses?

One of my wife's favorite stories is *The Swiss Family Robinson* by Johann D. Wyss, where a family finds themselves shipwrecked on an island in the Pacific. Shortly after landing on the island, Mother

Robinson is thinking to herself that her family must find a more secure and hospitable shelter than their canvas tent on the open rocky beach. "The longer we remained in this enchanting place, the more did it charm my fancy; and if we could manage to live in some sort of dwelling up among the branches of those grand noble trees, I should feel perfectly safe and happy."

There is something of an adventure when one considers tree houses, and I don't think there is a kid who has ever shirked from adventure.

I must confess that I frequently like to climb high among the limbs where I can better view the countryside and feel the gentle swaying inspired by winds. I have looked forward to the day when I could once again build a tree house. As adults, we often use our children as excuses for building tree houses or doing the childlike things we still yearn to do. But as adults, we may be reluctant to let out the child in us.

The tree we chose to build in was a burr oak that grows along an old fence line between our small field and the woods that once pastured my grandpa's milk cows. For years, the tree stood upright, but then I suspect it was a strong west wind, maybe brewed from a summer storm, that blew the tree nearly to the ground.

The roots held, however, and the tree continued to prosper, even though it is now more horizontal than vertical. At the tree's base is a hump where the roots and their cap of earth were forced up as the tree tipped.

The oak has changed its orientation, and the main trunk looks like a Christmas yule log, with the branches resembling candles as they assumed a vertical stature. In its struggle to thrive, the tree produces growth-regulating hormones and forms new wood to send the leaf-bearing limbs skyward to catch the sunlight needed to manufacture those sugars that ensure the tree's existence.

I pulled the cart with its load of odd-ball scrap lumber, jars of nails, a saw, and a hatchet. Britta carried her green-eyed, yarn-haired friend named Bevy Bernice, who supposedly was born in a cabbage patch.

Before nailing some steps on the leaning trunk, I took down an old rusted coil of barbed wire that hung on a distorted knob. I wondered how long the wire had been there. Had my father, grandfather or great-grandfather first stretched it out? At any rate, barbed wire and tree houses do not mix.

I had barely started hammering when Britta asked if I was done. I assured her it wouldn't take too long. It wasn't difficult working on the platform, because I could do most of the work with my feet still on the ground. The deck of the tree house is perhaps five and a half feet up—plenty high for one who hasn't yet seen four summers.

Finally, when the last board was nailed in place as a hand railing, I told Britta that the job was finished. Her wide eyes, smile, and bubbling giggles were all I needed as far as compliments on a job well done.

With a bucket and an attached rope, we made an elevator so Bevy Bernice could be pulled up to the fort to join us. Britta climbed back down and gathered some leaves that were to be the makings of a licorice pie. Britta, Bevy, and I sat on our crude floor contently nibbling on leaves.

The early evening was cool, and I'm sure the sunset looked especially picturesque from a slow-trolling canoe on a lake. But this was one view I would never forget. It wasn't easy coaxing Britta out of the tree, but I promised her that she could return tomorrow. So we lowered Bevy down in the bucket, left the little piles of wilting leaves on the plywood floor, and climbed down. Britta jabbered all the way back to the house.

With the taste of young oak leaves in my mouth, I silently hoped that she would try a different pie tomorrow. I never have liked licorice.

# "Here snipe . . ."

The wind carried with it the scent of rain, a much-needed rain.

On hands and knees, I followed a thin, powder dry furrow across my garden, tucking pea seeds into the soil. With a sense of hope, I patted the covered row firmly into place. Behind me, over along the neighbor's field in a flooded patch of greening canary grass, the spring peepers and chorus frogs were singing their own phrases of hope.

But it was the odd quavering whistle back over the slough, nearly half a mile away south of me, that caught my attention and made me pause. There is only one animal darting through April's skies that can produce such a tremulous sound, and that is the snipe. After listening to the bird again, I considered a break from gardening to head back to the slough for a snipe hunt.

I know I am not alone in recalling taking part in a "snipe hunt." Such an expedition generally takes place when one is not much taller than a snipe, and maybe not much smarter.

My futile attempt was not undertaken alone but with a patrol of fellow boy scouts on a camp-out. Of course, it was blacker than the ace of spades, and older, more experienced scouts had assuredly pointed us in the right direction, toward a thick overgrown swamp where the shy, mysterious bird was said to thrive. It sounded simple enough, all we had to do was carry a sack and quietly call, "Here, snipe . . . here snipe."

An hour or two later, we returned to the campfire, flashlights dimmer, wet to our middles, and worse yet, snipeless. We had been initiated into the rites of the snipe hunt, and in the following years we did our best to pass on encouraging words to other potential snipe seekers.

Not until my father took me along to the wild rice beds out at Grandpa's for some duck hunting did I think there really was such an animal. There we would often flush the bird from the lake's edge, and it would zigzag away, giving a sharp raspy call.

It took several years and far more shotgun shells before I downed one of the elusive birds. Though they aren't very large, maybe a third the size of a Cornish game hen, they are quite tasty.

A snipe flying high over spring-flooded meadows and marshes can lead the patient stalker to the area of its nest. The strange sound of a snipe is usually given by the slightly smaller male and is referred to as winnowing. On rare occasions, the female will also winnow. Other than their size, both sexes are similar in appearance. The winnowing sound is produced in flight and is most often heard in early morning or at dusk. The bird will climb to a height of 300 to 400 feet and then go into a dive. At such a height, it is difficult to spot the small bird as it moves back and forth.

As the snipe drops, it spreads its tail feathers. The two outer tail feathers are distended, and as the air rushes over them, it produces the quavering whistle. A yakking call is heard between winnows, as the bird climbs to repeat the display.

Winnowing in the snipe's territorial flight serves to warn the other males of territorial boundaries. At the same time, it is directed toward a prospective mate on the ground. After mating, the winnowing is often continued over the nest, which holds four well-camouflaged eggs.

The nest is on the ground, often on a hummock of grass or perhaps sphagnum moss in a wet meadow, marsh, or bog. As with all ground-nesting birds, the structure is well concealed. I have yet to find a nest, but I am confident that someday I will. The important thing to remember in searching is to follow the call of the snipe rather than pleading, "Here snipe . . . here snipe." As with all snipe hunts, wet feet and pants are the norm.

It was for that reason, along with the smell of a coming rain, that I instead busied myself with peas.


# The Cane Poles

An old weathered shed sits under a massive white oak. On its south-facing wall hangs a trio of equally grayed bamboo fishing poles. The three long poles hang wired together by a rusty wire under the shed's sagging eaves. One of the tips is broken, and the other two droop wearily down, permanently bent after years of fighting the tug of gravity.

I would guess that the only time that life has pulsed through the butts of those old slender bamboo shoots in recent decades was when an early spring phoebe found the bamboo ledge. The canes and the shed wall provided a dandy platform to build its handsome nest of mud lined with the greenery of moss.

Just down the hill, behind the long-silenced barn, is a body of water too small to call a lake yet too large to label a pond. The poles hanging on the shed would have been perfect for reaching out to the cruising schools of sunfish that could have cared less whether this hole of water was deemed pond or lake.

Though it seems that these lofty poles are relics of the past, they are effective tools in filling a frying pan with sunnies. A large area can be covered without any casting. Instead, one can quietly drop a baited hook into the smallest openings in a thick bed of pondweed and pull the hooked fish straight up without disturbing others in the school.

As a kid, when I walked the main street sidewalk on the way to the drugstore soda fountain, I would sometimes pause at the bundle of new, towering, bamboo poles that stood leaning against the front corner of the hardware store.

It was fun to grasp the thick end of a pole and give it a firm shake. The shake would travel up the whiplike pole to the fine tip, where it clattered against the others. Some of those poles were not much higher than a basketball rim, but others seemed at least half the height of the village water tower.

Day and night, the bundle of poles stood out front of the hardware store with their butt ends resting on the sidewalk, waiting for someone to come by and give the shafts a hearty shake. On a rare occasion, someone must have bought one, because some days the clattering wouldn't be as loud and there were fewer tips to knock about.

Seven days a week and even on holidays, the poles braved the weather on the sidewalk. Rarely would a pole be missing when the store opened up in the morning. It seems times have changed. In those days, there wasn't even a "Sheriff's Report" in the local newspaper.

I never owned one of those canes, though I did use one on occasion at a friend's cabin in Wisconsin. From the end of the dock, it seemed we could reach halfway across the lake. We pulled many sunfish out of the open water pockets in the lily-pad beds.

The long cane poles seemed best for learning the value of patience, which is what the sport of fishing is all about. Most of the time, these long reachers are in the hands of kids or old folks. I suspect that the fumbling coordination of youth and the stiffening joints of aging make the simple cane pole, with its lack of moving parts and ease of handling, so popular.

My first fishing pole was a bamboo pole. It came in two sections that when put together would have reached maybe a little better than half the length of those wall climbers in front of the hardware store. My pole was a birthday present, along with a kapok-filled life jacket, that my parents gave me during my sixth or seventh summer. I always considered it an advantage to have a July birthday, for I could usually count on getting something that dealt with two favorite summer pastimes—fishing and baseball.

I don't recall my first fish with my birthday pole. It was most likely a sunfish or a bait-stealing perch. But I can clearly remember my first trout taken with that piece of sectioned bamboo.

It was the trout opener in early May, and I was poised on the bank of the flow called Beaver Creek. Below me, in the water, was a tangle of willow branches that swept over the surface. It was midday, and the spring sun had caused the brook trout to pull back into the shady retreats created by bank cuts and sweeping willow limbs. I remember reaching out with my pole and quietly dropping the hooked worm just upstream from the sweeping willow. The worm bounced on the bottom and then disappeared as the current carried it under the branches into the shadows.

The unseen trout took the worm as if it hadn't seen nourishment in days. Few moments are more thrilling than a battle between fish and angler, where line is given and line is taken. This trout, however, never had the opportunity. As soon as I felt the tap that signaled a bite, I lifted my cane pole in a quick sweep. A ten inch trout lifted out of the shadows, flew in a circular arc skyward at least fifteen feet high, and then dropped at my feet. It flopped on the grass maybe once before I jumped, straddling my speckled beauty between my knees.

Like a first kiss, one doesn't forget one's first brook trout.

That two-sectioned birthday pole has long disappeared, but not before it succeeded in igniting a spark to pursue the finned creatures that move mysteriously in our streams and lakes.

Since those earlier days, I have used poles of stiff steel, colorful blanks of fiber glass, and now the more responsive graphite. Yet I am told that if I want the ultimate fly rod for sensitivity, fine casting, and exquisite beauty, I should return to bamboo. After all, it is bamboo, the fast-growing, treelike grass of the Far East, that the space age synthetics such as graphite and boron try to simulate.

The problem, however, is cost. The eighteen footers that leaned against the hardware store cost eighty-nine cents each, a far cry from a top-of-the-line split bamboo fly rod. Those in the know of such tackle will speak reverently of such rodmakers as Leonard, R. L. Winston, and Thomas and Thomas. These are considered the cream of the crop and can run as high as two thousand dollars.

For a lesser amount, one could consider a cane pole crafted by Mike Spittler of Minneapolis. According to those who know a good cane pole's qualities, Mike builds one of the very best four-piece quadrate cane poles in the country. To own one of Mike's rods, you may have to wait a year and be willing to loosen at least seven hundred dollars from your fishing budget.

How could a fishing pole, especially one made of a stout grass, cost so much money? The answer is simply craftsmanship. The builder must scour through a supply of bamboo and select those pieces where the power fibers are densest towards the cane's surface for better casting power and accuracy. Each of the four, narrow strips are split from a piece of cane and hand fitted by tapering before they are glued together. Mike estimates that he has at least forty-five hours of time invested in each rod.

The most sought-after cane for rod building comes from select tonkin cane grown in the Kiangsi province in China. Of the 1,000 or more species of bamboo in the world, there is no finer for crafting split bamboo fly rods.

For the time being, I will continue to fish my fiber glass and graphite rods. But I have filed Mike's phone number should I ever want to heft one of his works.

As the lake waters warm, the bluegills, pumpkinseeds, green sunfish and various mixtures of each will make their annual pilgrimage to the sand-bottomed shallows to spawn and guard their saucer-like nests. Perhaps I will take my girls out with a long switch of bamboo to reach those sunnies.

The problem is that the front of the hardware store has only lawn mowers and tillers on its sidewalk these days. And a phoebe that prefers the taste of insects to fish has dibs on the only other long pole I know of.

# Home Roots

Not long ago, I found myself standing with a handful of strangers at the curb of a busy intersection in Minneapolis. Each of us stood alone in thought, silently staring at the opposite semaphore, awaiting our permission to proceed across. The traffic was heavy, the air faintly scented with exhaust, and a block away the sound of sirens wailed as a pair of fire trucks dashed through an intersection.

I was wondering if the light was ever going to change and allow us across when I heard a familiar chord of robin music behind me. I turned, and in a small patch of green grass bordered by sidewalks and buildings, a male robin scurried in short dashes, as robins do, nervously chirping. It appeared that no one else had noticed the unsettled robin because the rest of the waiting pedestrians were still hypnotized by the red light.

As I watched the bird, it occurred to me that this robin doesn't have to be here on the corner of a hectic, noisy intersection. To me it seemed ludicrous that such a bird would even consider pausing here.

Why had this bird claimed a piece of city real estate as its territory? Certainly, it has no idea of the monetary value or the taxation of the ground. Is it the convenience and multitude of worm-producing city lawns that cause it to stay? Maybe it's the countless window ledges, nooks, or boulevard trees that beckon a robin to nest here. Most likely, this particular robin hatched in a nest not far from a city street light, and now it faithfully heads northward every spring to return to its home turf.

There are city robins and country robins. Nearly as adaptable as humans, robins can be found just about anywhere. I admire the ability of the robin to fit in so well in the shadow of skyscrapers, yet it's the robin that nests on the edge of the northern tree line, where forests give way to the tundra, that I envy more. Perhaps what I really envy are the wings that carry the bird over barriers and

92

beyond semaphores.

In appearance, the city robin is no less colorful than the country robin. However, it is their memories and where they have been that are so dissimilar.

The light changed, and the throng of people that surrounded me thinned out as we each chose our own pace in crossing the street. I had intended to stay in the city a while longer to run some errands, but I was restless and getting edgy. It seems to always be that way for me—I get to the point where I can't wait to leave it all behind me. Like the robin, I feel more at ease in a familiar setting where my roots were planted and nurtured.

I found my car among the hundreds in the parking lot, steered it northward, and joined the current of automobiles that were headed in the same direction. As I traveled the interstate to the country road and finally the sandy township road, I thought about the city robin. Such a bird is a touch of rural life and to some people a hint of wilderness, a thread that links man to bird. The robin becomes a symbol, an escape from that which is artificial and mechanized.

As I turned into a driveway with a grass stripe down the middle of it, I realized the importance of the city robin and no longer questioned its choice of homes. I also wondered why a robin has never, over the course of seven springs, built a nest in our yard. Maybe my yard is worm poor, or the nesting ledges are too few. Or is it that all the country robins I see are simply commuters from the city? At any rate, it was good to be home.

# Aromatic Antiques

Creaking windmills, sagging, grayed barns, or perhaps an old leaning silo are clues of once-thriving farmsteads. Eventually, these momentos of days gone by will succumb to the pull of the earth and disappear. When they are gone, strangers will probably pass by unaware of the toiling labor once performed there.

Sometimes the clues are less visible, like the patch of sunken ground now overgrown with brush and trees. The oversize dimple is

93

all that remains of a cellar that once housed bushels of potatoes. Or perhaps all that remains is a few moss-covered blocks of sandstone that once provided the foundation of a building. These clues will eventually disappear and become a part of the landscape.

Many farmsteads, however, will not be forgotten, for there are persistent, living clues. There may be an old, gnarly apple tree or a straight row of giant cottonwoods. But none thrives as well as the dome-shaped thicket of ever-spreading lilacs.

Hardly a home was without its wonderful smelling thicket or hedge of lilacs. These shrubs provided color to rest the eyes, smells to savor, and a thick fence to catch the blowing winter snow.

For over three hundred years, lilacs have graced the dooryards of settlers in this country. No one knows for sure when the first rootstock made the Atlantic crossing, but it was probably lifted out of English soil.

In 1767, Thomas Jefferson penned in his "Garden Book" of lilac plantings and their abundance at his home, Monticello. Later, another amateur gardener, George Washington, wrote in his diaries of transplanting lilacs. Eventually, as pioneers pushed west from the East Coast, so did the lilacs.

This showy shrub, which to some is the fairest call to spring, evolved in Asia and southeastern Europe. It shares characteristics with other plants in the olive family. The word *lilac* is derived from the Persian word *nilak,* meaning "bluish."

By the middle of the sixteenth century, the lilac was transported to Austria, and from there it spread rapidly throughout Europe, becoming a favorite planting in British gardens.

One would be hard pressed to choose a best quality of the lilac. Both the spring color and the spring scent are equally restful.

In earlier days, pioneer women hold dainty bouquets of lilacs, called tussie-mussies, to mask the stinking smells of catch-all street gutters.

As a grade schooler, I can vividly remember the huge lilac hedge that bordered the road and old farm across the road from our house. The old hedge, planted in the late nineteenth century, stretched for a couple hundred feet and stood nearly fifteen feet tall. We cherished a northeast breeze in May, for it would carry the luscious smell of lilacs to our place.

The air around the sweet smelling blossoms fairly hummed with the sounds of thousands of bees seeking the flower's nectar. Bees were not the only creatures attracted to the lilacs. Their thick, shrubby network of branches provided secure nesting sites for robins and catbirds.

On weekends, it was not unusual to see cars parked along the hedge. Like the bees, folks from town were drawn to these flowers to pick a fragrant spray for the kitchen table.

That magnificent hedge, the old farm as well, was claimed by progress. The road, no longer the sandy lane it was, has been widened and paved to accommodate the increased load of traffic. There are now three homes whose front yards take in what was once an incredible lilac hedge.

When lilacs don't have to contend with the bite of steel, they are quite hardy and can withstand the temperature extremes of the Upper Midwest. It seems that all you have to do to grow this shrub is to pull a young suckering stem out of the ground with a section of root, dig a hole, stick it in, add some water, and watch it grow.

In the past 125 years, agronomists have developed many lilac hybrids. There are now several hundred varieties to choose from. These colorful shrubs can display a variety of colors—white, rose, pink, violet, magenta, and everyone's favorite, the purplish lilac color.

Early colonial women captured the lilac tones for creating lavender-hued clothing by dying fabrics in a bath of purple dye created by boiling the lilac leaves.

Lilac blooms were believed to hold special qualities of enhancing one's beauty if certain rituals were maintained. One of these was to wash your face with dew collected from the lilac blossoms on May Day. Doing so would make you beautiful for the rest of your life. Or if a young woman wished to marry, she should cut a dormant, leafless lilac branch on December 4 and place it in a water-filled vase. If the branch greened in leaf by Christmas, the young lady knew her wedding day was near.

In Germany, it was customary to affix a spray of lilac flowers to the roof of the house to fend off lightening. Or if a household was smoked out with lilac blossom incense in a prescribed manner, the home would be free of mice and rats.

Old-timers often watch for natural events in governing their planting, harvesting, and other gathering activities. These sages of nature lore, for instance, claim that it doesn't pay to search the spring woods for the highly palatable morel mushroom until the lilacs are in bloom. Lilacs and morels show their respective beauty at nearly the same time year after year.

The lilac's beauty bears a personal memory for my wife, Susan, and I. We were married on a sunny day in a church where the heady aroma of lilacs mingled with the hopes for a happy life together. I know a lilac bouquet will be received with a special smile.

There is a patch of feral lilacs that stands just outside the slumping remains of the decrepit old outhouse at the old Kelly place, about a mile from our house. The Kelly house is gone, as are the other outbuildings. The lone outhouse and the flanking lilacs are all that remain of a family's history here.

I wonder if the lilacs were heeled into the ground before or after the outhouse was erected. Was the shrub's purpose to provide a masking fragrance when the spring warmth inspired insipid odors from the lower levels of the two-holer?

Or perhaps while paging through the remains of the Sears and Roebuck catalog, the users enjoyed cocking an ear towards the hedge to listen for the melodious mixed-up song of the catbird or the hum of fat bumblebees.

There is something soothing about a thicket of lilacs.

**UPDATE:** The Kelly outhouse collapsed in the spring of 1987. The lilacs, however, have expanded and are intent on erasing any remnants of a homestead.

# The Preacher Bird

Last week, my sidewalk was littered with tiny petals that had fallen from nearby black cherry trees. No longer are they white; they are dried and stained the color of weak coffee. I consider these dainty petals as spring's last hurrah—the fallen confetti of May's vernal celebration.

I realize that the true entrance to summer lies three weeks distant, but with the passing of the sweet smell of cherry blossoms and finally their dismantling, I know that summer is here.

Most schools are out, and so are the hordes of mosquitoes. To most people there is no need for further evidence that summer is upon us. But if you doubt the demise of spring, leave the comfort of your bed at the moment of dawn and stroll into your yard or nearby woods.

The crescendo created by the multitudes of birds we heard only weeks ago is already lessening. Individual songs become easier to pick out; no longer are they all jarbled together.

By mid-morning, the yard or woods starts taking on an almost eerie silence. Even so, there are birds who remain persistent with their song.

Even in the heat of the day, I can hear the occasional drawn-out whistle of a wood peewee calling from high in the lush tree canopy. Less frequent, but far louder than its peewee cousin, come the whistled *wheep* notes of a great crested flycatcher.

But the most tireless of all songs comes from another bird that is nearly as adept at staying to the treetops as the peewee. The caller is a male, red-eyed vireo, known to some as the "preacher bird" because of its habit of going on and on and on with its message.

The red-eyed vireo is the champion bird songster when one considers endurance and the number of songs uttered in a day. One patient observer counted 22,197 songs from one male in a ten-hour day!

The vireo's song is somewhat robinlike, but it is made up of short phrases seemingly repeating the following declarations: *See Me— Here I am—Up here—Do you hear me?*

Even if you spy the bird, it is inconspicuous in its spring plumage. From the ground, we most often see its white undersides or perhaps its flanks, washed in a tinge of yellow-olive.

If you should glimpse its head, easiest with the aid of binoculars, you will see its white eyebrow edged on top with a border of black. An excellent view would betray the red eye found in the adult.

Immature birds-of-the-year have a brown eye.

When the male vireos first arrive in early May, they start singing to establish a breeding territory. When the females show up several days later, their singing ground shrinks in size to an acre or two.

After mating, the female builds—in my opinion—one of the handsomest of birds nests. It is a beautiful suspended cup of woven grasses, fibers, rootlets, and even spider webs. It hangs from the fork of a small horizontal branch five to ten feet off the ground. Even after the female starts incubating her four or so white eggs, speckled with brown, she may add extra building material to the rim or outside of the nest. In our region, I have never seen a vireo nest that was not graced with some strips of white birch bark.

Apparently, brown-headed cowbirds find the nest equally hand-some, because they often deposit a heavily speckled egg in a vireo nest at dawn's early light. Being a good parental bird, the vireo will unknowingly incubate and care for the cowbird nestling as if it were its own.

While the female is tending her clutch of eggs, the male is singing proudly from the nearby treetops. Once his mate starts incubating the eggs, his tempo picks up, and he may sing as many as fifty to sixty phrases a minute.

If he should pause, the female becomes restless with his silence. He then may come down near the nest, and she will leave her setting duties briefly to join him for a bite to eat. For these birds, the preferred food is insects. The female may find her own food, or the male may feed her. After this brief luncheon date, she returns to the nest.

So while the bird world becomes quieter as the sun climbs ever higher towards its rendezvous with summer, the male vireo tirelessly prolongs the season of spring with his monotonous up-and-down notes.

From inside our church, I can be assured of hearing a great crested flycatcher singing his own sermonette from the large oaks that shade the cemetery. With a little more effort, I can always count on hearing the buzzing notes of a clay-colored sparrow that sings across the road in a cutover Christmas tree plantation. To the south, perhaps a quarter mile at best, roosters of various hues crow their challenges—even on the sabbath.

And though my ears are aware of these various Sunday callers, it is the "song" coming from the white, perchlike pulpit that dominates. I must confess that although the preacher's words dominate, they don't always make me sit up with the same straightness that the unseen birds do.

I suppose I should feel guilt for wishing I were outside the church walls rather than within, but at those moments guilt often dons wings.

On a warm, sunlit Sunday morning, one can usually witness a number of squirmers within the various "houses of worship." I'm not one to fidget that much. Instead, I find myself staring out the windows, hypnotized by the blue sky and the lazy motions of a summer breeze playing over the oaks. Invariably, it is on such days that the preacher sounds amazingly like a vireo.

# JUNE

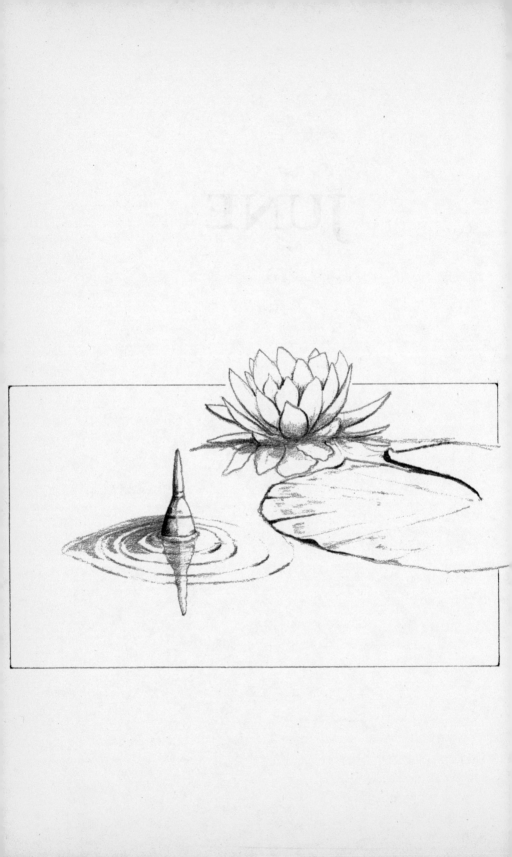

# Swallow Envy

As much as I enjoy the silence and grace of canoe travel, I must admit I rarely wet a paddle for the sheer joy of canoeing. A canoe best provides me with a means to pursue a task. Perhaps *task* is the wrong word. Such a word conveys a chore, and chores often give rise to tedium and sweat, neither of which I am particularly fond of.

I would hardly consider a north-bound canoe, ladened with full packs and a map, traveling from campfire to campfire, worthy of being labeled a task. Perhaps an adventure, but never a task. Nor is it a task to experience the quickening of the heart and the accompanying rhythm of galloping waves, surging eddies, and racing current when I commit myself and the canoe to an upright ride through a lively rapids. Sheer excitement, but never a task.

There is no finer craft built for stealth. I can quietly drift over the mirror surface of an early morning lake toward a raft of lily pads. My date is with an early morning largemouth bass. I don't need to catch a fish to call the dawning a success; all I ask for is one explosion of a bass striving to become airborne as it erupts under my cast. The canoe is a fine fishing partner rather than a taskmaster.

The only time the canoe comes close to creating a chore is when it is removed from its watery pathway and hoisted onto my shoulders for an excursion between lakes or episodes.

Last week I kept a morning appointment with a canoe and paddled away from shore toward a yellowing sky. Joining me was a nine-foot fly rod substantial enough to battle a bass in its protective maze of lily-pad stems.

Not far from the put-in point, I started fishing, casting fore and aft, delivering a favorite beat-up, black, deer-hair bug. The first few casts are most intense, for the outing is fresh and hopes high. Nothing happens, so I begin to concentrate on improving my casting distance.

The day lightens up quickly, and soon the sun is sending its first rays of the day over the treetops and on to me. Gradually, the air warms, and the layer closest to the ground warms first. These heated air particles are less dense than the upper ones, and they rise. Soon the warming and change in air can be seen in the trembling of the aspen and birch leaves that grow along the shoreline. A gentle breeze awakens.

Without an anchor, the light canoe skittered slowly out toward deeper water, away from the lily-pad bed—the target of my casts. I had purposely positioned myself in the front, or bow, seat facing the stern so that my weight was more in the middle of the canoe. If I had sat in the stern seat, the front would have risen out of the water, making the canoe less controllable and creating a sail to catch the wind.

Repeatedly, I found myself sailing out of position, so I paddled for more sheltered waters. After I moved, the breeze turned into a wind, and it seemed I was handling my paddle more than my fishing rod. Overhead, the tree swallows were making a mockery of my canoe pirouettes.

Shorebirds—sandpipers and plovers—are often referred to as wind birds. No other family of birds average such great distances during their spring and autumn migrations. It is during such epic journeys that they become one with the wind. But on this morning I assigned that title to the swallows. While I struggled to maintain my position on the lake, the swallows arced the sky with graceful swoops. They make hunting insects look like fun. It seemed like the wind was their playmate. Over the water, with their wings scarcely a hairbreadth over the lake, the swallows raced and chittered. Occasionally, I would witness a quick dodge to the side, followed by a swoop upward as the swallow found its prey.

At one time, a swallow passed a small damselfly to another swallow as they momentarily hovered beak to beak. The recipient raced off with the offering—perhaps to one of the many drowned shoreline trees that were graced with holes. Such trees offer not only cover for the lurking bass, but also nesting cavities for the swallows.

104

By this time, I had given up fishing. Besides, it was getting on toward the start of a workday. It took more effort to paddle back to my car, as the wind tried its best to make me late. The wind, however, felt good as it helped cool my sweating brow.

Sometime during the morning, the wind had stolen the fishing and carried in a task.

# The Puddle Calling

It could lie in your driveway, on a rutted field road, or just a low spot in the yard, pasture, or field. We all know a mud puddle that might leave for a while but, in due time, always shows up again.

Puddles and mosquitoes are inevitable in June. Though they are absent from our eyes for a short time, they will return. Some would argue the benefits of a mosquito, but those people are ignorant of the minnow, dragonfly nymphs, and other predators that feed on them. And if we are to neglect the needs of a simple minnow or dragonfly, we eventually will put ourselves closer in line to the exit door.

Like mosquitoes, mud puddles are often scorned. Not only do they serve as nurseries for these pesky insects, but they are a source of mud, which makes its way into our homes, cars, and sidewalks by clinging to our shoe soles.

This spring, I watched a small flock of cliff swallows encircle a small mudhole. With their wings held high over their backs fluttering like the leaves of an October popple, they dabbed beaks full of mud.

Their elevated, applauding wings always amuse me and for a moment the swallow seems more butterfly than bird. Supposedly, by raising their wings, they don't muddy them. After all, no one likes to track in unnecessary mud.

As if on cue, the birds all took to the air and headed for a destination that was to remain their secret. Several minutes later, the same birds, or perhaps another shift, settled down to stab their loads of mud.

Both male and female will fashion a flask-shaped nest of mud

105

pellets on a cliff or, more likely, under a bridge or beneath the eaves of a barn or other outbuilding. Some people aptly know this bird as the "eaves swallow." Well over a thousand tiny mud balls will go into the building of the nest.

As the puddle comes and goes with periodic rain showers and following dry spells, mud dauber wasps will make a less noticeable visit to the muddy water's edge. They, like the swallows, will be gathering mud for their respective nests.

These solitary wasps will leave a gift of tiny, paralyzed spiders alongside the wasp's egg within the mud chambers. After the egg hatches, the developing pupae will feed on the entombed spiders.

Puddles will always be the casual bathing stops for the blue jay, robin, and sparrow. But if you are a patient puddle watcher, you may catch a glimpse of the more shy but flashy scarlet tanager. All of these birds seem a picture of bliss as they fluff, shake, and wriggle with seeming joy in the water.

I have a bird bath. I admit it has a crack and is not as dependable as a mud puddle, but even when filled with clear, earth-drawn water, it seems the birds prefer the browned waters of driveway puddles.

By August, the swallow's mud nests will be empty and silent. The young swallows of the year will have been weeks on the wing, strengthening themselves for their upcoming journey south. The mud puddle where the swallows had gathered their pellets of mud will most likely be long dry after the work of the July sun.

But should we feel the relief of a summer rainfall, the dry grasses and the curled corn leaves will know the salvation of water and a puddle will once again beckon a visitor.

This time, the puddle may be wreathed in a flutter of orange-yellow as the sulphur butterflies take a moment from the alfalfa and clover fields to sip moisture from the puddle.

Some folks know of this butterfly only as the "puddler" or the "roadside" butterfly. Even with the disappearance of the water, these butterflies will continue to gather together as long as there is mud.

These obscure "wetlands" fall in a straight line, like a string of shiny coins, down the driveway. Though they may block my path, I tolerate and even enjoy them. Their appeal today is not the same as when I was a youngster and found puddles more fun to pass through than bypass. The joy now comes in watching the puddle and seeing what it calls.

Just remember to wipe your feet or take off your shoes.

# "I ain't such a somebody"

*The whole night seemed filled with the small whining of their wings.*
*"They'll quiet down some, if it cools off."*
*"They don't serve no purpose, unless to remind a man he ain't such a somebody."*
Jim Deakins and Boone Caudill in A. B. Guthrie's *Big Sky*

There is something soothing about the rhythm of a gentle rain. As I write this, the drops are sounding off the windowpanes and roof. Creeks, sloughs, and strawberries are full and flourishing as a result of the June rains. But the numerous puddles and pools are but a prelude to the song of another sort—one that is hardly comforting.

Rain does not lull the mosquito but inspires it to increase its kind. Without rain, the blood-seeking insects have no nursery to lay their eggs and start their life as an aquatic insect.

Millions of dollars are spent every year in battling mosquitoes to make life more pleasant for people. Hardly a stone lies unturned as far as unlocking the secrets of the life of this pesky insect. Yet by sheer numbers and tenacity, it not only exists but thrives.

I recall one of the first humid nights of the newly arrived summer. I lay in bed sweltering, unable to sleep. On such nights sleep becomes a chore. Not only was sleeping difficult, but every so often my ears detected the high-pitched whine of a mosquito that insisted on a late night snack on my vulnerable, sheetless body.

I swung wildly at the sound. I even slapped my own head repeatedly as one of the insect vampires bobbed in a dancing flight just outside of my ear. No doubt it was reminding me that "I ain't such a somebody."

I am convinced that one of the most effective tortures in the world

107

is the incessant, high-pitched screaming of mosquitos. Yet it is that same seductive drone that brings the two sexes together and assures us of future nights of agony.

Most of the time male and female mosquitos are found in their own respective swarms, with the females staying closer to the ground. The male mosquito is attracted to the sounds made by the female while she is in flight. Generally, the male has to be within a foot of the female or she is ignored.

The antennae of the sexually mature male are very bristly and resemble feathers. Antennae, under a microscope, remind me of the *Equisetums*, or scouring rushes, with their branches growing in a whorl from the stem like spokes off a hub. Antennae differences help in identifying the many species of mosquitos.

Such multispoked antennae gives the male better reception of the female's wing music. Confusion between the sexes is prevented because of the males' inability to hear their own wingbeats, which hum at a lower frequency than the females'.

After mating, the female lays her eggs singly or in raftlike masses on the surface of still water. Ponds, marshes, swamps, a water barrel, a discarded tire, a water-filled hole in a tree, or a persistent mud puddle all make for ideal mosquito rearing.

My only complaint is with the female mosquito. She, rather than the male, is in need of a blood meal. If she finds a blood donor, she may lay two hundred to four hundred eggs in each floating mass. But if she is unable to drink the needed blood, she may lay only forty to eighty eggs. A very few species are able to lay eggs without the nourishment of blood.

After the eggs hatch, the various larval stages are best viewed as they wriggle just below the water's surface. Their snorkellike trachea draws in oxygen, and the tiny bristles encircling their mouthparts collect algae or other floating organic bits for their food. After three or four weeks, the mosquito has gone from an egg, through four larval stages, a pupal stage, and finally transforms into an adult.

So thoroughly are the ways of the mosquitoes known that the media has been warning us on the nightly news that due to warm weather and wet conditions, a large hatch can be expected on the coming Tuesday. (If you are reading this, you have survived "the hatch.")

Really now, what are we supposed to do? Perhaps we should leave the state or stay indoors until a September frost. Some folks may cancel family reunion picnics over such news. Others may buy cases of the most potent insect repellent available.

Could it be that the mosquito control folks are seeding such dire forecasts to initiate a public outcry demanding that more must be done to provide a welt-free summer? Would not an increased budget be suddenly more acceptable and likely?

I thought we were a strong people who took pride in our ability to survive the hordes of mosquitos. We proudly wear shirts and apply bumper stickers that place the mosquito over the loon as the Minnesota state bird. Our heritage is rich in tall tales, where gigantic 'skeeters have been known to carry off babies and livestock.

I admit my tolerance of the incessant whine of mosquitos lessens as I grow older and perhaps more tender. At the same time, I have also gained a greater respect for their value.

There are, unfortunately, other nonpesky sorts of insects that fall victim to the blends of malathion, parathion, and other equally tongue-tying chemicals that are aimed at mosquitoes. The slough, a half mile behind our house, would not be as rich and diverse as it is without the mosquito and the many other marsh insects. In their various life stages, these insects provide the needed food for countless life forms such as the bottom-dwelling dragonfly nymphs, schools of minnows, leopard frogs, swallows, and the little brown bat that courses the evening sky.

Removal of mosquitos would result in a chain-reaction disappearance of many other animal species. I can appreciate a stilled and silent January slough but never a quiet June marsh.

One reason the far north remains a relatively unfrequented wilderness is due to the legendary populations of black flies and mosquitos. Wet conditions throughout the summer make this northern frontier a testy place to live or visit. The long daylight hours also warm the countless ponds, ensuring mosquito development. With the long northern winters, the ground never completely thaws, and the permafrost, coupled with the poor drainage of the land, provides ideal mosquito habitat.

One memory I'll never forget is of a canoe trip into the Canadian barrens. In the evening, we sought comfort from the bugs in our tents. If there was no wind, we could hear the ever-present, high-pitched whine just beyond the nylon walls. Sleep, however, usually came quickly and we were spared the torturous drone.

I recall awakening one morning and hearing the sound of rain-drops pattering against the tent. But as my head cleared itself of sleep, I realized that the sun was shining and that the outside of the tent was dry. The pattering was caused by mosquitos and black flies dancing on our tent.

No one was in a hurry to leave the tent, and we wondered aloud if the pests ever slept. Eventually, we had to emerge, and the bugs were waiting. Needless to say, we prayed for winds—gentle enough to paddle in yet strong enough to erase the bugs.

I have learned to use the mosquito's tenaciousness to my advan-tage. It so happens that brook trout and mosquitos share the same shadowy haunts. To pursue the trout, I must withstand the guardians of the stream. It seems that the best fishing often coincides with the time when the bugs are most determined to feast on me. It's not surprising that I very rarely come across another trout fisherman, so I am assured of undisturbed riffles, pools, and beaver dam waters. However, I admit that the creek and its pools lose a bit of their charm when viewed through a head net.

I recently finished stapling the last screen in place for a long overdue screenhouse. It seems I may have finished just in time for tomorrow is "mosquito day," according to the pest prophets.

Beyond the security of my screenhouse, I can only grit my teeth and apply bug repellent laced with a high percentage of DEET, wear long sleeves and perhaps a head net, and wait for the kiss of frost that will spell freedom from the untiring, whine of wings.

It appears that we're in for a long bout of summer.

*"Maybe the pesky little bastards is asking themselves what God wanted to put hands on a man for."*

*"Maybe they're thinkin' everything would be slick, except their dinner can slap 'em."*

*"Maybe they got as much business here as we have. You reckon?"*

# What's in a Name?

The clusters of small greenish white flowers were quite handsome but almost unnoticeable among the more typical splashes of yellow-orange, purple, and blue of a late May prairie.

However, someone in our group did notice the obscure tiny blossoms and asked if I knew what they were called. I was almost embarrassed to answer. I wished I had known the scientific name instead of the more variable common name. Why couldn't this plant have more than one common name, like the marsh marigold alias the clowslip?

I had no recourse but to give the only name I knew for the unpretentious little plant. "Bastard toadflax" was my quick reply. A moment of silence was followed by a horrified, "What an awful name for a flower!"

I had to plead ignorance, for I had no explanation as to how a petaled work of nature could be stricken with such a disgusting name. Since that encounter, I have learned that bastard toadflax is a semiparasitic plant that obtains some of its nourishment from the roots of trees and shrubs. Years ago, rural English folk would use the word *toad* to describe something undesirable. The plant only resembles a true flax and hence is an imposter.

That incident amid the prairie colors got me thinking about the names of particular flowers and how some seem so fitting because they are as phonetically attractive as the flowers they represent. And then there are those, like the toadflax, that the tongue stumbles over when reciting. Names, whether of flowers or people, sometimes give a false impression about the real identity of the subject.

There is a man who lives alone in the north woods and earns his keep by logging, real estate, and being a jack-of-all-trades. His name is Olor Snevets. When I first heard his name, I nearly caught myself responding with a "Gesundheit."

I know of no other Olors, and I suspect that there is almost no chance I will ever come across the name again. On the other hand, there are eighty-one Tom Andersons in the current Minneapolis and St. Paul phone directories, and who knows how many more are found throughout the rest of the world.

Rumor has it that Olor Snevets came alone to the north country years ago, having walked away from a less-than-perfect marriage. In order to cover his tracks, he started a new life under a new name. How could he ever come up with such a jumble of letters of a name you ask? Simple—he took his real name and spelled it backwards.

If by the some remote chance a vindictive Mrs. Rolo Stevens reads this and wants to know my source, I plead the Fifth Amendment.

There are other flowers that have disgusting sounding names. For example, there are louseworts, bladderworts, and spiderworts, and these are but a few familiar plants that end with the suffix -wort. Wort is pronounced like wart, and we all know that warts are small fleshy knobs that we cover with Band-Aids or Compound W or find on toads. Unfortunately, toads and warts have an image problem.

In reality, wort is not wart. The word wort is derived from the Old English word wyrt, which means potherb or plant.

Lousewort is a particularly noxious name, for it is comprised of two supposed outcasts, the louse and the wort. Apparently, it was believed, centuries ago, that if cattle fed on this yellowish flower, they would become infested with lice, rendering them "lousy." Lice are considered vermin and therefore unclean and most undesirable.

Bladderwort is another yellow flower that has a name one would rather whisper than shout. I wonder how many folks on hearing of this plant for the first time shrink away in embarrassment. The thought of a bladder wort is something only doctors should consider. This aquatic plant does, in fact, have many tiny bladders attached to the submerged leaf system. Their purpose, however, is not to store waste products before they can be rid of them. Instead, the tiny bladders trap minute aquatic insects to obtain the needed nitrogen for their growth.

Spiders, like lice, warts, toads, and bladders, are not cherished subjects among most folks. But spiderwort is a beautiful blue flower often found along June roadsides. When one of the long fleshy leaves is broken, it reveals a mucuslike sticky juice. If one slowly draws the broken leaf pieces apart from each other, the string of plant juice stretches to a thin strand resembling a spider web, and only then does one realize the aptness of the plant's name.

I've always felt that the dainty flower fleabane was named by the same folks who labeled the "worts." The word *bane* is derived from an old Anglo-Saxon word *bana,* which means murderer, destroyer, or poison. In other words, when you break the word down into its two parts, you realize that the flower was used as a deterrent against fleas. Fleas, like lice, are vermin and avoided if possible.

Interestingly enough, there are other flowers ending in *bane.* Wolfsbane, dogbane, and bugbane are plants that were used to keep away the subject of their prefix.

Another evil-sounding plant that does, in some respects, live up to its image is the thistle. Utter the word *thistle* and it sounds like a snake with a lisp. Everyone, whether a snake lover or not, respects a hiss.

But not all is forbidding and creepy in the plant kingdom. Many flowers are nearly as beautiful to name as they are to witness. I especially enjoy saying lily and laurel. And then there are trillium, violet, clover, and I can't omit lady's slipper.

It is sheer poetry and music to speak these words. Perhaps it is the gently rolling of the *l*'s that makes these most pleasant sounds. Other words loaded with *l*'s, such as *lovely* or *lullabye,* are likewise soothing.

Perhaps it would be best if we just walked among the flowers and did not learn their names, instead admiring them for what they are. After all, the honeybee and hummingbird know more about blossoms than we ever will, and they don't ponder the names or how the names sound.

I wonder if I could ever get used to Mot Nosredna?

**UPDATE:** Regretfully, the north woods has lost another of its unique characters. Olor Snevets passed away on July 6, 1986.

# Ripening of the Spears

No one forgets their first dog. The second or third may become somewhat foggy in the memory bank, but the first is indelible.

"Pokey" was his name, but in name only. He enjoyed racing our car from the neighbor's house to our house, some 300 yards or so in distance. I always wondered if somewhere in his cluttered lineage that there weren't a few greyhound genes floating around. He was deep in chest, thin of waist, and though his legs were lean, they were well muscled.

One of his trademarks, beside his Holstein coloring, was his tail, which looked like a perpetual hoop—describing it as a curl would not do it justice.

But no matter how fast he was, he could not avoid the annual, early summer hunt when he became the prey and we kids became the hunters. In late June, Pokey was no longer a dog but an imaginary woolly mammoth of preglacial days. We became twentieth century "cavemen," equipped with spears to hurl at this harried, hoop-tailed, ancient elephant.

The reason that the hunt took place in late June was that our spears were not available at any other time of the year. Our supply of weapons came from a patch of tall grass that grew just north of our garden. At this time of the year, the grass was perhaps three feet tall, and the stems were flaxen colored, like a yellow-gold straw. The tips of the grass stems were heavy with long-tailed seeds, causing them to gracefully bend over and sway in the faintest of breezes. If we grasped the five-inch "tails" of the seeds and they pulled out easily, the seed was ripe, and they were no longer seeds, they were spears.

The grass is known as porcupine grass or needlegrass, and it is considered a prairie grass. Indeed, that patch north of our garden kept company with other prairie plants such as big bluestem grass and prairie smoke, also fondly known as grandpa's whiskers. This tiny remnant of prairie is gone now. Instead, a neighbor's yard of Kentucky bluegrass and red fescue covers the ground in a monotonous carpet.

Needlegrass was once quite common throughout the Upper Midwest, but much of it has been erased by the bite of the plow or the cow. Sometimes, however, the speared grass would have its moment of vengeance when a cow would swallow the bristly spears and experience choking or other mechanical problems.

The seed of porcupine grass is the feature that gives the plant its name. Not far from our current mailbox is a strip of ground flanking the road that is host to a number of prairie plants, including porcupine grass. The stems are now bleached the color of summer, and the seeds are ripe and full.

I pulled a few seeds from a clump of the grass and brought them up to the house for a closer look. Under a hand lens, the hard, slender seed closely resembles the armament of a porcupine. The tapered seed comes to a bristly point, with nearly microscopic barbs surrounding the seed's tip. As with a fishhook, penetration is made easier with such an arrangement of barbs but withdrawal is more difficult.

The shaft, or the tail, of the miniature spear is a slender, terminal bristle, technically known as the awn. When the spearlike seed ripens and falls to the ground, the seed tends to screw itself through the ground cover into the earth. The awn is responsible for the self-planting movement. As the humidity or moisture changes, the awn twists in a spiral manner, forcing the seed into a boring motion. Such a method of seed propagation assures future stands of the grass.

One of my pet projects at home is a plot of former yard, measuring about twelve feet by twenty, that I am restoring into a miniature prairie. I have gathered seeds and plants from other nearby locations to sow into my plot. It's been about three years since I first planted, and now it is beginning to look like a real prairie, with an accompaniment of prairie flowers that bloom throughout the summer.

In a few days I will toss gathered porcupine grass seed into the air over the plot and let it journey on its own toward a natural germination. With luck, in two or three years I will have my own stand of needlegrass growing in the company of my Indian and bluestem grass.

Patience is needed more than a green thumb when planting a prairie, for the bulk of the early growth is downward not skyward. One reason these grasses and forbs do so well under the heat of the sun, even during dry years, is that the plants have deep, extensive root systems to prevent drying out.

Dogs and kids have a special partnership, and it never seems more intense then during summer days when kids explore the countryside. The shadowing canine chum is never far from the young summer explorers. Pokey, likewise, followed us everywhere, even when we headed out north of the garden during the latter days of June. After fortifying ourselves with our tiny spears, we would practice our marksmanship on Pokey's back.

In short order there would be a dozen or more spears sprouting from his coat. He never yelped in pain as the seeds never could get through his thick covering of hair. Usually a hearty shake would dislodge all the tiny annoyances from his hide. To get a better, more vocal reaction, we would end up slyly sending one of the green, tiny spears into the back of one of our fellow cavemen. Sometimes, if our T-shirt was tight against the skin, we would emit a yowl of pain.

The drama would be played out with a following counterattack. In the meantime, our object of attack, the black-and-white, hoop-tailed mammoth, would quietly move toward the house to retreat into the shadows behind the spirea hedge. There Pokey would wait for us to evolve from cavemen to twentieth century youngsters.

I recall several battles where we resembled pin-pricked voodoo dolls, but we always had a universal pact that no one was to aim their throws above the shoulders.

I'm not so sure that I will show my children what wonderful spears the grass seeds make. When they are old enough to hurl such spears with any accuracy, our dog, Jenny, will be nearly ten years old—too old to play the part of a mammoth.

# A Fisherman's Toast to Midsummer

Fishing and summer provide the perfect marriage. The two are meant for each other. It's not unlike the relationship that puddles and kids have. Some folks would argue that the best of all combinations is a golden ear of hot sweetcorn and fat slabs of melting butter that refuse to stay on top of the cob. Puddles though, are not restricted to summer, whereas the blissful union of corn and butter is usually an August celebration.

But no alliance seems more true than fishing combined with the slow days of summer, when the buzz of the cicada tries to outdo the drawn-out, lazy whistle of the peewee. So it only seemed natural that friend Charlie and I should usher in the coming season with some fishing on summer's first morn.

Though this first day of summer, renowned by fellow Swedes as "midsummer," is predictable every year, it unfortunately has to wait several years before falling on a weekend. This past year, the solstice fell on a Friday, so our pursuit of largemouth bass had to be a meeting before eight in the morning, when wages are earned.

Charlie, being a salty blend of Scottish-Polish blood, disapproves of the title midsummer. He can't understand how you can have *mid*summer when we have barely had time to taste new sweet peas and radishes. I forgive his ignorance, however. After all, he is foreign to the quivering platter of lutefisk and the bowl of rice pudding that are found on every good Swede's Christmas Eve dinner table.

The sun rose earlier than I did, but as it was the longest day of the year, I knew there would be ample time to hook a bass before going to work. As usual with early-morning rendezvous, I berated myself for not getting up early every morning to witness the quiet period of awakening. Though my intentions are good, I too often find another ten minutes on my snooze alarm to be irresistible.

Our planned early start was just as well though, for it seems that bass are more shallow-shy during the brightness of midday. These explosive predators make their forays in the shallows best during the red-to-gray-to-black skies of dusk and then again during the black-to-gray-to-red skies of dawn. Since we were to try and fool the bass with flies, we also preferred the stillness of morning air to cast the fluffs of colored, trimmed deer hair.

With the sun climbing, I pulled out of the driveway. Just across the road, I noticed feathers from yesterday's pair of drake mallards floating on the temporary pond in the rain-flooded soybean field. Soon, like the strawberries of June, the mallards will be gone. They will retreat to more overgrown cover to shyly finish molting their colors of courtship and take on the quiet, subdued patterns of summer.

Charlie was already in his hip boots and in the water by the time I pulled up to the lake. As I walked down to the lake, gear in hand, I could see Charlie and his reflected duplicate casting their fly rods back and forth with long loops of line extending far out, where they hardly paused before shooting forward. From my vantage point, it looked like Charlie and his upside-down partner were connected at

117

the knees, making a formidable looking predator of fish.

It seems like Charlie always casts too fast. Rather than working into the rhythm of the picture-perfect four-count cast, he condenses his efforts into a two-count cast resembling a gladiator whipping his chariot team on to victory. Charlie gets so wound up with a fly rod in his hands that all else is forgotten. Rather than have the fly pass gracefully back and forth over his head before shooting it out to a pocket of open water in the lily pads, he wants the bug on the water instead of in the air, where bass are only dreams. Hence the hurried two-count cast.

As I made my way through the wet grass to the lake's edge, I made a comment to Charlie that his image had far better casting form than he had. He loudly countered by asking where I had been and that, as usual, I was late. It didn't help matters when he informed me with deliberate pomposity that he had already fooled two nice bass.

When I suggested that we use the canoe that lay overturned in the grass to get out to those hard-to-reach lily-pad beds, Charlie quickly made his way toward the canoe through the man-high canary grass that flanked the shoreline. Had it not been for his extended hand holding the antennalike fly rod, it would have been difficult to tell the difference between him and a not-so-quiet Cape buffalo.

The lake was like glass as we paddled slowly along the lush shoreline, casting into the clear blue reflections of wild iris. Back and forth we waved our slender rods in casting, almost as if we were orchestrating the wild bubbling music of the nearby bobolinks and the closer red-winged blackbirds.

More graceful than our casting was the pair of tree swallows that played tag out over the lake's calm surface. The duo barely skimmed over the water, twisting and turning as only a swallow can. It could mean rain later, for they say when the swallows fly low, the air pressure is dropping, forcing insects and consequently insect-eating birds closer to the ground or water.

Our casting efforts were not unrewarded. Twice that morning we each had leaping, head-shaking bass on our lines at the same moment. The fish were far from trophy size, but they performed well and provided nearly constant action. We carefully unhooked each fish and placed it in the water. Peering down through our grinning reflections, we watched as the bass hung momentarily suspended, unaware of its freedom, before giving an indignant splash of the tail and disappearing into the depths of the still lake. Hardly an appreciative adios for its release.

The action slowed down as the midsummer sun began its long march up into the June sky. It was just as well, for we knew we had better leave the lake, the bobolinks, and the blue-petaled iris or risk losing our jobs.

As we pulled the canoe up onto shore and stowed our fishing gear, Charlie and his stomach both grumbled about his predawn meager breakfast of a half a piece of toast. The other half he had shared with his dog and predawn breakfast companion, Cisco.

But I knew Charlie's love for a fresh pastry—nearly equal to mine—and I had also known we would be hungry by midmorning, so I had stopped at the bakery enroute to our fishing hole.

Bakeries, like bass, seem particularly active just after dawn. I had stood in line behind an electrician and a carpenter as they fortified themselves with the sinful likes of raised doughnuts, fruit-filled rolls, and frosted, chocolate-filled eclairs before heading to their respective jobs.

I had picked out two obese cinnamon rolls from the bottom shelf of the glass case and tucked them into my pack, where they would remain unseen until the right moment.

It's hard to say what got Charlie more excited that morning—the bass strikes that he missed or that oven-warmed roll covered with soft, sticky, white frosting.

I don't pretend to be much of a coffee drinker but there are exceptions, especially when one considers the likes of sweet rolls. We boiled up yesterday's coffee in a small saucepan and poured up a couple of mugs of the inky brew. I've seen creosote oozing from stovepipes that seemed pale by comparison. After muddying the potion with milk, we sat down with our butter-soaked rolls, reflected on the fine morning, and toasted the beginning of summer.

I raised my cup and exclaimed a hearty "Skol!" Charlie only raised his cup and muttered something about the mixed-up Swedes.

# JULY

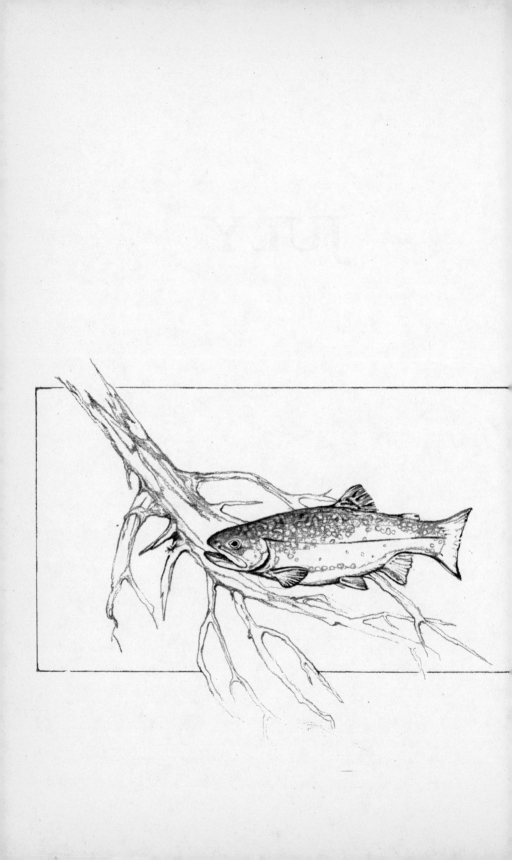

# What Good is a Deerfly?

My dog, Jenny, came dashing by me, ran into the tall grass, rolled on her back, and wriggled back and forth like an oversized, beached tadpole.

Then she got up, ran across the yard, passing under the picnic table before she dove under the overturned boat. But the boat's canopy didn't fill her need, so she scooted out and ran by me again, tail tucked between her legs and jaws snapping futilely at the air about her head.

She seemed crazed, as if she were pursued by an unseen horror.

She made her way for the open garage and entered in search of comfort. Then she sulked in the dark, still, and sultry corner of the garage. The building at least, was somewhat free of the annoying deerflies. Needless to say, she does a lot of sulking these days.

As I stood there watching Jenny's complicated avenue of escape, a fly was burrowing into my hair while a trio of its green-eyed brethren raced around my head. No doubt the three in flight were distracting me while the chosen one was tunneling closer to my scalp for a meal of blood.

Unfortunately for the fly, I felt the intruder before it bit, pulled it through my tangle of hair, and without any compassion whatsoever, rolled it in my fingers and dropped it to the ground.

I swung wildly at the air about my head and taking the same action as the dog, I went for the house. Typical of many Junes and Julys, I find a hat and a nearby building a necessary part of my daily survival.

With deerflies it seems that mental survival is more difficult than staying free of welts. I have seen many grown men and women, normally calm under pressure situations, reduced to babbling idiots

123

after five minutes of deerflies making laps around their heads.

Unlike most flies, these black and green nuisances fly silently. Their tactics seem simple—circle the target however many times is necessary to confuse the host, then light quickly for an equally quick bite.

As with the mosquito, it is only the female deerfly that pesters and bites. When she bites, the blood does not clot, due to the fly's saliva, which acts as a thinning agent, making it easier to draw up a meal. She needs to gorge herself with blood in order to lay the custers of glossy black eggs on the leaves and stems of plants growing just above the water in swamps and ponds.

The male needs only to feed on the juices of plants to nourish himself for his role in mating.

After the eggs hatch, the predaceous fly larvae feed on other aquatic larvae. Finally, the larva is ready to pupate and leave the water. Emergence as a fly usually takes place in a thick mat of floating vegetation or in moist sand or mud at the water's edge.

When the wetlands are full of water, conditions are ripe for a boom deerfly year. It seems every year I hear someone declare, "This is the worst I've ever seen them!" And next summer, they will probably say the same thing.

Frequently, on outings, I hear cries of "What good is a deerfly!?"

As I pull another ensnarled fly from my hair, I usually halfheartedly mutter something about the numerous insects, birds, fish, and frogs that feed on the deerfly and how by eradicating them we would severely disturb a complicated food chain. No one argues with my answer, but there is usually more muttering.

As kids, we were told by someone wiser than us, probably a grown-up, that we should shove fern fronds down the backs of your shirts so that the tall lush fronds would project above our heads and lure the flies away from our scalps.

To a certain extent, it actually worked, though it was uncomfortable having the ferns work their way down our shirt. The problem is that deerflies and ferns are not always close associates, so there were times when we were fernless.

It seems that deerflies are attracted to movement, and they always go for your highest point. The ferns become a decoy of sorts—

though a poor one at best.

I've been on some hikes where kids will walk along extending their hands high over their heads to draw the flies away. I find this technique tiring, and I am forever thinking that the whole group has a question to ask me as they parade through the undergrowth with arms reaching to the sky.

But I have learned there are ways to minimize the deerfly's attacks. There is no need to raise hands, use a headdress of ferns, or stay indoors for two months.

First, a hat helps keep them out of your hair, and a head net does an even better job. I have seen folks wrap their heads in towels, bandannas, hoods, and even paper sacks, such is the fury of the deerfly. Insect repellents seem hopeless unless you lather your hair with Muskol or Cutters.

Through the years I have learned some effective tricks, though I feel reluctant to share them for fear of having my image tarnished. But when faced with circling squadrons of deerflies, my survival instinct is most keen, and all stops are pulled. Anything goes.

When walking with a group, you will find it to your advantage to let someone else go first. It is an ego booster, and it gives the person a sense of being the bold and adventuresome pathfinder.

Deerflies will boil out of the undergrowth and, for the most part, will form a living helmet around the trailblazer. As the harassed leader is waving his or her hands and muttering how bad the flies are, it is wise to make a few perfunctory waves and agree that you've never seen them so bad.

If the front person stops to look at something of interest, make sure you do likewise. Don't become too eager and find yourself at the front of the pack. If you do, you are doomed.

It is best if the tallest person in the group is up front. If that is not possible, walk alongside someone taller than you. They will draw the bulk of the pests. If you happen to be taller than average it might be wise to forget the hike, or walk stooped over and explain your posture by claiming you have a sore back.

I must confess that when I have had an overly loud and rambunctious twelve-year-old in the group, I offer him or her the highly sought position of being the lead person. Funny how a mere insect

LEARNING NATURE BY A COUNTRY ROAD

can take the starch out of the "terror of the block."

I have always been a believer and follower of the principle of "survival of the fittest."

Recently, while adding some finishing touches on a screen house, from which I can enjoy the "lazy, crazy days of summer" without the accompaniment of deerflies, I watched a dragonfly perch on an oak leaf next to me. A closer look showed that the winged predator was manipulating a deerfly in its grasp and slowly but surely the fly was disappearing.

Need I ask the dragonfly the value of a deerfly?

# Learning Nature by a Country Road

Upon stopping at my mother's recently, I noticed that the road going by the house had been widened and repaved. The dull black surface is now smooth, without a blemish and a comfort to drive on. I'm sure that everyone living up and down the road is pleased, for the time being there are no craterlike potholes to slalom by or to jar one's teeth.

For a moment I really enjoyed the smooth ride, until I reflected back a few years when the road was truly a "country road." With the black, hard and unforgiving surface, the road has lost a bit of its original character.

Years ago, it was narrow and without ditches. The woods and brush grew right up to its edge. On a May Sunday afternoon, it was not unusual to see several cars parked along the neighbor's ancient lilac hedge while their owners picked fragrant bouquets. And on a fall Indian summer Sunday, those same folks would stop once more, further down the road, to gather the reddened vines of bittersweet to bring a touch of October into their homes.

A massive red oak stretched its reaching limbs over the narrow road. By day it was harmless and harbored scurrying squirrels, but at night its silhouette seemed formidable and oppressive as it lurked over the road.

I recall several summer evening hikes returning home from town

126

with my younger brother, Scott. As we approached the eerie form of the dark tree, I often wondered aloud what it would be like to spot a dead man hanging by his neck from the limb that stretched over the road. At this point, Scott would plead in a quavering voice, "Tom, shuuuuut up!" But the more I tried scaring him, the more frightened I became, and soon we showed our heels to the heavens as we raced under the tree, down the hill, to the safety of our beckoning yard light.

In the winter, the snow-covered road would become packed ice hard from passing traffic. As there was no salt or gravel spread on the road, we sometimes had our own skating rink lane. Up and down the road we skated, watching closely for traffic and the occasional exposed rock or patch of sand.

Since those winter days, I've never known the effortless glide of a downhill stretch like the one provided by the slight hill just south of our driveway.

Change was inevitable as the Skoogs, Harders, and Schmidts sold portions of their woods and fields. Stakes denoting surveyed or measured lots started showing up. Basements were dug, and new homes seemed to pop from the earth. Traffic became heavier, and there was pressure to upgrade the narrow road. First, roadsides were cleared, ditches cut, and the road widened. The lilac hedge, the bittersweet, and the spooky oak all stood in the way and were erased. The road is safer now—even if there are far too many yard lights to make scaring younger brothers worthwhile.

But it is the sugar sand that I remember best. A fine sand that thousands of years before had tumbled and sorted as it settled on the bottom of a misdirected Mississippi River. The original river course was temporarily dammed by a massive lobe of ice extending to the northeast, and the widened flow of meltwater was rerouted miles to the east of its present channel.

I like to think that we grew up on a river bed, long extinct perhaps, but nonetheless an actual river bottom.

It was a sand so thick and fine that it literally swallowed my bicycle tires. To forge through the sand, it seemed that we pedaled from a standing position more than from a sitting one. Coasting was a luxury, while strong calf muscles were the norm.

In the spring the sloppy road was made up of meandering ribbons of ruts that formed temporary rivers that we kids would dam to create pools until the next passing car would destroy our efforts.

And what a thrill it was to read the daily chapters authored in the sand by the crossing doe and fawn, the marauding fox, or the grit-seeking pheasant. Tracks left in the sandy road provided countless mysteries and puzzles. Only after seeing a plodding June bug swimming through the sand did I realize what had left the pair of squiggly lines across the road. What a treat to follow the shuffling tracks to the shy turtle burying its nest of eggs on the road's edge.

Dirt roads can be an improvement over books rich in natural history. If I can personally witness the clues, I will better remember that May and June are the months to watch for turtle tracks and nests. The pheasant leaves a chapter telling that it needs to bathe in dust or seek gravel bits in order for its gizzard to render the beans or corn to pulp.

Asphalt, however, leaves no tracks. The nighttime travels go unnoticed and the mystique is gone. I wonder how many kids on that road even know what a fox or raccoon track looks like.

As we accumulated new neighbors, daily traffic increased. For convenience and ease of maintenance, the road was coated in a layer of asphalt. The problem of blowing dust billowing up as cars sped by was ended. Gone were the muddy springtime ruts to contend with. The newly paved road increased the appeal of those acres adjoining it, and still more houses were built.

Oh sure, there are many benefits to a paved road. The question of paving a road or not paving it is a sore spot among county board members. The success of county commissioners is measured by how much money they can save while providing the maximum services to their constituents, which includes paving roads.

In the decade from 1967 to 1977, over thirty million acres of land were paved or built on in the United States. For every mile of interstate highway that stretches across the state, thirty-three acres of land were consumed. Prime farmland, wetlands, forests, and meadows were not immune to that reach of the freeway.

I enjoy a smooth ride as well as the next person, but perhaps we would lessen our traffic accident rate and better enjoy the countryside if we weren't in such a hurry to get where we are going. Sandy roads have a way of slowing one down.

I don't live on that road anymore but I do live on another unpaved road. It has enough sand to make "reading" worthwhile and biking a bit more work. I look forward to the day when my daughters will learn to read the daily journal of the road. They will learn, as I did, to ride a bike in the sand. I can be sure that they will each have a strong set of legs. There will be some spills during those first wobbling moments of the solo ride on two wheels, but the pain shouldn't be too bad. Whoever heard of someone skinning their knee in the sand?

# A Breach of Manners

To some folks, insects are simply bugs. I accept that premise, but then it seems awkward to label a butterfly a "bug." Their colors, fragility, and graceful manner of flight seem beyond a mere bug. Butterflies, to many, most resemble flowers in flight. In fact, one can hardly envision a meadow of flowers without the bouncing flight of a butterfly.

Among August's blue spikes of blazing stars, I can be assured of finding nectar-thirsty monarchs. Or if there are round, blue thistle blossoms, I will likely see the smaller, less colorful butterfly called the painted lady.

Bugs, on the other hand, are often depicted as offensive, six-legged beasts that might pester us for a taste of our blood, eat our gardens, get in the flour bin, or writhe as they scavenge a rotting carcass. In other words, only bugs seem capable of utterly despicable acts.

Yet recently, as I nosed a canoe onto the muddy shore of a local lake, I caught a butterfly in the act of being a bug. The offender was an eastern tiger swallowtail, a favorite of mine in its scale-garb of pale yellow and tigerlike black stripes and tailed hind wings.

As the bow of the canoe furrowed into the mud, bringing the canoe's momentum to a stop, the swallowtail fluttered up from the water's edge and reluctantly circled. It was obvious that the but-

129

terfly had been disturbed, and now it boldly showed in its circling that it wasn't about to leave the spot. But instead of a flower, the attraction was a runny streak of white on the black mud. The long-toed track of a heron, still fresh, identified the guano maker. Without acting the least bit embarrassed or shy about its intentions, the butterfly gently touched down on the heron droppings and uncurled its long, rolled-up proboscis and started feeding.

I sat and watched as the butterfly tentatively walked across the stained mud and feasted on the morning offering. How can such a gentle, floating symbol—one of nature's beauty marks—have such an attraction to the bodily wastes of another animal? Everyone knows that such duties are relegated to loud bottle flies, seething maggots, and other bugs.

I can prove that this was not the appalling act of a degenerate butterfly. Somewhere in one of our closets, in a paper sack filled with boxes of slides, is a photograph taken of a pile of northern Minnesota bear droppings. The feces were not so much my subject as were the dozen tiger swallowtails that covered and fed on the bear scat—a moment of beauty and the beast. Such a seemingly deviate behavior in which an animal feeds on excrement is referred to as coprophagy.

Rabbits, those innocent symbols of Easter and spring, often engage in this distasteful practice. However, they are more fastidious in that they eat their own pellet droppings. Two types of droppings are expelled by rabbits—a night pellet and a day pellet. The rabbit prefers the soft green pellet that is usually passed during the daytime loafing period. These pellets are formed of plant foods that are only slightly digested. By eating them a second time, the rabbit is recycling its own food, enabling it to make use of any remaining nutrients left in the pellet. Such strange eating habits are beneficial when pickings are lean for the rabbit, especially during winter's lean days.

Before we start changing our opinions of the grace and beauty of a butterfly, we should understand that swallowtails and other dung or carrion-seeking butterflies—yes, there are others—are primarily nectar feeders. However, swallowtails find the scat a readily available source of nitrogen and amino acids, all necessary components for growth and development.

The swallowtail I watched was large, with a wingspan of at least four inches. I guessed it to be a female because among swallowtails she is the larger of the two sexes. Likewise, she is most apt to be the more ardent scat-seeker. She is the egg layer and most in need of nitrogenous compounds for the development of her eggs. The droppings also provide a needed source of sodium for these colorful insects.

Unlike the fly that delights in finding a decaying animal or pile of droppings to use as a nursery for its eggs, the female swallowtail will likely lay her eggs on the green leaves of a cherry or ash tree. After the eggs hatch, the caterpillars, or larvae, will spend their days doing nothing but eating the leaves on which their lives started.

The butterfly I watched was especially bold and most reluctant to leave its heron treasure. Several times it flew within an arm's length of me. It would have been an easy catch had I been armed with a butterfly net. Often these same strong-flying butterflies are observed twenty to thirty feet off the ground, keeping company with the treetops. Hence they are difficult to catch.

My patience was no match for the swallowtail, so I placed the paddle's blade into the mud and pushed off, leaving the butterfly alone with its secret.

On second thought, maybe it was a bug that I left behind.

# Summer's Arena

Though parades and lemonade stands draw well in the summer, they don't have the same magnetism that a beach has.

Recently, on a hot, muggy day, we wove our way among a clutter of spread beach towels and partially clad bodies to stake our claim on a piece of a lakeside beach. We found ourselves settling close to the waterfront, where most of our neighbors, like ourselves, were toting children's water wings, beach balls and float tubes bearing smiles of Mickey Mouse and Papa Smurf.

After a much-needed, cooling dip in the lake, I felt rejuvenated as I made my way back to our small pile of familiar towels.

Behind our vantage point on the beach was the unmistakeable

131

booming of a suitcase-size radio. Spread out near the music maker were three copper-skinned fellows tossing a frisbee back and forth, trying their best to make spectacular, leaping contorted catches.

Between throws they would comb their fingers through their hair or toss their head back to put their locks back into place. This was all very serious business as there was no smiling.

This seemed most peculiar, because I know I can raise a smile from my preschool daughter if I suggest an outing to the beach. She equates beaches with fun, and something fun will bring out a smile.

As I watched the young men perform, I noticed there were several clusters of similar-aged, bronzed females intently watching the frisbee performance. It was apparent that the lean Olympian frisbee throwers were showing their skills, and to smile would not be cool.

A short distance away was another radio thumping out a beat, only this one was slightly smaller than the first. This radio also had a covey of young folks clustered around it. All were well tanned and suited in loud splashes of color.

I became curious about what I was seeing, so I strolled along the beach and found similar isolated focal points of radios, coolers, combinations of the two, another less skilled group of frisbee throwers, or groupings of beach lovers sitting and laughing on ruglike towels.

What proved interesting was that each radio, cooler, and blanket grouping was spread out rather nicely, almost in a territorial arrangement.

Immediately, I was reminded of several past predawn outings to a Wisconsin grassland to witness prairie chicken booming grounds. Such an area of communal courtship is known as a lek and is derived from the Swedish word *leka,* which means "to play, gather, or assemble."

From inside a plywood blind, several of us had watched a gathering of male prairie chickens dance and give their resonant booming sounds from their inflated orange air sacs found on the sides of their throats. Female prairie chickens are attracted to the dancing and booming. If a hen should stroll within the arena, nearby males become more excited, and the intensity of the dancing and booming is accelerated.

132

Though such booming grounds are rarer today than before the plows of early settlers turned the sod, the male chickens still practice the same courtship tactics that they have successfully used to attract the female birds.

Similar dramatics were obvious at the beach: the arena of dancing males and females leaping for frisbees, the booming stereos, the curious onlookers, the shy smiles, and the spacing of blankets and towels. There were obvious locations on the beach where more traffic was directed, hence better potential of being viewed. Such an area played host to the most skillful of the frisbee throwers, who coincidentally had the loudest music. Is it just a coincidence that this same stretch of turf is often controlled by the best of frisbee tossers?

I smiled, remembering a few years ago when similar displays were carried out with a different group of participants and different tunes. I suspect many of those adults who were now stationed along the waterfront chasing windblown water wings and the Mickey Mouse tubes had similar smiles as they remembered their own displays and antics.

Only a few days prior to the sweltering visit to the local beach, we were exploring a different sort of beach. This one bounds a small northwestern cove on Lake Superior. The water is too cold to swim in and is composed of rocks rather than sand grains.

It is no surprise, in fact it was comforting, to find this beach without radios or their bearers. There are no territorial displays here, just the lake, its rhythmic wash, and a beach of stones. Such beaches are more popular for those who are beyond the interest of displaying and attracting attention.

On hands and knees, my wife, eldest daughter of four years, and I ran our hands through the depths of pebbles in search of an agate or other pretty rock. We talked of how these rocks were smoothed and rounded by strong waves rushing onto the beach and then washing more slowly back to the lake. Back and forth, year after year, century after century, the water has tossed these pebbles about, wearing them smooth. Someday these pebbles will become grains of sand and maybe give rise to a beach of sand.

As we searched, our daughter Britta stated that the best beaches have "lots of little, pretty rocks."

"How many pebbles do you think are on this beach?" I asked. Without any deliberation to compute such a problem, she firmly declared, "fifty-one hundred, fifty hundred, eighty-one rocks." I wasn't about to argue because she may have been correct.

For the time being, I'm going to cherish our agate searches, because there will be a day when sand beaches, frisbees, nonsmiling guys, and radios might have more appeal than two parents crawling around on their hands and knees.

# Sheltering Hedges

I was a good half mile from a sheltering roof when the sky quickly darkened and a mist of rain started to fall. I was caught in the open in an overgrown, grassy field. Nearby was a lush belt of shrub and thicket, so I set my course for it to see if it offered a bit of cover.

Bent over, I twisted and turned to penetrate through the tangle of stems and branches as I entered the dark heart of the thicket. For the moment, I was dry, while above me, the uppermost roof of leaves fluttered in a quiet hiss as the rain hit. I knew that if the rain continued for any duration, the lower leaves would soon be soaked by the runoff from the thicket's canopy. Eventually, my dry hideout would become a wet one.

A quick flash of gray feather just ahead of me betrayed the presence of a catbird, another shelter seeker. I was the intruder, for thickets and hedges are home grounds to such birds as catbirds, song sparrows, and brown thrashers. Even though these birds were momentarily quiet and out of sight, their clues were evident. Many of the green leaves were splashed with the whitewash of bird droppings.

If I'm ever pressed to find a bird nest, I will first investigate such a hedge. Many birds choose to raise their broods there.

Slowly, I crept along a fallen, rusty barbed-wire fence that the thicket now hid from view. Lying under the old fence, partially covered by years of accumulated leaves and twigs, was a slight ridge of softball-sized rocks. I paused as I imagined the drudgery of the annual spring job of picking the frost-heaved rocks from the field and dumping them along the fence line. Plows and rocks have never been compatible.

Here and there among the rocks were pieces of old broken bottles, mostly in shades of amber and blue. Occasionally, pieces of clay-fired crockery could be seen among the rocks. Not only was this a shelter for birds and myself, but I was in the midst of a history book.

It was no accident that this hedge grew here. Many years ago, a farmer stretched this barbed-wire fence around his property. It's unlikely that he had any idea that the birds of his fields and woods would create a living fence that would one day entomb his strands of steel.

Most wire fences serve as convenient perches for passing birds. In pausing on the fence, birds often defecate the seedy remains of juicy berries and fruits that they had gleaned from distant fruiting shrubs. The hard, undigested seeds fall beneath the fence, and if given ample space, sunlight, moisture, and time, they will sprout. A neglected fence line eventually becomes a hedge.

Rather than spend dollars on "wildlife plantings" offered by various conservation-minded organizations, wouldn't it be simpler to let the birds plant a hedge of their own choice?

Simply stretch a single wire along the route where you want your future hedge and let the birds do the rest. One can be creative and provide more cover by routing the wire in a series of curves. To hasten the hedge's progress, I would work up the ground directly beneath the bird perch, exposing bare soil to reduce the struggle between competing plants.

Most hedges, including the one I took refuge in, are not pure stands of shrubs. Instead, they are hybrids—a mixture of species that make the thicket more diverse and appealing for wildlife. In this particular sanctuary, hazel was predominant, followed by dogwood with its white fruits forming. Along the outer border of the hedge, where the sun shone brightest, a living version of a barbed fence, the arching thorned blackberry canes, made this thicket truly a refuge.

Some hedges have particular attributes. As youngsters, we used to crawl under the drooping, skirtlike branches of whitened spirea bushes that encircled my grandparents's big front porch. From underneath the spirea, we quietly watched the goings-on of the farm without being seen.

Often, one or more of the cats or the dog would be rousted from a midday nap as we scurried under our hideout. To this day, the smell of a May spirea evokes memories of that front porch hedge.

Sumac thickets were also great arenas for play, because their spreading canopy of leaflets provided us with a tent of shade in the clear, grassy understory. Winter cottontails also frequented the copses of sumac. Though they were rarely seen, we followed their trodden paths among the freshly gnawed and girdled sumac stems.

Thickets of wild plum were difficult to penetrate, with their miserable maze of branches. Perhaps that is why the gawdy autumn pheasants often hang out in such places. It's as if they know I am reluctant to invade such a tangle. That is one of the reasons I own a dog who is curious about the hot odor of pheasant.

I am more apt to brave the plum thicket in the spring, when the white-petaled blooms create the heaviest of perfumes. Once inside such an aromatic thicket, I am reluctant to leave, even if I must keep company with a leap-frogging orchestra of honeybees and bumble-bees.

There is something unexplainably comforting about standing in the midst of a thick hedge. Perhaps it's the shade, the darkness, or the quiet sense of security. Even after the rain shower quit and the sun shone once again, I found it difficult to leave the strip of wildness.

A small flock of cedar waxwings landed very close to me but quickly left when they spied me. Then off to my right came the catbird's alarm call meowing from the thicket. Obviously, I was out of place—the trespasser. Reluctantly, I crept back into a world of sunshine.

# Beating the Heat

Driving to work, I passed several hayfields streaked with long windrows of yesterday's cut hay. Over the field and road, there was a tinge of bluish haze, the kind that forecasts a muggy day.

The voice over the radio did not have to tell me that even though it was only 8:00 a.m., it was already eighty degrees Fahrenheit. The haze and the lazy, shade-seeking cattle along my morning route were indications of an upcoming barn burner of a day.

When I got to work and got out of my car, I noticed that even the rocks on the drive were sweating. The humid woods were quiet without bird song. On those days when the mercury climbs into the uncomfortable range, it becomes critical that the parent birds brood their young, shading them from summer's hot sun. Without feathers, the nestlings cannot regulate their body temperature and depend on the umbrella wings and body of their parents.

It would be one of those days when I would let the sun and humidity chart my tasks for the next eight hours. Like many of the creatures of the desert, I was going to survive best by avoiding the heat rather than coping with it. In other words, it would be best if I didn't move much, stayed in the shade, or retreated underground.

As the sun climbed and that overall feeling of stickiness took hold, the phone rang. So as not to increase my metabolic rate any more than I had to, I moved in slow motion to the phone.

Upon answering it, I was challenged with a single, deliberate question, "Do birds sweat?" Before I had time to answer I could feel the clammy earpiece of the phone receiver stick slightly to my ear.

"No," I answered, "birds cannot sweat. They don't have any sweat glands."

We are capable of shedding as much as a gallon of sweat onto the surface of our skin in one hour. Under somewhat dry conditions, much of this salty moisture will evaporate, thus cooling us off. To increase the rate of evaporation and cool off faster, I can direct the wind driven from a fan towards me or create lesser air currents with a fanning hand or newspaper.

To avoid overheating, birds and many mammals will pant. Panting is simply rapid, shallow breathing that flushes out excess heat. Some birds will triple their breathing rate while panting. With more air passing over the inside of the mouth, tongue and nasal passage, heat can be more readily lost. Birds are equipped with a number of air sacs inside their body. Not only do they hold air to maintain a light body for flight, but it may serve to cool the body. Evaporation is increased internally, thus cooling the bird. The blood flow in a dog's tongue can increase up to six times the normal flow at the onset of panting to better flush out the surplus of heat. Though panting may appear uncomfortable and strenuous, it has an advantage over sweating in that there is little loss of much needed salts.

I remember as a kid, walking down the main street sidewalk on a very hot summer day and coming upon a couple of folks leaning over a fallen person. Lying on the sidewalk in front of the grocery store was an older man. The man was flushed, and his movements were slowed. In a few minutes, after word traveled up the street, nurse Dottie came hurrying across from the doctor's office. With the appearance of the nurse in her white uniform, hat, and socks, the crowd parted and let her through. Through the encircling fence of legs, I heard the word "heatstroke." Dottie gave the man a salt tablet or two and some sips of water and had him rest in the storefront shade.

In short order the man was up. The crowd dispersed, and I hurried home with a story that would be worth repeating to my family and friends for at least another week.

If you raise chickens, ducks, or watch a resident robin or grackle patrol your yard, take a close look at them on a hot day. Chances are their bills will be gaping open. Unlike dogs, their tongue is not very fleshy. Nor does their tongue hang well out of their mouth, slobbering all over everything.

Unfortunately, when the humidity is high neither sweating nor panting is very efficient. The only way to beat the uncomfortable humidity is to become aquatic and take to the water or to follow the ways of desert animals and stay low in the shade and plan activities in the cool early morning or evening hours.

The inquiring woman on the phone was satisfied with my answers and perhaps a bit jealous that birds didn't have to contend with sticky clothes that show dark perspiration streaks or patches. She thanked me for my help, and as I hung up the phone, I thought I could hear the unmistakable rhythm of panting on the other end.

# AUGUST

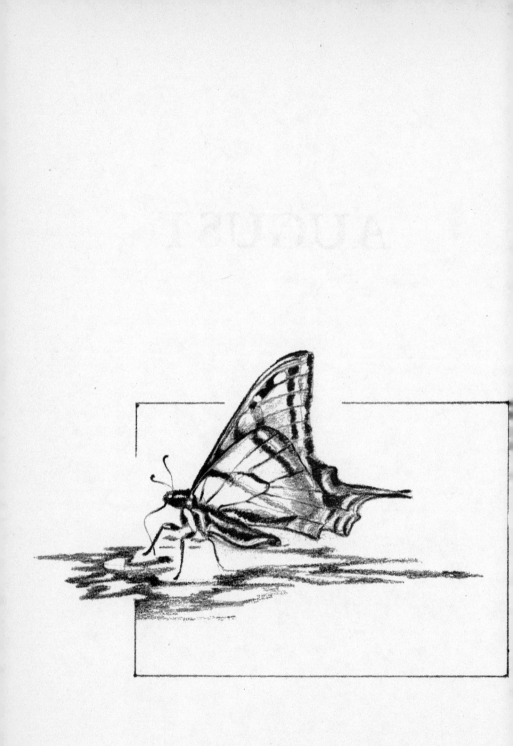

# A Creek's Power

Moose Creek, Murmur Creek, Kimball Creek, Hay Creek, Indian Creek, Irish Creek . . .

There are certain words that I cherish. They have the power to fuel daydreams and rekindle memories. There is a lilting music in their assemblage of consonants and vowels. One word that stirs my innermost feelings is *creek*.

As a youngster, I would play with my friends for hours down by the "crick." We built forts and friendships along its banks. The crick, a half-mile from my folks' place, was a summer spot—a place to swim, float in inner tubes, hurl pitchforks at wallowing carp, and to catch long-legged leopard frogs. But that was a crick, not a creek.

A creek should be born from the earth—spring fed, pure, and cold. It is a place where I can lay on the bank, lower my face and peer through the crystalline water at the stone-strewn bottom while I draw in a refreshing drink. With my dripping face barely off the water, I may spot a mass of glued-together pebbles and sand grains, resembling an underwater cocoon, crawling along the bottom. Upon closer inspection, I may see tiny insect legs sticking out at one end of the stonework. This is the larval home of one of the many caddis flies.

Unable to swim, the larvae slowly crawl along the bottom carrying their protective housing. After a year or so of growing and retrofitting its stone coverings, the larva pupates and finally matures to an emerging adult caddis fly. Quick on the wing, the caddis fly is easiest observed when it is bound to the creek.

The brook trout that live in the creek are more interested in the caddis fly than I am. Brook trout consider this insect food, as I consider the trout sport and delicious. A creek is not a creek without the brilliantly flashing colors of a brookie. It is not just the color, the sport, or the taste of the fish that I love, it is their haunt that absorbs not only the trout but my total self.

Every creek must have overhanging trees to cast sun-dappled shadows over its surface. The tree's shade keeps the water cool, ensuring the brook trout its preferred waters. Some of the overhanging trees will have fallen across the creek. Others growing at the edge of the creek will have had their roots washed free by the water's flow. Either way, the tangly mass of limb and roots provide a secure hideout for the creek's trout. My dwindling hook and fly supply is proof of the protection given by submerged trees and roots.

From the shadows run shallow riffles sprinkled with scattered boulders. Some of the higher rocks are moss covered, and the black, tapered scat left on a flat-topped boulder prove that a mink also has feelings for the creek. In the spring's high water, the boulders are awash or drowned by the March and April snowmelt. By early summer, these boulders will inspire the water to chuckle and make music.

At the end of the singing water, there should be a dark, nearly black, pool. The water here is quiet while it swirls in short-lived whirlpools, slackens, and pauses before it races onto another set of riffles. The water will not be denied its rendezvous with a river or lake and ultimately the sea.

Water flows more slowly through a pool, and it is easier for a trout to lie here and collect any drifting insects or minnows that gather. The deeper pools are too dark to see the bottom, and it is such pools that haunt me with visions of large trout.

These creek holes are magnets for trout, and it is no wonder that the flanking fisherman trails are often most heavily trodden and littered with empty worm boxes here. There are various degrees of creeks, and those flowing too close to a road are usually heavily traveled. If the muddy paths dwindle to faint trails, I know that I am returning to a "true" creek. A creek should be a Brigadoon of sorts, a magical getaway where wonderful things happen.

I was raised just northeast of North Branch near Beaver Creek. Most of the local folks never called it Beaver Creek, it was always "the trout stream." Since the 1940s, the state fisheries people had made April pauses there to dump thousands of various-sized brook trout into the creek's waters. Though there were some stretches where the fish reproduced, the hatchery fish bolstered the population.

During those growing-up years, I remember biking to the creek under the hot summer sun on an overly sandy road. With my brother or neighbor chum, I never enjoyed the luxury of coasting on that road as we toted our fishing gear to the creek. Tackle was simple—just one two-piece cane pole carried across the basket of my bike.

In the pasture below my great aunt and uncle's farm, there was always a pitchfork stuck in the soft ground to use for digging worms. An empty coffee can left at the fork held our wriggling bait. A short hike from the fork was the creek. The field road crossed the creek there, and it was always a highly prized fishing hole. At the crossing, the narrow creek disappeared into a brush-screened, rusted culvert. We used to call dibs on the culvert because any pasture worm drifted into the black, swirling entrance almost always encountered a hungry trout. There was no need to dally at the culvert. It was only good for one trout on each outing. From the culvert we would move upstream or downstream to other familiar runs and pools.

The hot August sun usually drove the worms deeper, so we often scoured the grassy ditches, jars in hand, to catch the "tobacco-spitting" grasshoppers. Hooked carefully on a hook, the grasshoppers would frantically kick. Placed in the water, the insect would kick and swim as only a grasshopper can. Playing out line, the bait would drift unseen through a tunnel of canary grass that arched over the creek as it cut across the pasture. Unable to see our sacrificial offering, we would listen for the sudden splash that foretold of a taking trout.

In those days, I didn't know there was a difference between hatchery-raised and native trout. For a twelve-year old, it didn't matter, because any landed trout was a prize worthy of admiration.

Beaver Creek had a problem, however. It's true identity was a mystery. According to the books at the county courthouse, the creek was known as County Ditch #3—a source of embarrassment for the creek's trout.

In recent years, pressure has been applied to county officials by folks who have an interest in the rich, black fields of peat that bordered much of the creek. Peat, like a sponge, has the ability to hold a large amount of water. If the water can be removed, the agricultural potential is great. The easiest way to get rid of the water is to carve ditches across the peat-land.

Miles of straight, lateral ditches entered the little trout creek. It was argued that more land could be made tillable if the main ditch, ditch #3, was widened and cleaned of any clogging brush or trees. A clean raceway could more effectively carry off a greater flow of water.

After several heated public hearings, the promise of an increased tax base won out. Officially, the creek's flow was a county ditch and not a designated trout stream. It wasn't long before draglines and other heavy equipment were moved in to do the job.

Fields of corn, sod, carrots, and radishes have a monetary value to the farmer, his family, local businesses, and the local tax base. No revenue is taken in when the creek entertains a kid watching the splash of a rising trout or spying on a streamside mink. Nor is the county any richer for the vision of a boy churning through the sand as he pedals his bicycle home toting a stick from which hangs a trio of brookies.

Except for perhaps a haphazard stray, the trout are gone now. The state no longer finds it a worthy place to pause in their April hatchery trucks. There is no cover under which to hide, keep cool, or sulk. No longer is there a Beaver Creek, and I submit it is indeed a county ditch.

Besides draglines and chain saws, I must contend with another scourge of the creeks. Swift running water carries a continual supply of oxygen for both trout and water-borne insects such as blackflies.

The trout benefits best from the blood-seeking creek mate. For the fish there is nourishment in the tiny flies that feed on me. Nothing tests my fishing perserverance greater than a June-hatch of blackflies.

I recall a day of trout fishing on a northern Minnesota creek. The sky was clear, too clear for the best fishing, and the scent of fir and cedar mingled in the air. Also mingling in the air were goodly numbers of blackflies.

144

I felt smug, however, because this time I carried my beekeeping helmet and net to keep the bugs from feasting on my face. The only problem was that while the mesh of screen kept the mosquitoes at bay, the tinier, more persistent blackflies could squeeze their way in. Repeatedly, I had to rub my hand over my netted face to smash those flies that fancied it. To lunch in comfort, I climbed a tumble of boulders to sit at the base of a falls. Here the cascade's mist cooled my brow and held the blackflies back. The deep pool below the falls held my interest, and after eating a damp sandwich, I cast into the deep, frothy water and caught two wonderfully colored brook trout.

That evening I went to a wedding with my face and neck bearing the reddened welts of forty-two bites. I counted every one of them. But it didn't matter, because I had also carried out six plump brookies and the memories of a very special creek.

# Backwater Mysteries

Many folks who don't really know a river consider its backwaters to be akin to the "other side of the tracks." After all, it is the hearty flow of a river that beckons travelers to ride its current and poets or balladeers to write of its energies.

A backwater is that part of the river that is hidden in the closet, often unseen, beyond the main river channel or tucked in the shadows of flanking trees. A backwaters could be the remains of the overflowing spring runoff. It may be the track of yesteryear's river, where the current had once coursed. Eventually, its persistent energy cut a new, shorter, more direct route. The backwaters are clues of the river's past travels and past immensity.

Upon hearing of a backwaters, one often conjures up images of alligators, blanket of rolling fog, bloodsuckers, or an enfolding tunnel of overhanging trees. In a backwater, the river is quiet. There is no hiss of current or cadence of a rapids. One expects to hear junglelike calls of unseen birds or hear whispered tales of bloody murders. Indeed, Huck Finn lived in such a backwater, where he staged a gruesome scene to fool his drunken pappy.

The St. Croix River has a hard time living up to such an ominous reputation. There are no gators, no Huck Finn shacks, and certainly no jungle birds. However, a barred owl with its varied vocabulary presents a respectable "jungle bird." And foggy nights, misty mornings, and hidden caves or arching trees are all part of a St. Croix backwater.

On the contrary, a backwater is home to far more life than the main avenue of the river. To cope with a strong current, one must be either well anchored, streamlined, or very strong. In the lazy flow of a backwater, plants thrive. Plants attract insects which feed on each other or dine on living or rotting plants. Birds and fishes are enticed by the insects, a host of mammals, reptiles, and amphibians get their share as well.

Recently, while exploring such a side channel with a group of kids, we came across another backwater product. The intent of our adventure was to learn the ways of river fish and how to tempt them to take our baited hooks. As with all fishing, it has its slow moments, and soon several of the boys were off wading into the backwaters, climbing over washed-in silver maples. The moment could very likely have been a peaceful summer scene of the sort that Tom Sawyer or Huck Finn might have known.

All of a sudden, one of the boys yelled for me, with a hint of fear in his voice. I made my way through the knee-deep water and over the fallen river maples to join the cautious group of boys. As I peered into the water where they were pointing, I heard comments about a "rotting body," or "looks like brains" and "ooh that looks nasty." Affixed to a submerged maple branch was a series of large, melon-shaped balls of a gelatinous consistency.

I assured them it wasn't a body as I carefully pulled at the branch, drawing the whole mass closer. Now that the initial apprehension passed, the boys became bold and helped me ease the limb and its mysterious cargo into the shallows.

Rather than finding the fetid remains of some animal or a large cluster of frog eggs, there were colonies of moss animals known as bryozoans. Each round mass is made up of thousands of microscopic individuals. Unable to grow in fast moving water, the colonies are found in the haunts of backwaters or in ponds where the current is slowed and shaded.

A closer inspection showed that the mass was very slippery yet firm. The species we looked over was the genus *Pectinatella,* which is derived from the Greek word *pektikos,* "to coagulate." During the peak growing season, each colony is capable of creeping several inches every day over the limb, stick, or whatever object it clings to.

Each mass or colony is made up of thousands of individuals called zooids that lie at the surface of the jellylike matrix. A crown of fine tentacles encircles the opening of each zooid. These hairlike structures are nets and filter out food particles such as microscopic algae, diatoms, and protozoa that drift over the colony. Few animals bother the assemblage of slippery animals.

By fall, the colonies start to disintegrate. Countless tiny winter buds are released and float downriver or are carried by a heron's muddy feet to a distant backwater or pond to begin a new colony the following summer after a winter of dormancy.

Though a bryozoan's appearance may seem disgusting, it is an indicator of a good water quality. These animals cannot flourish in polluted waters.

After we inspected the globes of *Pectinatella* and boy had touched or prodded the colony, I got the feeling that the boys would have rather found a body or some other gruesome backwater treasure. It's hard to get too excited about things that are microscopic or don't move.

We left the dark cavern of trees and waded back to the sunlit world of a flowing river—a more comfortable place, at least for poets and balladeers.

# Crickets Warming Up

In the darkness, there were two sounds: the quiet hum of a fan and the ring of cricket music. The fan was unwavering in its feeble attempt at providing any sort of soothing comfort to us. The air was heavy, too heavy for the fan to effectively push away.

On this night, Susan and I abandoned our overheated, upstairs bedroom. We opted for the somewhat more tolerable lower level for a night on the fold-out couch in the living room. Here there is a battery of windows to catch the relief of a wandering breeze. Upstairs, our bedroom is stifling with trapped heat and has only one window, facing south, to catch the limited wind offerings.

As the sun melted into the hazy, western horizon, all of our windows had been pushed open to invite any accommodating breeze into the house. However, the wind was elsewhere on this evening, and the only entry through our screens was made by the notes of the crickets.

I closed my eyes, remaining as still as possible and listened to the crickets' untiring calls. Their music pulsated, giving the night's darkness an eerie, high-pitched heartbeat.

While we tend to falter and slow down in the heat, crickets seem to accelerate as the mercury climbs. Crickets and other insects are cold-blooded, and as temperatures rise, so does their metabolic process, which includes chirping. Likewise, as temperatures drop, the cricket slows and chirps become fewer.

Somewhere in my file, I have some notes giving a formula to gauge the air temperature by noting the number of cricket chirps heard over a certain period of time. After the chirps are counted, a constant, fourteen I believe, is added. There may be another function of multiplication or division, but I don't remember it, and it's far too hot to ferret out the correct formula. Crickets may do well in the heat, but the virtue of patience has a lapse.

As with the previous muggy evenings, the night belonged solely to the crickets and the occasional erratic buzz of other evening insects. None of the other typical nocturnal noises could be heard. The local accompaniment of barred owls were silent, as were the distant farm dogs, who usually barked for the slightest of reasons. It was too hot.

I am not ashamed or embarrassed to admit that our home is without an air conditioner. We could go out tomorrow and buy a window-unit type, or we could scrimp or borrow the money and have a central air-conditioning unit pump a current of wonderful cool air throughout the house.

I'm hesitant to make such a purchase because part of me would rather spend the money on something that builds memories, like a fishing boat or a dreamed-about trip. Air conditioners are not the usual cause of such reminiscences. Another part of me clings to the old-fashioned. I am reminded that years ago, folks fared without air conditioners and even electric fans. These sturdy folks had no choice in the matter. Yet I sometimes wonder if these people really were made of tougher stock.

So in pursuit of memories and a stoic mettle, my family and I must suffer in the summer heat.

As I lay listening to the crickets and wishing for greater things from the fan, I seriously considered buckling to the heat and modern day conveniences. Maybe I would at least check out the prices of such promised comfort. I convinced myself that past generations of my ancestors would likely have installed air conditioners if given the choice. After all, the twin-holed outhouse that had once stood in the company of a spreading apple tree was all but forgotten when running water and toilets made their debut.

For several sleepless minutes I weighed the pros and cons of buckling to luxury. And then in a moment of realization, I considered the crickets. Ever since humans and crickets first started sharing homeplaces, generation after generation of people have listened to singing crickets. Yet I wonder how many folks still listen to and ponder this evening pulse of cricket noise.

It's really a matter of tunes. Do I want to be lulled to sleep by the drone of an air conditioner or the bell music of crickets?

I can't help that I have a weakness for things that go chirp in the night.

**UPDATE:** Today the windchill is minus forty-five degrees Fahrenheit and the summer fan is hibernating under the workbench in the basement. With the short days and long cold nights, I find more time to search for the correct cricket-thermometer formula. I've come across two different formulas in predicting air temperature. Both formulas require that one count the number of chirps in a fifteen-second span. The difference between the two formulas is found in the next step. According to one formula, add fifty, while the other equation calls for an addition of thirty-seven.

To make things easier, I'm going to take an average of the two constants and use it. Therefore, number of cricket chirps in fifteen seconds plus forty-three equals the air temperature in Fahrenheit degrees.

# Sand—the Good and the Bad

What do Christmas trees, potatoes, pocket gophers, sand burrs, burr oaks, and my late great-grandfather Anderson all have in common?

They all prefer or preferrred to set their roots down in sand country. Not only have they preferred the sand but they have flourished on the sand.

The potato's affinity for growing best in sandy soil was directly responsible for a state fair medal won by my father for his potato entry. It was earlier responsible for the success of not only great-grandpa John Eric's farm but also for the farms of many of the other early immigrants who cleared the land in order to till it.

Seven miles northwest of his farm was the town of North Branch, self-proclaimed "Potato Capital of the Midwest." Indeed, the town boasted two potato starch factories and at least a dozen potato warehouses during the spud-rich years in the early decades of this century.

Stories passed on by old-timers tell of mile-long caravans of horse-drawn wagons waiting all day to unload their cargo of potatoes. Old black-and-white postcards showing doctored scenes such as a man at a wheelbarrow with its full load of *one* gigantic potato bragged of the region's potatoes.

My great-grandfather and his four big work horses—Nellie, Dolly, Blaze, and the cantankerous Cap—no doubt found it much easier to pull stumps, turn the sod, and later cultivate in sandy soil rather than in the heavy soils less than ten miles to the north. The potatoes he planted found the sandy loam easy to stretch in so that their tubers could grow. Many long-abandoned potato cellars near old farms are mute dimples on the landscape. In their sunken forms, they bear testimony to the benefits of sand.

The sand my great-grandfather built his farm on was left behind approximately 12,000 years ago during the last advance and retreat of the glaciers. The last of the four great ice sheets reached as far south as the Des Moines, Iowa, area and covered much of Minnesota. Born off the main southerly thrust of ice was a smaller arm of ice that in its short life grew towards the northeast to the Grantsburg, Wisconsin, region.

At that time, the Mississippi River was much larger than it is now as it carried the meltwater from the huge mass of melting ice to the north. As the river flowed, it was diverted by the damming action of the smaller arm of ice. The river was rerouted and flowed over much of east central Minnesota.

Finally, after thousands of years, the ice dam melted and the rerouted river settled back into its original course. Left behind was a vast plain of sand that had settled to the bottom of the broad river.

Winds later sculpted the sandy barren landscape a bit to make it more rolling. Eventually, grasses started to grow, and in doing so, their fine network of roots held the sands in place. On came the big and little bluestem grasses, the pasqueflowers, the burr oaks, the prairie chickens, and finally my great-great-grandfather and his sons, including John Eric.

In the heat of summer, when the rains seem nonexistent, we curse the sand. Crops, gardens, yards, and shallow wells suffer the consequences. The coarse, gritty particles of sand do not hold water very well as there are larger pore spaces between the sand grains than there are in a heavy soil with a blend of clay. The fine, microscopic clay particles and pore spaces have better water-holding properties.

Advantage . . . heavy soils.

After the recent rains, many new ponds have been created in the low spots of bean and corn fields, especially in those found on the heavy soils. Some basements, particularly those wrapped in clay, have felt the prescence of these same rains. Most basements surrounded by sand, where the water is easily drained, remain dry.

Advantage . . . sand.

Water trickles downward more rapidly through a sandy soil. One drawback, however, is that the percolating water flushes the bits of organic matter, rich in nitrogen and phosphorus, deeper into the ground—a process county agents refer to as leaching. During a dry spell, these important food stuffs do not move to the roots fast

151

enough for the plant to use. As a result, a lack of nitrogen is a major problem in dry weather.

Both sand and clay travel on the soles of our feet, especially when wet. When dry, the clay becomes hard. The sand becomes the greater culprit, in its abrasive manner, when it finds its way into our homes to collect on the floors.

In strong winds, the blowing sand can sting one's face and pelt a building with sandblasting results over a period of time.

Advantage . . . heavy soils.

But digging in sand is wonderful. I wonder if the pocket gophers dig their meandering tunnels just for the sheer joy of easy digging. I doubt it, but a look at the many gopher mounds would seem to indicate so.

A good friend and I each helped one another dig our respective house footings. My house is in the sand, and all that was needed was a shovel and an afternoon. On the other hand, my friend built on a firmer bed of clay. Besides shovels, we needed a grub hoe, a pick, more time, and strong backs.

Even the roots of lamb's-quarters, pigweed, quack grass, and other evils of the garden relinquish their holds more easily in the sand.

Advantage . . . sand.

With the nutrients being flushed through in the sand, there is a tendency for the soil to be more acidic. For those farming such land, it is often necessary to "sweeten" the soil by applying lime. But there are those plants that prefer to sink their roots in an acidic environment.

A half-hour hike from my house will take me to a pine plantation, where I can witness over a hundred pink lady's slipper blossoms growing from the needle-covered duff.

Adjacent to the pines and in nearby woods, I can find plump blueberries in July. There won't be quarts by any means, but enough to grace a fine dessert if they make it back to the house untouched.

Flowers of the prairie have evolved to grow in areas where water is not readily available. These plants send their roots deep into the ground. Some will plunge to depths greater than a spade's length in their search for water. Thus, I can be assured that the blaze orange butterfly weed, the golden puccoons, and the blue wands of blazing star will continue to flower, even during the dry times.

Advantage . . . sand.

Like those who came before me, I have come to live on the sand—an old outwash plain. I do not depend on it for a living, as my great-grandfather did, but I do gain much-needed nourishment. The varying products of sand bear fruits that fulfill physical and mental needs.

Advantage . . . sand.

# In the Heat of Summer

The day started harmlessly enough. The early morning sun was filtered by a quiet fogbank to the east. The orange ball rising in the sky was easily viewed without squinting and appeared more lunar than solar.

It would only be a short time before the sun would burn off the opaque screen of fog.

The upcoming day had all the promise of being one of those perfect summer days that inspires musicians to write the likes of "those lazy, hazy, crazy days of summer" or "summertime—when the living is easy . . . fish are jumpin'" and on and on.

As I reflect on that day, I am convinced that there was no fog at all and that the sun, in its summer deviltry, was steaming the countryside as it crept westward.

Not a puff of breeze could be had to offer a moment of relief, and unless one surrendered as a hostage to the air conditioner, there was absolutely no escaping the wet heat. It's hard to be patient and logical in such weather.

Even as I sat and did nothing but daydream of October days afield in the crisp autumn air or wish for a blast of bone-chilling January arctic air, I sweated . . . and sweated . . . and sweated.

I've noticed that erratic behavior also seems more evident when the wrath of July and August is upon us. How else can a friend explain why a great blue heron landed next to his bird feeder on his

153

deck outside his dining room at ten in the evening? I know for a fact that his feeder holds no fish and that it is impossible to view a slough or pond from the deck.

Such is the way of the summer's sun.

Or how, at high noon, could I explain why a lone holstein cow should be running back and forth in the pasture? Cows generally are not known to be overly ambitious animals, yet here was one trotting through the tall thistle and milkweed on a hot, cloudless day.

The reason for the midday run became clear when I saw a panting red fox lope across a break in the thistles and milkweed. The fox moved lightly and easily on its feet while its black and white pursuer lumbered right behind. Back and forth the duo ran until they dropped out of sight beyond a slight rise.

The pasture was empty except for the flash of a goldfinch busying itself in the white fluffs of thistle heads—nothing out of the ordinary.

What I had just witnessed was not a mirage, and I swear that I didn't imagine it. Besides, I was standing in the shade of an old oak; the two beasts were the ones without the protection of shade.

Such is the way of summer's sun.

Then there was the day recently, when I was transporting a caged raccoon in the back seat of my car. The raccoon had been a neighbor's short-term pet. Seems it was becoming more wild than tame, as raccoons usually do. I was to bring the animal to the nature center, where it would be released.

It chattered and chirred in protest as I drove, but I ignored it. After seven miles of driving the back seat became strangely quiet.

I felt something brush my shoulder, and in the next instant I was wearing a live raccoon hat—Davy Crockett style.

It jumped on the seat, scooted over my lap, and shoved its head out the window. I pulled the car off the road and after a bit of a scuffle, I managed to get the escapee back into the cage.

Such is the way of summer's sun.

No one is immune to the heat's distractions. My wife, Sue, was putting together a batch of pickled beets for canning. I hardly dared ask what was wrong when I heard her muttering in the pantry. She has no love for beets, and every year I manage to sneak a row in the garden. For some strange, unaccountable reason she had used chili

154

powder instead of cinnamon in mixing up the ingredients. Luckily, the beet slices hadn't been added yet.

I made light of the error by remarking that the concoction might make an interesting hot pickle. The look I received was icy enough to send a shiver down my back even in the heat of August.

To remedy the sticky temperatures, we are loading up the canoe and heading north for a week. With a bit of luck, this weather may cause a walleye or two to act irrational and take our summer offerings of bait.

Such is the way of summer's sun.

# The Unlucky Catch

Face it, for most types of fishing, luck plays a major role in the outcome if the success of an outing is measured in the catch. You can invest hundreds or even thousands of dollars in equipment to pursue the fish of your dreams. Or you can pick up fishing accoutrements at a garage sale for a little more than two bits.

On a given day, the economy package may bring home the fish while the amply geared, sophisticated angler will be counting unpaid bills rather than fish.

I have been accused by a close friend and fishing companion of being a disgustingly lucky fisherman. Admittedly, I'm not overly skilled in fishing techniques, but I do know how to tie several of the necessary fishing knots. I know how to hook a leech and rig up a slip bobber. I've learned the virtues of patience and endurance when standing waist deep in April's icy water as they rush downriver to Lake Superior to beckon a spring run of steelhead.

I know well enough that when winter camping on a lake trout lake, you had better bury your container of minnows deep in the snow if you hope to have lively bait the next morning.

Though I've never caught any record-breaking trophies, I've had my share of respectable fish. This past spring, I even accidently hooked a very nice muskie when I wasn't in quest of one. I consider that lucky when it has been estimated that it takes thousands of casts

155

from muskie enthusiasts before they hook one of these fresh-water tigers.

But last week, I caught a fish that will live as a constant memory. It certainly wasn't the size of the fish that left the impression on me. After all, eleven and a half inches of fish will only take the edge off my appetite.

The prize was a trout, a brown trout whose ancestors were European imports to the East Coast back in 1883. Like the carp, this alien brown trout never had to pause for scrutiny at Ellis Island under the statue we call Liberty. Since the arrival of those first fish, we have learned it was our mistake to allow the carp's entrance and our good fortune that the brown trout accepted this new land as home.

What makes a fish not much longer than my hand so special? It was the fact that I had to use a fair amount of skill rather than luck to catch it. Luck did, however, play a role in that it was lucky for me that Charlie had convinced me to take a particularly sunny, yet cool, afternoon off from work to join him on a special stream.

I suspected something very special about this stream when I realized there were absolutely no deerflies flying laps around my head or mosquitoes boiling out of the shady thickets. The water of the stream is too cold and too fast for the likes of these winged pests, who prefer still, stagnant water to lay their eggs in. Instead, insects like caddis flies and mayflies thrive here, and in turn, the gayly spotted brown trout also thrives.

The stream where we fished meanders through pastureland where even the holsteins seemed relaxed, unlike the "tail swingers" that stand closely bunched in my county, where potholes and sloughs are many and spring-fed streams are absent.

Not only were buzzing insects nonexistent, but the only other competition for taking trout that I saw was an indignant kingfisher that rattled its protest over our brash trespassing.

Charlie not only shared this stretch of stream, but he handed me a fly to tie on my line that he insisted I try. The tiny imitation, called a hairwing caddis, would barely cover Abe Lincoln's face on a penny.

To you and me it resembles a minute tuft of different colored hairs and thread rather than an insect. But to a trout, if correctly tied and presented, it is but another newly emerged caddis fly resting on the

156

water's surface before it takes to the air in search of a mate.

Charlie, I'm sorry to say, is a purist. He openly scorns the use of any fishing gear unless it is a delicate fly rod tipped with an artificial fly. In fact, I wouldn't be surprised if it was his old spinning gear that you could pick up for a little more than two bits at a garage sale.

When I mentioned that I might have to kick up the earth under the alders in search of a fat night crawler if his fly didn't work, he shook his head and muttered something about having a lot to teach me. Though I have fished trout off and on for years, I had, up to now, caught ninety-nine percent of my trout on worms. If a bait is productive, why switch?

Never had I caught a trout on a floating fly—sinking or wet flies yes, but not on a dry fly.

Within minutes after stepping into the stream, Charlie showed me how to place the fly on the water, and within a few casts, he caught a decent trout. It looked altogether too easy.

We separated. Charlie worked upstream and I walked across a well-manicured pasture to intercept the stream below our starting point.

It didn't take long to realize that this was not like fishing sassy sunnies over their spawning nests. It took some accuracy and thought about where to cast the fly so that it floated serenely, like a live caddis fly about to take to the air.

Like a November whitetail buck, brown trout are far too wary. If a poorly cast fly rides over them, they will dart under a dark brown undercut or retreat to the shadows under a tangle of water-logged roots, where they will sulk until long after the intruder has passed. Even the faint shadow from the floating fly line gives them the jitters.

I found that even if the fly floats as it should and a trout comes up to sample the offering, one has to have nearly troutlike reflexes to set the hook. After two hours, the kingfisher and I were still fishless. Unlike me, the bird was not enjoying itself, as indicated by its occasional scolds directed my way.

I could tell by the bulging dimple on the water that it was a pretty nice fish that was feeding on drifting insects of some sort. It rose every few minutes from under a large spreading willow and just a

157

few feet downstream from the fence of a cattle crossing. Like a heron, I ever-so-slowly walked upstream so that I could position myself within casting distance of the upstream-facing fish.

In my mind, I made a checklist of what I had to do: cast the fly with delicacy so that it landed ever so softly just upstream from the trout's lie, don't hurry and keep the slack out of the line so that I could quickly set the hook.

A sidearm cast would be needed with the guardian willow leaning over the stream. I grasped the bend of the tiny hook and blew the fly dry. With several delicate strokes of my finger, I fluffed it up so that it would sit proud and dry on the water for a better float. So I edged into position, the fish rose again, and my blood pressure followed.

My first cast caught the bush behind me. After I dislodged the hook, I put my second cast in the tall canary grass, ten feet to the left of the fish. Sidearm casting could use some practice. With a gentle tug and a prayer, I popped the fly free from the bank.

I won't bother you with the details of the third cast, because a description could be found in hundreds of how-to books on trout fishing. Besides, I've always told myself that in my writing, I would try to stay away from stories of the "see-what-I-caught" sort. But, like I said, this was not an ordinary fish and I was not lucky to have caught it—I *earned* this fish.

Compared to my brown trout, the St. Croix muskie—had I landed it last May—would have been far the lesser prize.


# Plumes of Gold

If I were to choose a color that best represents August, it would undoubtedly be yellow. Buttery sweetcorn, late-nesting goldfinches, aging milkweed leaves, tall regiments of sunflowers, and perhaps most showy of all, those plumes of gold—the goldenrod.

Just as flits of warblers and the alfalfa-field woodchuck are intent on putting on their stores of autumn and winter fat, the goldenrod seems to grow heavy with sunshine. Finally, the summer sun has ignited the open places and the goldenrod bloom is upon us.

It must have been an August goldenrod that inspired fellow-Swede Carolus Linnaeus to ascribe this group of plants to the genus *Solidago*. Indeed, they seem to be fragments of "ol' man Sol." However, the prefix is not derived from the word for sun but from the Latin word *solidus,* which means "whole" or "to make whole."

The Ojibway Indians aptly referred to the plant as the "sun medicine." Although it was not a cure-all, it certainly was an important plant to have in one's medicine bag. It was used in treating fevers, sprains, lung problems, sore throats, backaches, and even hair problems.

Yellow dyes from goldenrod blossoms added color to clothing for the Indian and the settler.

My attraction to the August yellows is not so much for medicinal reasons but for entertainment. I really enjoy walking into a tall clump of goldenrod to inspect the compact golden flower heads more closely. Each plume is a bouquet of tiny flowers, all resembling each other. The goldenrod is of the family Compositae, an aptly named group because their bloom is a composite of many individual flowers.

Bending over to peer more closely at the host of tiny flowers, one can witness dramas that make the glory days of Rome seem pale in comparison. This is where the action is. The numerous orange and black leatherwing beetles, along with the black, antlike foliage beetles, seem to be living the Babylonian life of milling about, eating, and fornicating.

Butterflies, bees, wasps, and a host of other flying insects are probing the flowers for the sweet nectar. The honey my bees make now will be a darker-colored stock. Little do these insects realize the important role they are playing in carrying the sticky pollen grains from flower to flower, thus ensuring the goldenrod's future.

The yellow pollen grains can only be carried by the insects, not the wind, as many hay fever sufferers mistakenly believe. I pass a short-lived meadow of crowded goldenrods every summer that is never allowed to go to seed. At the peak of its bloom, the landowner hooks up a sickle mower behind his small Ford tractor and cuts the goldenrod flat. I suspect he or a family member knows the discomfort of hay fever and feels he is doing what he can to bring comfort. Nearby, all along the shoulder of the gravel road is a hardy growth of

159

the probable culprit—ragweed.

Among the flowers, there is also the drama of the hunt and death. The yellow crab spider, a small predator, blends in with the blossoms as it waits patiently for a nectar-seeking insect. The spider has the ability to change to a white color if it should happen to haunt a white flower such as a yarrow.

One must have a sharp eye to pick out the yellow-green assassin bug that tucks itself quietly amidst the flowers, waiting to ambush an unsuspecting insect. At the right moment, the hunter, resembling a miniature praying mantis, unleashes its powerful front legs and grasps the unlucky prey. It pierces its catch with its short, stubby beak and draws out the juices of the captured insect. It may seem gruesome, but most predator-prey meetings follow a similar pattern, and only the fittest survive.

Unseen, but more tied to the goldenrod than the flower-top insects, are those tiny dwellers that live within the walls of the stem—the gall makers. Galls are those curious, distorted swellings, lumps, or knobs found on a plant's stem or leaves that have formed as a result of an insect "injection." This injection may be an implanted egg or secretions from the developing insect.

A walk among the goldenrod in a nearby fallow field yields four different kinds of galls. Each type of gall is specific to a particular insect. The goldenrod ball gall, most common in my patch, is the nursery for a tiny fly that is a close kin to the fruit fly. The gall provides both food and shelter for the larva.

In groupings here and there, one can find goldenrod plants that appear to be tipped with multipetaled green roses. The roselike growth is actually a tuft of goldenrod leaves all growing close together from the tip of the plant. Known as the goldenrod bunch gall, this deformity is formed when another gnat-sized fly lays its egg on the growing tip of the plant. The gall forms after the egg hatches and the larva starts secreting a chemical irritant of sorts that prevents the tip from growing skyward and causes the leaves to bunch.

Another stem gall among the goldenrods is the elliptical gall, which resembles a stretched-out ball gall. Rather than a fly, a moth is the culprit. After the eggs hatch from the dead goldenrod stem in the spring, the tiny caterpillars journey to a tender, new plant and eats its way into the buds before tunneling into the stem. The gall forms, and as summer gives way to fall, the moth emerges, mates, and lays its eggs before dying.

Similar to the elongated shape of the elliptical gall is another, only this one is not smooth skinned. Instead, it is furrowed and ridged as in a build-up of scar tissue. Aptly named, the goldenrod scarred gall is the product of another moth in the larval stage. The entry hole in the stem is near the base of the gall, while the exit hole will be bored out the top.

According to the monotone voice on the radio, the economic future appears questionable. Most of his report is simply noise to my economic-poor ears. And when I hear that gold has dropped to $435 per troy ounce, I wonder to myself how many people are rushing to a broker. Instead, I find it easier and more relaxing to take a stroll through a nearby meadow or roadside ditch and find a patch of goldenrod. If I squint my eyes, the plumes of gold become merged as one huge gold nugget. These are riches beyond measuring and weighing, and there is enough for all. We just have to look for it.

# SEPTEMBER

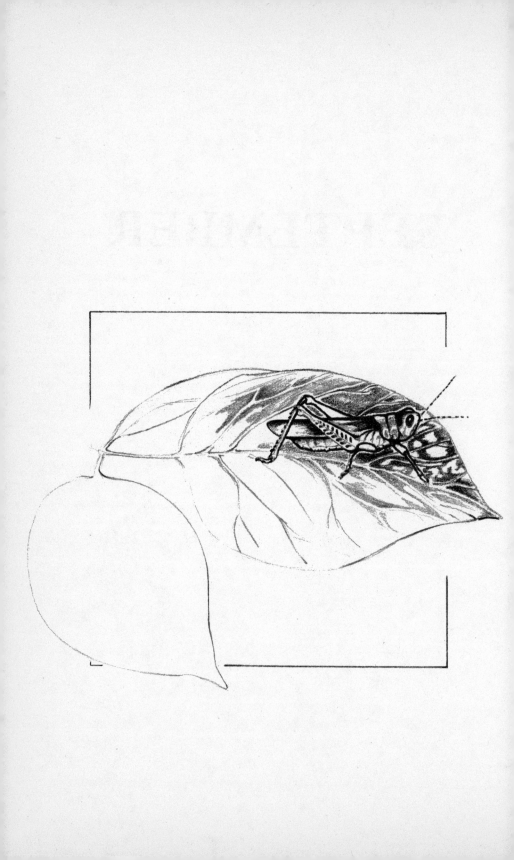

# The Fall Planting

Our garden is played out, and it has not taken as keenly to autumn as the flanking stands of sumacs and oaks have. From one standpoint, the vegetable patch is a bleak picture of desolation. But underlying the air of carnage is a subtle smugness, a declaration of "See what I can do."

Rather than wear autumn's bold splashes, the vegetable leaves have wilted and browned under the touch of several recent light frosts. But in their defeat, the fallen leaves reveal the colors and forms of summer-lost fruits.

Squash, in greater numbers than I ever imagined, appear where I thought there were no squash. And though I had planted none, there is a renegade pumpkin in the midst of the limp vines. It must have volunteered from a forgotten jack-o'-lantern of last year. In the spring, it was turned into the soil as my neighbor's plow made its seasonal mark.

Fallen banners of stalks and leaves cover an occasional bald knob of a potato. It's hard to believe that only a short time ago, there were lush rows of potatoes here. Their stems and leaves grew so thick that the four rows merged into one big patch. Those spuds that grew close to the surface and that I had neglected to hill with a protective screening of dirt have been colored a sickly green by the summer's sun. Instead of wintering, busheled in my basement, they will stay in the garden and add nourishment to next year's crop.

What the garden leaves may lack in brilliance is made up for by the ripened fruits. Squash, pumpkin, and especially the many tomatoes are more ablaze than ever now that their leaves have bowed and shriveled.

165

It seems such a waste to leave these plump, fist-sized tomatoes. But we have only so many quart jars, and those are now adding the robust color of tomato to our cupboard in the pantry. The tabletop on the back porch is crowded with tomatoes of various hues of pink and red as they ripen under the window-cast sunlight.

Though we lessened the waste by giving away a couple bushels of tomatoes, there seem far too many left. These softening tomatoes, like the sunburned spuds, are part of our offering to the garden for a job well done. Somehow, with that thought in mind, leaving the produce seems easier.

Not only is the garden a scene of defeat, but it is altogether too quiet. Two weeks ago, a flock of bluebirds found the garden and surrounding alfalfa field to their liking. Now they are leaving, in search of more southerly gardens and meadows.

Of all the noises, the one most strangely absent is the insect music. There is no constant chirping of crickets from under the mulch of straw, nor is there the metallic clacking and crackling of wings as startled grasshoppers avoid my starts and pauses as I move through the garden.

A couple of weeks ago, when the sweetcorn hung heavy on the stalks, I had managed to cup my hand over an escaping grasshopper. Carefully, I grasped it by the armament of the thorax and brought it close to my face for a better look. Typical of struggling grasshoppers, it proceeded to spit out its "tobacco juice." Perhaps the brown spittle is the insect's feeble attempt to get me to drop it. I'm not sure why grasshoppers have this seemingly revolting habit, but I have seen enough people drop the disgusting insect to make me believe that there is some escape advantage to the act.

I refused to let go, and as the grasshopper spit and kicked its overdeveloped hind legs, I inspected it. The "thigh," referred to as the femora, were sharply patterned in a black herringbone. Below the femora, the leg was a shade of August yellow. The legs and the long, folded wings projecting beyond its rear are clues that identify the red-legged locust—an altogether too common garden dweller.

On warm days of sunshine, the garden had been loud with grasshopper and cricket songs. Most of the time, these notes are performed by a lone male or a group of them. The song's function is to attract a female. She is likewise capable of answering a male's pleas, but for the most part is a silent partner.

One hot day as I was kneeling in the garden, busying myself with some hand weeding, I heard a nearby insect trill. The noise came from the opposite side of the tattered bean row that I was working on. Slowly, I peeked over the top for a look. Sitting on the hot sand, paying no heed to me, were three grasshoppers. One of them seemed to be the source of attention of the other two. As I watched, two of the insects faced the third and briefly serenaded. Entomologists believe that when two males are near a female, they will alternate their songs in a "rival duet."

The ability of grasshoppers and crickets to make their August chatter is widespread among these insects. However, each species carries its own unique sound, an important prerequisite to prevent mating between nearby grasshopper species. The trills and chirps are not utterances from the mouth. The production is similar to a violinist drawing a bow across the strings. Grasshopper noises are called stridulations. The insect produces them by drawing its wings together or by rubbing the inside of its femora against the edge of its wing. The noise-making instrument on the leg is a hard ridge of tiny pegs that resembles a file. The wing instrument, known as a scraper, is also a hardened ridge, but without the teeth. When the "file" is drawn across the "scraper," the result is grasshopper music.

The cricket's tools of song are on the wings, never the legs. The male's scraper is on the upper edge of the left wing and its file is just under the right wind edge. The wings are rubbed against each other at a speed that makes an eye-blink look slow, the cricket shrugs its bell-like trill. Crickets are more secretive about their romantic notions. They make their music under the cover of darkness or a blanket of straw mulch. Either way, they're hidden from my prying eyes.

The grasshoppers of August seemed even more abundant than the prolific green beans of July. The hoppers seemed particularly fond of our single row of beans. The heart-shaped leaves have been transformed into works of lace by the cutting insect mandibles. It hardly mattered. We had eaten plenty and frozen enough of the string beans to be well reminded of their untiring efforts when we serve them

167

next winter.

The hordes of grasshoppers are creatures of the hot summer sun. They fare poorly as the days shorten and chill. Some insects, however, handle the cooling days better than the grasshopper. The monarch butterfly finds its way to the mountains of Mexico for the winter. And the woolly bear caterpillar hurries, like no other caterpillar, through autumn in search of a nook or cranny to shelter it from winter's snows. The butterfly leaves winter behind, while the woolly bear overwinters in a dormant stage, not unlike the chipmunk, who likewise is fond of nooks and crannies.

But the grasshoppers, like fall's colored leaves, are doomed. They cannot follow the monarch's trail, nor can they slow down their metabolism so that their bodily functions are barely running. Instead, they will freeze and die, leaving all gardens and fields without the tickings, clacks, and trills of grasshoppers.

Before the grasshoppers die, they will know the fulfillment of mating. After courtship and mating, the female will lay several hundred eggs by depositing them into the soil in clusters of ten to twenty. Under a thin layer of dirt and a thicker layer of snow, the eggs will overwinter until late spring, when they will hatch into tiny grasshoppers. Unlike most insects, grasshoppers do not go through several odd-looking larval stages before taking on the appearance of an adult.

I stood outside on a recent night and looked up into a cloudless sky where the stars seemed especially bright. Without the haze of humidity and summer's heat, the stars seemed far closer and livelier. A trace of steam escaped from my mouth and faded into the night as it climbed skyward. I forced a blow of air out to prove that the first wasn't an illusion. Somehow, the first see-your-breath-night of the fall is a familiar spectacle that is worth repeating.

On this night, I knew that there would be a heavy frost before morning's light. In the darkness, I heard the hoots of an owl from back by the slough. Otherwise, it was perfectly still and quiet.

There were no whimperings or screams of frost-driven pain coming from the garden and field. But I knew any surviving grasshoppers were slowly dying as they clung to familiar grass stems. I couldn't help but wonder if they felt the touch of death's chill and, if so, why they didn't seek refuge to avoid it? Surely they could forestall their death by days or perhaps even weeks if they crawled under the cover of dried leaves and grasses. Instead, they choose to share a grass stem with heavy frost crystals.

These insects are incapable of complaining, and I suspect that they will die gracefully, for they know no difference. Besides, they have served their need well by planting their own "seeds" into my garden. Thus, I am assured of exquisite doilies in next summer's bean leaves.

# Pull of the Roadside Tree

In our travels, there are special trees that grow as close to the road as they dare or, more aptly put, as close as the road crews allow. For the best roadside trees, one has to forget the tedious interstates and the busy state highways and follow the quieter roads.

The best backroads for tree viewing are those that are covered with sand or gravel, and they must never have a black hose stretched across them that leads to a metal box that mysteriously clicks every time a vehicle passes over it.

It is over such roads that limbs are allowed to stretch out. On hot summer days, the limb casts a full shadow to cool the hot sand, and if you travel the road barefoot, such places become familiar stops. Some roads become dark tunnels in summer's lushness, as they pass through arching crowds of trees.

In October, the shade of the leaves lessens as the leaves fall to the road, where they may lie undisturbed for hours on end before they briefly swirl skyward every time a car passes over.

There is a certain white oak I've come to know that in an act of boldness has sent a strong reaching branch out across the road. It is just high enough so that the plow in winter can pass cleanly underneath. The stout horizontal limb seems to grow faster than the rest of the tree, not skyward as trees generally do but south in quest of the sun.

The road, built years ago, has created an opening that not only attracts oak branches but also blackberry and sumac, which find the

169

opening more to their liking than the shade a short distance from the road.

Perhaps it was the warmth of the sunlight that the female hornet sought early last spring when she decided that this limb of oak should support her future nest and colony. Was her choice haphazard or planned? Did she know that in the cool of early summer mornings the sun would race down the road from the east and shine on this bold branch? Unmolested by the screening of other oaks and maples, the sun would warm her colony and inspire them to get an early start on their daily duties.

A few years back, while fishing brook trout on a small creek, I discovered a huge ball-shaped paper nest hanging over the water near a small shaded pool that undoubtedly held fish. The creek, like the road, provided an occasional opening where a bit of sun could warm the nest over the water. I also remember that the pool under the guardian nest remained unviolated from the drift of my carefully hooked night crawler. Relunctantly, I gave the trout hole a wide berth and moved on in search of hornetless pools.

After a summer of laying eggs and increasing the numbers of her kingdom, the queen's nest in the oak has steadily grown larger. The oblong nest is mostly gray, but a closer look shows it is girdled with fine, irregular belts of browns, rusts, and tans.

To create the nest of paper, the hornets make their own pulp by chewing bits of wood and mixing it with their saliva. A small pellet of mashed fibers is carried back to the nest, where it is spread out almost like butter. The various colors in the nest come from the different varieties and ages of wood that the insects have gathered. The rust color so commonly found is most likely from rotting red oak.

Several layers of this "hornet paper" cover the layers of brood cells that resemble honeycomb. The larger the nest, the more levels of horizontal cells. Hundreds of cells are built to accommodate the queen's eggs and larvae.

Those hornets born female—but unable to reach the status of queen because of their infertility—hold the position of worker. Throughout the summer, they build and tend the nest, care for the larvae, guard the nest, and hunt for food. Though these insects are often scorned for their damage to fruits and vegetables, in summer they feed primarily on other insects, especially caterpillars—caterpillars which do far more damage to crops than hornets do. On a diet of high protein "insect meat," the larvae grow fast.

Recently, I came upon a hornet straddling a small but lively dragonfly. It was hard to believe that this insect speedster, with its two huge eyes of thirty thousand lenses, was unable to escape the hornet's grasp. The dark, husky hornet held the larger insect still while it frantically worked its mandibles back and forth behind the dragonfly's head. In a matter of seconds, the head dropped from the body of the winged goliath and fell stilled to the sand.

I was somewhat shocked and moved my face to within inches of the occupied hornet for a better look and to await the killer's next move. But the hornet preferred to be alone and after a couple of attempts to get its burden airborne, it managed to slowly fly off with the decapitated dragonfly.

Since then, the days have become shorter and are cooling. The queen has or will soon halt her egg laying. The worker hornets will then seek fruits rather than insects—for a sweet liquid diet. There are days in the fall when the fruit-littered ground under an apple tree seems alive with hornets, wasps, and yellow jackets.

Ultimately, frost and snow will cover the oak limb and the nest of gray paper. No longer will the hornets busy themselves at the entry hole on the bottom of the nest. The queen and those fertile females destined to be next year's queens will be gone, seeking underground shelter from winter. The workers who served the queen so fervently will die under the touch of Jack Frost.

The white oak over the road will surrender its leaves, and no longer will the empty hornet nest have its leafy protection. Perhaps, other hornet nests will be discovered along the road when the curtain of fall is dropped. Then it will be a naked limb with a harmless ball of gray paper hanging over the road until the snow, sleet, and cold winds cut through the layers reducing the papery globe to shreds.

Several winters back, there was a hanging hornet nest conveniently constructed in a red maple that was easily viewed from the kitchen window. The bountiful months just prior to this particular winter had been lean of acorns. Squirrels, feeling the pinch of winter, became more resourceful and certainly more determined in their efforts at the bird feeders where riches of sunflower seeds lay.

One particular squirrel in its foraging discovered a stilled hornet nest. With no appreciation for the work that went into the nest's construction, the squirrel tore the layers of paper off until it reached the inner combs. Tearing out chunks of the brood combs, the squirrel carried the pieces to a favorite perch and proceeded to feed on the hornet larvae that had frozen, cutting short their destined metamorphosis into hornets. It matters little to the squirrel in what form its calories come—acorns or hornet embryos, both take the squirrel towards another spring.

By spring, the limb of oak will take on a soft green hue, and folks passing underneath will once again ooh and ah over the tree's beauty. And maybe the south-reaching branch will entice a searching hornet queen to start a tiny nest of gray at its tip.

**UPDATE:** Three Septembers have passed since I wrote about the hornet nest. In the summer of 1987, a new one was discovered hanging in an oak that is the closest neighboring tree to the roadside white oak.

# Together They Fly

From a distance, it looked like a dark smudge, a blemish on a clean morning sky. As I got closer, there was movement to the smudge. It slowly flowed just above the distant treetops, and then suddenly it surged upward like a cresting wave before dropping down to its original level.

Finally, the smudge became obvious; they were birds. Blackbirds by the hundreds or, more likely, the thousands were clustered together in one large flock that stretched nearly a quarter of a mile.

These migrant birds were followers, not individuals, going this way and that. They seemed to share the same pulse, as if the flock had a life of its own. The path of the blackbirds carried them over a yellowing cornfield. Though there were no obvious obstacles, the birds in front would, for no apparent reason, swoop up. Those birds following would follow the move in the very same manner at the very same point in space. It was like watching a well orchestrated game of crack-the-whip, only in slow motion.

I wondered what triggered the response to swoop, turn right, turn left, or settle down in an instant in the field of corn. Is it the same message that a cruising school of minnows feels when a shadow passes over them and they all, in amazing unison, dart erratically to safer water? Well-practiced school fire drills are far more chaotic than a spontaneous exit made by fish or birds.

How well I remember when I was finally of age to join my father in the rites of the annual duck hunting season. There was one particular day when the skies were empty of passing ducks. I had wandered down the shoreline of the lake in hopes of jumping a teal, or better yet, a mallard.

In short order, I spotted a flock of a couple dozen mallards loafing on the water up ahead of me. As a hunter, I had yet to bag a mallard, and to a first year waterfowler these birds were the prize. This was the bird that, in my eyes, would christen me as a worthy duck hunter.

Behind a screen of cattail and willow, I crouched over and slowly moved toward the unsuspecting birds. I was nearly within range of my single-shot 20-gauge shotgun, when one of the ducks raised its glistening green head up high. Had the out-of-place splash from within the cattails put the bird on the alert?

In the next instant, there wasn't just one head-raised duck, but nearly two dozen. The lake erupted in a rush of mallards. So flustered was I that I never lifted my gun. In a matter of seconds, it was only myself and an autumn-busy muskrat left along this shoreline.

Now, years and several mallards later, I have come to appreciate the magic of how a flock can mysteriously respond in what seems to be only milliseconds. Those birds that hestiate, like the heavy mallard drake that I finally bagged in my second year of hunting, are most apt to die by the claw, fang, or gun of a predator.

I once watched a hawk, a sharp-shinned or Cooper's—it was too far for me to tell the difference—fly purposely at a strung-out flock of blackbirds. As the speedy raptor closed in, the flow immediately pulled their ranks together forming a ball of birds that flew in a swirling mass. The hawk stayed with the boiling blend of feather for a while before it dropped with empty-talons back to the treetops. When a flock tightens up its formation and the birds fly erratically within the group, it becomes far more difficult for a predator to select a target. In fact, sometimes a flock can become the aggressor and mob the predator to turn it away.

Even if an avian predator makes a kill, it can only catch one bird at a time. Therefore, each individual flock member is statistically less apt to be caught than if the bird were flying alone. If a bird should stray from the flock, the predator closes in and often makes a successful kill. Such ways of survival were practiced long before the first birds took to the air.

We can witness the same strategy in a simple game of tag. Imagine being "it" and the game begins with everyone scattering in every direction. Usually there is a moment or so of confusion and a feeling of "Who do I tag?" That slight moment of hesitation has often temporarily saved someone from getting tagged early in the game. Most likely, the first person you catch will be someone you have judged to be slower than yourself or someone who has strayed from the departing cluster of folk who are heading for the maze of trees in the backyard.

There is no doubt that the behavior of one bird in a flock may influence how the others act. Birds, fishes, insects, and others are able to recognize, in a fraction of a second, a change of behavior in their companions. More amazing is their ability to quickly react to that change of mood.

But who determines when the horde of blackbirds will rise, fall, or turn? Some biologists believe that there is a lead bird that is the catalyst. But the role of lead bird may change many times in a day and the flock still moves as a whole. So for the time being, the question is without an answer. I, for one, hope that some of these vexing questions are never fully understood. We need to have unsolved mysteries in the natural world so that we never loose that sense of awe and wonder.

Besides it keeps us humble as we follow distant tumbling smudges or try to figure out who to tag next.

# Holding onto Autumn

Ask me my favorite season and I will unhesitantly utter "fall" before the question mark can be put on. We are only days from October, and in my opinion, no year would be complete without these thirty-one days.

I recall reading once of the perfect year. The months would fall like so: October, November, October, October, October, October, April, May, June, October, October, October, and finally, what else, October. The composer of such a calendar year shares my passion for the "harvest moon."

Consider those mid-July days when even the wood-shaded rocks sweat and the early morning hours drip with heat. The deerflies and mosquitoes celebrate such weather by paying entirely too much attention to me. I dream of mornings with frost-covered windshields, wool shirts, and the calls of geese from high overhead.

I knew summer was doomed when I started seeing assemblages of swallows lining up on the roadside powerlines. At about the same time, nighthawks and monarch butterflies were moving in no great hurry towards the mysterious pull to the south. They all contend for the title of "the most graceful" of September's rush into autumn.

Even before my calendar told me that fall was officially here, there were other signals telling of summer's end. Sumacs, laden with their upright clusters of woolly fruits, are red with summer's blood. Soon other plants dazzle us with their end-of-the-summer fireworks.

In thickets and treetops, one can catch a glimpse of a flit or a flutter. It seems the green of summer is carried away on the backs of those warblers that all field guides assure us are "confusing." Now these energetic little birds seek subtlety rather than the attention they craved last spring.

Even the air is different now. Summer's heavy air, like a stout ale, has disappeared, and the days carry a touch of crisp urgency scented with molding leaves.

Just today I heard a lone cricket. It stroked a few cautious chirps—hardly the outburst I heard a month ago when the meadows and roadside ditches were loud with the wing music of many courting male crickets. The soloist I heard today sounded lonely and unsure, as

175

if it wanted to hang onto summer just a little longer.

All of a sudden I find myself feeling a bit like that cricket. Most years, I grow restless waiting for the act of autumn, but this year I wouldn't mind walking barefoot for a few extra weeks. It will always be my favorite of seasons, it's just that this year I think part of the problem is my attitude and the lack of being ready.

For one thing, I find myself looking past these glory days of fall toward a landscape of winter. Every day when I step out my door, I have to look directly at my wood shed, there is no avoiding its hollow stare. At the moment, it seems more shed than wood. My wife confidently assures me that we should have enough fuel for this winter as she reminds me of the several piles of oak still out in the woods. Though the scattered woodpiles will help fatten the shed, I'm still not convinced of a wood-fired winter.

I don't know why, but as we experience the passing of winters, it seems that I get a little edgier about my wood supply. Maybe one acquires the hoarding instincts of the wise ant who worked at readying itself for winter while its fellow insect, the grasshopper, basked in summer's sun without a thought of snow or ice.

Maybe I'm getting entirely too sentimental about autumn. Trees that had been lush with summer's foliage slowly become whittled by autumn's chilly winds, and soon they are but skeletons appearing more dead than alive. Indeed, if spring is rebirth, fall is a time of dying for many plants and creatures.

Perhaps the drudgery comes in the thought of upcoming winter chores. All too soon there will be shoveling, carrying firewood into the house, tending the stove, winterizing the house and car, hanging the canoe in the garage, and now there is a second child to bundle and boot before we can step out the door.

Rather than look weeks or months ahead, I remind myself to savor the moment and take a day at a time. There is no better season than the one we have now stepped into. With a little luck, we may even experience a bit of "Augtober." And there will still be a few days of racing barefoot through the leaves.

# Drumming an Old Tune

Note from the publisher:
Because of an unfortunate electronic glitch that occurred when the type was being set for this story, parts of pages 211 and 213 are not readable. We think Tom Anderson is a wonderful storyteller, and all of his essays are worth reading. Here those pages are reproduced—we know you'll enjoy "Drumming an Old Tune."

When I was a boy, there was a "cannon" in the pastured woods behind my grandpa's barn. The volleys fired were many but were heard only by those of us who armed and fired the cannon.

The armament was positioned back in the woods, a good distance from the barn and outbuildings. The closest building, or at least what was left of a structure, was the rotting framework of the old dynamite shed. My great-grandfather had kept his supply of dynamite far from the barn and outbuildings. Only when there was land to clear and stumps to dislodge would he visit the shed. Knowing that dynamite had once been stored there made the cannon's location more exciting.

This particular piece of artillery was fixed in position, always aimed south, and it could not be raised or lowered to adjust the trajectory of the next discharge. Years prior to my discovery of the fieldpiece, Grandpa had unknowingly created the fantasy cannon.

A stout red oak had had a feeble anchor of roots, and one day, with perhaps a stiff north wind blowing, the tree slowly leaned into the pull of the earth. The oak stopped its downward, gravity-powered flight when some of its outreaching limbs broke the fall. The sturdy branches held the trunk off the ground in a canted position, angling skyward.

When there is a nearby winter-hungry wood furnace to feed, such an oak is short-lived. The bowing oak was severed from its trunk about four feet from the ground. My guess is that two men pulled in musical rhythm on each end of a long crosscut saw. As a team, they sweated and stared in concentration at the growing cut and spilling sawdust as the saw steadily worked through the oak.

A chain saw might have been used on the tree, but the height of the cut, a comfortable one for a pair of sawyers, would indicate the work of a crosscut. A chain saw operator would have made the cut closer to the ground to get all the wood possible.

After the tree was cut, split and dragged to the house, only the angled butt of the oak remained sticking out of the ground, aimed at the low December sun in the south.

Several years later, on a Sunday afternoon, while the grown-ups for another reason. To the competition, other nearby males, the message is a declaration of territorial boundaries and that any trespassing by them would be scorned.

Spring drumming is a welcome sound, no less thrilling than the first returning bluebird, the first tentative chirps of a spring peeper, or the music of northbound geese. But here it was October, when bluebirds and geese have reversed their direction, and peepers have retreated undercover for the winter. Yet it was the unmistakable sound of a drumming grouse and not the firing up of an old John Deere tractor.

Though the annual ritual of mating is half a year forthcoming, the older male grouse often drum in the fall to reinforce their boundaries to other male grouse, particularly those young males who are trying to find their own piece of woods to settle in.

By early September, those grouse hatched last spring are fully grown, and it is time for them to leave the security of mother and the brooding grounds. This period of dispersal is often referred to as the fall shuffle.

Grouse researchers have found that young females tend to roam farther than their male siblings before settling down. Such dispersal practices help prevent siblings from mating with each other, assuring a healthier, more mixed gene pool.

The young male is more likely to finally settle down near the region he grew up in, if he can find a vacant territory. In order to let these wandering males know that a particular piece of woods is already claimed, adult male grouse will drum—not to attract a female but to express their dominance.

After the young birds have spread over the countryside, the young males may likewise drum on their newly claimed log to broadcast their territorial message.

As I have not heard a grouse drumming from this pasture-turned-woods for the past few years, I'm suspecting that this drummer is a young bird staking a claim.

I enjoy following my dog, gun in hand, through tangles, briars, and popples in search of an autumn grouse. However, more often than not, I end up doing a lot of following. There is no disguising the fact that I am less than a fair grouse shot. I'll lay my money on bringing

# A Season of Falling

*Fall* is quite an acceptable word for describing the months of September, October, and November. The person responsible for coining the term fall probably envisioned leaves of crimson, gold, orange, and rust falling erratically to the pull of the earth.

To fall is to drop or descend. Therefore, is it not correct to say that the wavering skeins and Vs of migrating geese fall to their southern wintering grounds? Birds go "down south" never "up south."

Even snakes and woodchucks fall to their respective hideouts to wait out the long march of winter. Above them, the tall brown grasses bend under autumn's winds and finally fall with the weight of winter upon them.

Now the hours of daylight are falling, and the creeping hours of night bring dropping temperatures. None of these phenomena would be possible if the sun didn't appear to fall away from summer's temperamental sky. The sun's path across the heavens appears lower every day only because of the tilt of the earth's axis. We in the northern regions of the globe are tilting away from the sun and will be farthest away from the direct rays of December 21.

But there is a creature of the marshes that is fighting the "fall" of things. With the passing of September and its accompanying loud flocks of blackbirds comes the rise of the muskrat lodges. No longer are the marshes so monotonously flat. Though, I must admit, the tall waving ranks of *Phragmites* and cattails add some relief to the lower expanses of sedges and bulrushes.

It seems inconsistent for something to rise in a season when nearly everything else is falling. Yet the muskrat seems to understand that a thick wall of mud and vegetation between it and the sub-zero temperatures, not to mention the winter marauding mink, may spell the difference between life and death.

On the way to work, I pass a small corner of wetlands that has so far escaped falling victim to the work of the dragline. In just three weeks time, four 'rat houses have climbed above the water to a height of three to four feet. Stems of rushes and cattail leaves are interspersed among the mounds of black mud that the muskrats dredge from the marsh's bottom.

The mud, a rich accumulation of past seasons of dead plant growth, is mined from around the lodge's perimeter. As a result, the moat of water is deeper here, lessening the chance of a freeze-out.

The winter lodge is much larger than the smaller, rounder, and more numerous feeder houses. These houses are used for feeding platforms and shelter away from the main lodge.

I started learning the ways of the marsh when my father let me join him hunting ducks. I often sought out a growing fall muskrat lodge among the thick belt of cattails that bordered the lake. From atop my perch, I could stretch up high enough to scan the dawning skyline for flocks of waterfowl on the move. The dog that joined me on those hunts would sidle up next to me on our 'rat island, watching my every move as she whined and shivered in excitement.

Over the years, I have learned and appreciated the efforts, trials, and tribulations of the muskrat. Consequently, I am not as eager to take refuge on top of the mound of mud unless I am sinking dangerously low with water rising towards my wader tops. It seems I have learned that there is far more to a hunt in a slough than bagging a mallard. There is an evolving awareness. An awareness of muskrats and their autumn efforts to rise above the marsh while the rest of the world "falls."

# The Web Maker's Lesson

It froze hard that night, hard enough to knock the summer out of September. Why is it that the first good frost is as sobering as it is beautiful? I realize there are fine days of Indian summer ahead, but somehow the seed of urgency continues to grow, and I know all too well that I will never be totally ready for what November or December brings.

There is wood to cut, haul in, and put in the woodshed. Storm windows must replace screens, and plastic must be placed over the back porch windows, where the cold northwesters of winter attack our house. Dull-colored spuds must be dug and put in the root cellar with the various colors of squash and pumpkins. The list doesn't end here, but why frustrate myself and bore others? Autumn is too short for that.

Unlike the wise ant that readies itself for winter, I all too frequently follow the "live for today" attitude of the carefree grasshopper. It was on the eve of the first day after the frost that I took a short stroll into a long-abandoned field that now produces fine crops of goldenrop, mullein, milkweed, and assorted grasses.

The touch of frost had not missed the meadow. Only days before, hundreds of grasshoppers had scattered before my feet as I invaded their realm. Now their numbers are fewer and their jumps less energetic.

I walked into a clump of browned goldenrod to cut open a few swollen goldenrod galls that interrupt the slender upright stems. There are those wise to the ways of winter sunfish who claim the fat little grubs that form within the galls make a fine bait.

In the middle of the patch, I nearly trampled a plant that was tipped with a small, tubelike tent of leaves. Closer inspection showed fine strands of silk drawing the leaves together like a tightly wrapped shawl. Inside the leaves, sitting still, was a robust spider.

It was a shamrock spider, one of the orb weaver spiders—those that make the familiar netlike webs with concentric strands of silk that make interesting geometric patterns. The spider was good sized, nearly the size of my little fingernail. The round abdomen was gray and flecked with four white spots and a middle row of smaller spots. Such are the markings of the female. The male is less than half her size and has an unmarked abdomen.

I gently poked her with a blade of grass, and she reluctantly backed higher into the leaf wrapping. This refuge of goldenrod leaves is her hideout while she awaits an insect to blunder into the web below her.

These spiders have poor vision and must rely on their fine sense of touch to tell them when a meal has arrived. From her tent to the center of the web runs a stout silk thread that serves as a trip wire of sorts. When a cricket, for example, hits the sticky cobweb, it struggles to free itself. In doing so, it only falls against other strands, making the situation worse for the ensnared insect.

The spider, facing downward in her hideout, keeps one of her eight feet on the signal thread to detect a faint vibration or change in

179

tension. When she feels the signal, she quickly crawls down the web, and if the prize is food, she quickly wraps it in a cloak of silk before biting it. Then the prey is carried back to her retreat, where she can eat it undisturbed. Anything that gets caught in her snare that is unpalatable is neatly cut out of the web and dropped to the ground.

When times are good and food is plentiful, a fresh web is constructed by the female every evening. The old one is not abandoned, it is eaten strand by strand so that the silk can be recycled.

Spider webs are perhaps best seen on mornings when the dew is heavy and clinging to every strand of the web, resembling a jeweled necklace. It is on such a morning that we marvel at the surprising numbers and beauty of the webs.

But those days are drawing to a close. Perhaps, like me, the fat female spider I watched feels the October prod of urgency. The webs, like the grasshoppers and crickets that sometimes find them and ultimately nourish the web maker, are less frequent now.

Soon the spider, as well as the grasshopper, will be claimed. The frost does not discriminate between those we call pests and those we label helpers. Before the shamrock spider I watched dies, she will lay hundreds of eggs near her leafy tent. The eggs of tiny spiderlings may overwinter and come out in the warmth of spring.

But if the days of Indian summer glow warm, the miniature spiders will release a delicate shiny strand of silk that will catch the October breeze and carry not only the spiderlings but the usual load of dead leaves and cast-off seeds to far reaches of the meadow and beyond. Thus we are assured of future webs graced with the dew of morning.

All of a sudden, it became apparent that my nagging list of chores was not all that significant as I watched the spider crouch in her simple wrap of leaves . . . and wait.

# OCTOBER

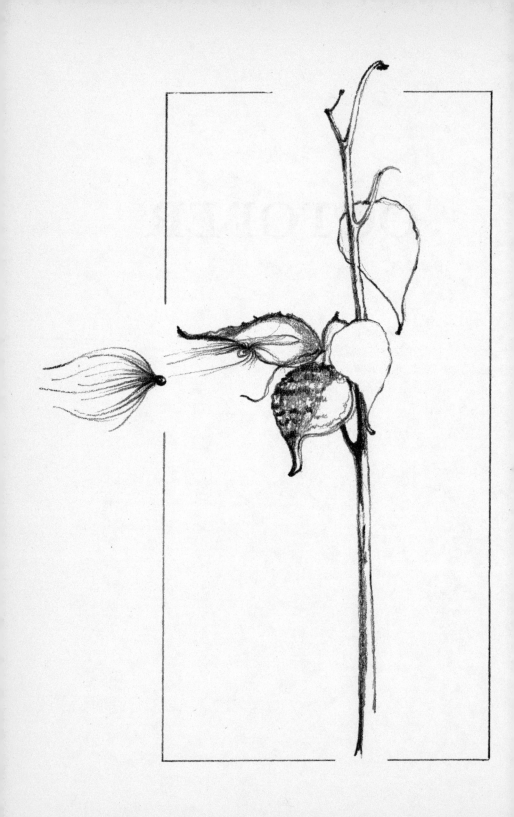

# Free-spirited Milkweed

White puffs of seeds betray the presence of dried milkweed plants along the roadside. Most are in the ditches, but some have withstood the onslaught of the cultivator and the herbicides and have succeeded in invading the monotony of soybeans and corn.

Many pastures have their manicured appearance interrupted by these scattered torches of white. Unlike the larvae of the monarch butterfly or the milkweed beetle, cattle and horses have not acquired a taste for this forb.

About a mile of milkweed ditches lies between our house and a fenced-in goat pasture. A score of tiny goats keep the pasture clean-cut except for scattered clumps of tall milkweeds. Even in the eyes of a goat, it seems a tin can has far more appeal than a milkweed.

Armed with tools of steel, herbicides, and the opposable thumb for better pulling ability, humans, more than any other mammal, threaten the life of the milkweed.

Several bold milkweed plants have found a niche in our garden. I've pulled many of these sturdy, sticky-stemmed intruders from the ground, but within days their spirits rise again.

The stout milkweeds in our township are blessed with a deep taproot that courses deeply into the sand. Growing off the mainline taproot are numerous lateral roots that are usually left behind when I pull a garden milkweed. From these offshoots, new plants will be directed by a hormonal message to charge into the airspace of my garden. And a few days hence, I will entertain myself by pulling more milkweed.

I have no desire to conquer the species *Asclepias syriaca*. My war is only with the garden vermin—those plants I label weeds.

In his book *All About Weeds,* Edwin R. Spencer defines a weed as "a plant out of place in the eye of man; in the nice eye of nature it is very much in place." I'm the first to admit that milkweeds have their place. Without milkweeds, there would be no monarchs to ponder. The milkweed is the fruit for the monarch caterpillar, the aphids, milkweed beetles, and others.

Now that the land has been touched by frost, the battle between milkweed and garden is finished. Vegetable produce has been toted, frozen, jellied, jarred, and cellared. Scattered along the garden's edge are dried yellow milkweeds waving their fluffy white flags of seed in surrender to an approaching "General November."

The dried pods, with their load of silky, fleece-adorned seeds, are waiting. One of these days, an autumn gust, perhaps from the northwest, will carry in the message that the chill of winter will soon be upon us.

Of the hundreds of seeds found on a plant, some will begin their skyward journey with an explosion as a rush of air prods them to leave their summer pods. Other seeds will fly only reluctantly as they seem to cling to each other before they are loosened.

Over nine hundred waxy, hollow hairs carry the solitary, brown, corky seed. With such a side surface area to catch even a whisper of a breeze, the light seed is easily lifted. Dandelions, thistles, and goatsbeard are a few of the other plants that follow the same tactics in sending off their seeds.

Once in the air, the seed may race along, float lazily, or dance and pirouette among the unseen swirling winds and thermals. Some of the seeds scoot along the ground only to be grabbed and clutched by seeds or branches. Other will rise higher and higher into the sky until finally they are lost to the eye.

Like flocks, many of the seeds will migrate noiselessly over towns, freeways, croplands, woodlands, and bodies of water. It makes no difference if they go south, east, west, or north—just so they spread out as far as their adaptations will let them. No respect is given to the landowner as the seed floats brashly and unhesitantly over property lines festooned with "No Trespassing" signs.

As I watch the aimless flight and daydream, I must admit I am somewhat resentful of the seed's carefree journey. I am jealous of its ability to ride the wind in a moment of total freedom with nowhere to go. These are truly autumn's vagrants.

According to Newton's doctrine, "What goes up, must come down." And eventually the fluff of seed must adhere to the rules. A settling down does not mean there is a fruitful future for the encased collection of genetic material. Some seeds may come to rest in the middle of the woods. However, this sunloving plant will find competition keen and the shade too great to even bother with sprouting.

Last week, while drifting in a canoe, I passed a crumbling lily pad that hosted a wet, bedraggled milkweed seed. I marveled at how the lone, marooned seed had just happened to land here. There would be no future for the lake-bound seed. Only the swamp milkweed can withstand "wet toes." Resting in a marsh or swamp is usually the beginning of the end for other milkweed species.

Who knows how many of the drifting seeds will finish their flight on the pavement of a highway, tennis court, or shopping mall parking lot. With thousands of acres being encrusted with asphalt every year, I suspect that the nomadic milkweed will not be the only organism to suffer from the lack of space to sink its roots.

Little by little, the pods are emptied. By November, they will stand rattling in the chilly winds, awaiting the quilt of snow that will cover the dormant seeds. Thus, the cycle begins once more, assuring us of future seeds drifting dreamily through autumn's artwork.

# Building an October Memory

A couple of Saturdays past, the sun was shining and the wind was blowing stiffly from the northwest, prematurely bringing down the tree's fiery cloak of leaves. It could have been just another October day, but this was the duck opener, and for some of us, it is autumn's answer to Christmas.

Though the acorn and wild grape crops are abundant this fall, the duck crop is not. Consequently, lawmakers have decided in the best interest of the ducks to shorten the hunting season and to lower the limit to four birds a day.

So the season is shorter, and I'm not able to bring home as many ducks. But how often do I bring home a limit of ducks anyway? The limit is not important—it is the experience that tugs strongest at my heart. Drop the season to a week and cut limits to one and I would still be out in the marsh building on a tradition that is as strong as the teal's urge to see South America.

As with Christmas, there are the little jobs to tend to for duck opener. Instead of decorating the tree, buying or making gifts, sending cards, or planning the Christmas Eve feast of boiled potatoes, lutefisk, sausage, and rice pudding, there are decoys to check over, duck calls to practice, and guns to ready. These chores are very much a part of the tradition, and they have a way of building the excitement.

Three days before the season, Nels and I thought we had better shoot our guns for the sake of calling it practice. Just as we were finishing our attempts to break clay pigeons, my Ithaca pump acted up, and I was unable to fire it. There was no way that I would be able to get it to a gunsmith and back in my hands by the Saturday opener.

I wasn't too concerned, however, because I could use my father's old Winchester—a model 12. Dad had been an avid duck hunter all his life up until a few years before he died. I can still visualize him standing just inside the woods along the bean field on the pass between the lakes at Grandpa's.

He had a real knack for dropping ducks with fair regularity with that old pump. As long as I hunted with Dad, I never could match his consistency. I looked forward to using the gun this year; it would be kind of like having a part of Dad with me for another opener.

Why, even to my dog, Jenny, Saturday morning was just the start of another fall day—perhaps a bit windier than most, but then there are great smells born on an October wind if you are a hunting dog. I let her out of the kennel and she followed me, as is her custom, with her favorite toy, a torn tennis ball. Her eyes begged for me to pause and throw the ball, but I had decoys to get down and gun and shells to load into the car. When she saw the cased gun come out, she jumped all around me and her tail banged my leg with more authority. You see, memories lie strong in a dog, too. And for her, October is the only Christmas.

It took no coaxing to get Jenny into the car. She settled down on the front seat with laughing eyes and a torn tennis ball still gripped in her mouth. Once on the road, she dropped the ball to the seat and stared out the window at the passing countryside, giving an occasional yawn. How could a dog repeatedly yawn when she is about to take part in another duck opener?

Then I remembered reading once that yawns are often emitted when a person is nervous. I thought back to my high school days sitting in the locker room before a football game, all geared up and ready to do battle. Even though I wasn't much of a football player, and never did play all that much, my stomach would flip and flop as we waited to take to the field. Amid the noises of scraping football cleats on the cement floor and the hushed words between players would come yawns. All around the room could be seen gaping, nervous yawns. I used to yawn a lot, and somehow seeing Jenny yawn now made me feel good.

In fifteen minutes we met Nels and his dog, Rusty, and loaded our gear into his truck. While Jenny is six years old and supposedly in her prime, Rusty is a grizzle-faced golden retriever whose age is in double figures. But on this day, the duck opener, she likewise seems six or maybe even four. Both dogs helped push the tail gate of the truck open in their excitement as we unloaded our gear. The tennis ball was forgotten in my car.

If Christmas is a compendium of memories, duck hunting openers are no less so. Nels and I took our gun safety classes together over twenty years ago. We both hunted ducks for the first time on the same opening day, and we both used a little, single-shot 20 gauge to bag our first duck on that day. Both our fathers were very strict on how we handled our guns, loaded or empty, and because of that, we hunt with each other without worrying about how the other guy handles his gun.

We've watched many sunrises together, gotten soaked and cold together, shared many laughs and thoughts with each other. We've shared so many moments in the marshes and woods together that we can clearly read each other's sign language and sometimes minds as we sneak up on a flock of ducks or geese.

Why, I've even carried him across a creek on my back because he conveniently left his waders back in the car. And he would have done the same for me had the forgotten waders been mine.

Now it was another year, and we had hiked along a cornfield leading to a flooded, low area where the water, now covered with a green coat of duckweed and flecked with shed curls of duck feathers, had flooded far into the woods.

In short order, we had the decoys in position and our colorful blinds of reddened dogwood, maple, and oak branches built. With a few minutes left before the noon opener, we sat on the hillside and savored the moment. We each cradled a model 12 that had once known the opening ritual with our respective fathers. The dogs sat anxiously beside us, shuffling on their haunches and giving an occasional toothy yawn. It all seemed so right.

These are the things that bring us back. Without them, we could just as well scratch October off the calendar.

# Prize of the Autumn Bog

My grandparents' large farmhouse, like so many of that era, had a surplus of bedrooms. There was one room however, that never did harbor a bed or have its plaster walls covered with paper or paint. But it was far from empty. It contained a wide assortment of items such as old rockers; camelback trunks; boxes of old clothes smelling of mothballs; multicolored quilts; old, elaborately framed photos of stern-faced relatives; set-aside toys and dolls; balls of rag strips destined to become rugs; and a little bit of this and a lot of that. This room, appropriately enough, was always called the scrap room.

But about the time of the year when the spuds were dug and the teal were starting to pull out of the lakes, the scrap room would sometimes hold another treasure—baskets of reddened cranberries gathered by my grandfather and great-uncle. They would pick their berries from the boggy sedge meadows that bordered some of the nearby shallow lakes.

If some of the scrap room berries were still wearing shades of summer's green, they would be spread out on the floor to ripen. Since the room was only a scrap room, it was closed off from the rest of the house and not heated. Such a room seasons both yesteryear's treasures and cranberries well.

Of course, there were years of scarcity, autumns when no baskets of berries brightened the scrap room, but many years there were filled baskets and the smell of sauce cooking downstairs.

Those shallow lakes that dimple the sand country of my grandparents' township were born from the great masses of ice left behind some ten thousand to twelve thousand years ago by the slowly departing glaciers. Eventually, these great lobes of ice melted, leaving water-filled, kettlelike depressions.

Over the centuries, tons of organic matter, the remains of dying plant and animal life, were left behind in these pothole lakes. Nothing is exempt from aging, lakes included. Since there were neither inlets nor outlets to these lakes, the decaying plant matter accumulated, making the lakes shallower. A floating mat of vegetation, tied together by intertwined roots, spread from the shoreline farther out into the water. The chemistry of the lake water also changed. A higher ratio of carbon dioxide to oxygen developed, and as a result, the waters became somewhat acidic.

Special plants thrive in such an acidic environment, such as the spongelike sphagnum moss that is typically found in a bog. Other unique plants are many of the orchids and insect-eating plants, including the vase-shaped pitcher plant and the tiny, glistening sundew. However, it is the cranberry that is the prize of the autumn bog.

Long before my great grandparents came from the old country, the Ojibway peoples waded into October's bogs to pick the fruit of the cranberry. They called the plant *mashkigimin,* or "child of the marsh." For early Native Americans, the cranberry harvest was a festive occasion, with much socializing. A good crop signified good times, or a fat autumn, a time to smile, laugh, and feel content before the lean of winter was felt. A staple winter food item for the Ojibway was pemmican—a blend of dried meat, usually venison, and dried berries, often cranberries. The cranberries were also of value to the Ojibway in making crimson dyes and in preparing a poultice to combat food poisoning. The small, oval-shaped, leathery leaves of

189

the cranberry plant were also steeped to make a tea to lessen nausea.

Early colonists in New England found this unique berry of the New World not only tasty but an excellent source of vitamin C. The berries have good keeping qualities, and barrels of the fruit were shipped to England without fear of spoilage. Whaling ships, often out at sea for several years, carried casks full of berries to feed the crew as a scurvy preventive. Cranberry juice was also often used in treating kidney stones, and it is still prescribed for urinary tract infections when more conventional antibiotics fail or are not desirable.

In colonial days, the berries were known as craneberries because of their pink blossoms, which bloom in July, have long, pollen-bearing stamens shaped somewhat like the head and neck of a crane. With the passing of time the word was shortened to cranberry.

If one wants to spy a cranberry blossom, you must be willing to subject yourself to summer's heat and mosquitoes. I prefer the October cranberries. The object of desire is the fruit, not the flower. However, one cannot speak of one without admiring the other.

As a kid, I did not appreciate the pungent taste of the cranberry sauce that graced our table alongside our Thanksgiving turkey, so I passed it up. I don't believe the word *tart* is in the vocabulary of youth—*sour* perhaps, but not *tart*. Perhaps, like the appreciation of lutefisk on Christmas Eve, an accumulation of years is needed to develop a taste and desire for the berries. Now I no longer find the berries sour. Definitely tart, but not sour.

Their tartness seems proof that cranberries draw their acidity from the very bogs in which they grow. To tame some of the acidity of the berries, one must use sugar. There are numerous recipes using cranberries, but by far the most popular—and my own favorite—is cranberry sauce. There is no prettier or tastier marriage of tastes than that of a slice of venison roast with crimson cranberry sauce.

It was on a golden Indian summer day that my great-uncle Eldo led my wife and I from the firm footing of a fiery October maple woods into a spongy, quaking bog. I took my time moving across the heaving meadow because I had the additional weight of our wide-eyed daughter on my back. The bog extended about one hundred yards out to the open water of a small lake. Once we gained the floating mat of vegetation, I finally spotted a few marble-sized red berries nestled in the green sphagnum. Immediately, my wife, Susan, started working her way towards me. In no time, she had water in her knee-high rubber boots. She never whimpered or complained, for she comes from her berry-picking fervor honestly. Her mother becomes giddy with enthusiasm at the prospect of filling a pail with these natural goodies.

Those berries that had already been touched by the chill of repeated frosts had turned a translucent red and were soft. We wanted only those that were hard and flushed with red, or nearly so. Old-time cranberry men claim that evening temperatures dropping to twenty-five degrees Fahrenheit are ideal for "painting a good red skin on a cranberry."

I sloshed further down the shoreline and soon found a greater number of berries. Here, tucked under the insulating blanket of grasslike sedges, the fruit had escaped the evening frosts. With my chest waders, I was able to kneel down in the soft, thick moss and pick the berries. I was also less apt to dump my napping daughter out of her backpack. Everytime I got up to move on, I found it worthwhile to look back at the pools created by my sinking footsteps. More times than not, several of the small fruits were bobbing in the water where they had been dislodged by my boots from their tiny, running vines.

We had not been the first to this berry patch. Here and there were small pieces of half-eaten fruits piled under the shrubs. I suspect that bog-lurking rodents visited this patch long before any of the early settlers did.

In the past there were others who lived in small farms near my grandparents, and they also anticipated the cranberry harvest. They had picked their berries in this very patch, as did others in the area.

Picking is always easier if you can kneel, but in a bog, such a practice can prove wet and chilly. One farm wife here used to fill burlap feed sacks with straw and kneel on them to keep dry while she filled flour sacks with cranberries. Then there were those good berry years when milk cans were hauled onto the bog and filled with the red fruit.

Another fellow, a confirmed lifelong bachelor, used to don long wooden skis to navigate across the undulating bog. Back then, most of the folks kept their berries for sauce or juice, but some would take their havest to town to sell to local grocers. Their labors sometimes would fetch them as much as twenty-five cents for a quart of berries.

Now, with the sun dropping and the cool of an October evening descending on us, we called it quits and bounced off the bog back to solid footing. We hadn't picked the great quantities that I remember seeing years ago in the scrap room. But it didn't matter, because my mind was already thinking ahead to the fresh cranberry sauce that would trim the brace of mallards that the slough out back had given up that morning.

# Chores of the Popple

There was no doubt about it, we were going nowhere. With Nels muttering at the wheel and old Charlie and I sitting glumly at his side, we listened to the telltale spinning of tires on frost-slickened bluestem.

Jenny, my staunch friend and dog, was sitting on the floor of the truck, grinning at the prospect of finally getting out of the stuffy cab.

Here it was opening day of duck hunting and we were stuck, fallen prey to an unseen dead furrow in a long-forgotten field, no doubt abandoned because it lay so far from human habitation. With that humbling thought in mind, and without a shovel or a decent jack, we knew we were in trouble.

Though the duck opener was several hours away, we had planned on spending some time weaving our way through thick popple stands in pursuit of grouse and woodcock.

We got out and stood around the truck, scratching our heads and slowly rubbing our foreheads while Jenny, oblivious to us, explored frosty hazel thickets at the popple's edge. Perhaps we believed, in the chill of the morn, that such scalp massaging might awaken our numbed minds to render a solution to the problem.

It has been said that we learn from past mistakes. Well, it was such a mistake that I suddenly remembered as I watched Jenny's thick, wagging tail course through the browned bracken fern under the straight popples. It wasn't the dog but the popple that provided the catalyst of recollection.

Years ago, two friends and I were heading down a washboard gravel section of the Gunflint Trail after finishing a canoe trip in the border country. Miles from help, we found ourselves with a flat tire and no jack to lift the car. What little traffic there was, passed us.

Soon, we found ourselves grunting while rolling a boulder the size of a clothes basket into position behind the car's bumper. We hastily cut and dragged a long popple log out of the woods. The boulder of granite provided the fulcrum and the popple worked as a lever.

A couple of husky rocks were wedged against the front tires to prevent the car from rolling forward. Two of us hung like last week's laundry from one end of the springy lever and pried the car's rear end inches off the ground. The car was high enough for the third member of the team to quickly change the tire.

Wouldn't you know it? Those two brothers now own a service station in town, though I doubt you will find a section of popple in their back room among the tools and jacks.

We decided that the popple lever was worth a try in freeing the truck. So with Nels's double-bit ax in hand, I headed for the nearby popple stand, eyeing the trees for one of stout, straight stature.

With morning's first breezes beginning to stir, the golden popple leaves shimmered overhead. Some call the aspen, or popple, the gayest of trees, because even on still days the leaves with their flattened leaf stalks catch the breeze's slightest stirrings, causing them to flutter. Hence, the names trembling and quaking aspen.

There are folktales that attempt to explain the origin of the shuddering leaves. It was believed that Judas Iscariot hung himself from an aspen tree after betraying Christ, and to this day, the tree trembles because of its ties to the crucifixion.

Another philosopher of generations past likened the fluttering movement of popple leaves to the "wagging of women's tongues." I have heard vague rumors that this particular great thinker mysteriously disappeared shortly after this bold declaration.

As I walked under the trees, I could have sworn that the leaves overhead were chuckling at our predicament. But the mood changed and the chuckles turned to trembles as the ax drove into the soft wood of the chosen tree.

I gave Nels some grief about his dull ax, but it didn't really matter. The wood cut easily, and soon the tree was felled, limbed and made into a pole.

After several attempts, the power of the popple pried the front end of the truck high enough to lift it from the culprit mound underneath. We were free.

Rather than discard the straight pole, we carried it back into the trees near the old beaver-cut area. The beaver, like the grouse, woodcock, deer, and numerous songbirds, finds the popple more valuable than we do in our efforts to pry trucks or cut for pulp. For wildlife, it is most valuable as food and cover.

Popple is the milkweed of trees in its tenacious drive to rapidly grow skyward. Those who are ignorant of tree values scorn the popple as a weed tree. Not surprisingly, these same folks are unaware of the goodness of weeds.

Few trees can equal the popple in its fast growth rate and ability to regenerate after a fire or a clear-cutting.

We set up a camp near a maze of old beaver-felled popple, with a new growth of supple saplings rushing upward to replace the old. Our shelter for the night was, at best, rudimentary. We lifted one end of the popple pry pole and placed it in the fork of a red oak and lashed the other end to a birch. Over the horizontal pole, we threw an old canvas tarp, bringing one edge to the ground and tying the other edge out beyond the pole in awning fashion. Our lean-to shelter was complete in short order, the truck free, and the rest of the day ours.

Later, with the orange sun disappearing through the popples to the west, Nels and I prepared our evening meal over the fire. Simmering in a pool of sizzling butter was a conglomerate of spuds, carrots, onions, and duck. The full pan was doomed to be short-lived.

Earlier, Nels had carefully driven Charlie out over the rocks, ruts, and through the waterholes back to Charlie's car. As much as he would have like to share the lean-to with us, Charlie was homebound. The following day, according to state dogma, was the final day of the year in which Charlie could stalk his favorite trout pools, and he had planned a day of worship on a favorite, lively stream.

After sopping up the bottom of the pan with a piece of bread, we rested under the lean-to, well satiated, and watched the brightly burning campfire. We had built up the fire with well seasoned, beaver-cut popple before crawling into our sleeping bags.

Jenny, tired and still wet from her efforts in the potholes, curled up between us. Her only movements were the slow but wet and noisy licking of her legs and flanks. She, like us, was tired and felt the fire's warmth and sounds work its magic. Soon we all slept.

I don't know how much later it was when we awoke to hear the drawn out howl of a nearby coyote. It yapped and howled from out in the dark popples for a short time, and then there was nothing except blackness, the glow of dying embers, and the overhead murmuring of unseen popple leaves that soon whispered us back to sleep.

Such are the values of popple.


# October's Crowded Skies

I don't believe there is a wind that has more responsibilities than one conceived in autumn.

Summer's air currents are hot, often dusty dry, and occasionally downright mean when they send towering thunderheads at us. Heat has a way of making things angry and short-tempered.

Winter's winds, by contrast, are bitter cold, which is no surprise as they are of polar origin. It is hard to feel any kinship with such icy blasts, and like the chipmunk and the toad, we hunker down and try to avoid them.

Some folks would disagree, claiming that the winds of March carry the greater load of chores. After all, the spring winds are able to carry the warmth that has the power to melt any remnants of winter's cloak. These are the breezes that carry the welcome noises of water once again dripping. And it is the drying winds, they say, that make it possible to get into the gardens and fields to get on with the business of putting seed into the ground.

195

Another convincing argument for vernal winds is their ability to hasten the northward progress of countless flocks of birds, who in the spring feel an unexplainable urge to homestead a piece of my yard, a corner in the woods, or a thicket of willow near the slough.

Youngsters don't even question which seasonal winds have the greater value, for there are long-tailed kites of every shape and color to send aloft to mingle with both the returning geese and the returning march of a summer-bound sun.

But it is in the fall that the winds most need to hurry and get their jobs done. The passengers on these winds are many. Sailing away are summer's dreams, while winter's promise rides the same wind.

As in the spring, the autumn skies reveal birds riding high and fast in pursuit of an ending summer. But the flocks are larger now, with many young birds coasting on their first autumn wind. Ask me to compare the gusts of spring and fall by watching a respective flock of bluebills in flight and I will not hesitate to say that a flock of November bluebills tumble, twist, and cut the skies more skillfully than at any other time of the year. But that is understandable when they had lead shot or driving flakes of snow prodding them on.

Without the breath of autumn, it would be impossible for the milkweeds, the goldenrods, and a host of other plants that are totally dependent on the wind to carry their fluff of seed to new grounds. And on those blustery days, the milkweed's flight is no less erratic and speedy than the bluebills.

The high flying wedge of geese or the solitary, fragile flight of the monarch butterfly prefers a north wind at this time of the year. While such a wind may cause us to turn up our collars, it is a wind that carries the migrants, making their journey an easier and swifter one.

Try as they might, the autumn breezes that ruffle the lakes and ponds eventually lose the battle to the cold and calm. As fall progresses and the days shorten and become cooler, the water loses summer's heat.

Then there will come a night so clear that the stars seem to mingle with the naked treetops, and on that night the wind will sleep. Lakes and ponds will stiffen and become silent. Without the wash of gentle waves, there seems a certain sadness—unless you own a pair of ice skates.

Large lakes, like Superior, are so great in volume that they do not give up their heat so readily. Instead, Superior will become more restless and alive during November's winds. The giant ore ship *Edmund Fitzgerald* has become a legend since it lost its challenge of Superior's waves and was broken apart. Talk to an old Norwegian or Swedish fisherman about Lake Superior and its November temperament and you will see a change in his stare and voice. There is respect, fear, and even sadness, for he undoubtedly has lost a member of the family or a dear friend to the waves born of an autumn wind.

Without the breezes of Indian summer there would be no flight of the spiders. Recently, on a warm cloudless day, I passed a few hours of fishing. The fish were not cooperating, so my attention toward them faltered and I found myself looking around and daydreaming. As I looked out over the glassy waters, I saw the shine of a gossamer thread. The silk line floated ever so slowly across the water toward me until finally I was able to reach for it. There, hanging on the bottom of the thread, was a speck of a spider. Actually, at this point in its life, it is not a spider but a spiderling.

I looked up and spotted another thread drifting just over the water. Soon I could spot several of the shiny threads as they floated from the far end of the lake toward me.

These spiderlings, like the milkweed, are traveling to wherever October breezes may carry them. In a practice referred to as ballooning, the spiderlings climb to the top of a twig, weed stalk, or fence post, face into the wind, and release a fine thread of silk from the tip of their abdomen. The wind pulls the thread farther out, and as it gets longer, it becomes a sail lifting the spider off of its perch and sending it kitelike into the sky.

Most of these spiders are from a group known as dwarf spiders. Many spiders in this group have been known to cross oceans or drift to mountaintops thousands of feet high. A few years ago, I saw a field of new rye covered with a gauze of silken threads from grounded spiders. The young green rye shoots shimmered with a covering of wispy, silver hairs. In Europe, this appearance during the warm sunny days of autumn is often referred to as "the old woman's summer."

Perhaps the strangest rider of a late autumn wind lifted off near Kitty Hawk, North Carolina, in 1903. It was the first manned machine to successfully take to the air. Since that day, the autumn skies have never been quite the same as they were when they belonged only to southbound birds, monarchs, falling leaves, floating seeds, and ballooning spiders.

# Reading the Wood

We learn from experience. Experience that may be generously passed onto us from others or that may be gained by repeatedly trying our hand at the challenges before us. Most skills in life are learned this way, whether it's casting a tiny, delicate dry fly, baking a blue-ribbon apple pie with a fine flaky crust, or creating a lifelike sculpture from a mound of clay. They all require practice.

Splitting wood is no different. There is something very satisfying about setting up a formidable chunk of wood and hearing the sharp crack as the splitting maul tears cleanly through it. It comforts me to add the split wood to the ever-growing pile knowing that eventually they will be properly stacked in the woodshed to await their turn in giving up their stored energy to heat my home.

I've helped split wood using a gas-powered hydraulic wood splitter, but it's not the same. The challenge isn't nearly as great. Admittedly, there is an advantage when it comes to wear and tear on my muscles and frame. But I find that sleep comes easier after a few hours of swinging a maul, and I like to think my muscles become more firm.

How well I remember my first splitting attempt, with an ax in hand and a piece of oak taunting me. It was a warm summer day, and my brother and I had just finished mowing the lawn at our great-grandparents' farm. When Great-grandpa Schmidt asked if we would like to try splitting some wood, we eagerly accepted the challenge.

We made our way out to the old woodshed that was set into the side of the hill. The back, or uphill, side of the shed was open so that as the wood was split just above the shed it could be tossed down onto the bark-covered floor.

Brother Scott and I took turns flailing at the stubborn wood while Grandpa, seated on a great chunk of oak, watched us and told stories. We loved to listen to his stories of skunk-killing days, of bears raising stolen human babies, and of his younger days in helping on cattle drives in South Dakota. We took turns hacking at the wood as Grandpa watched patiently. I remember thinking that the sun must be getting to Grandpa when he somewhat dejectedly reminisced about how much he missed hard work. Only now, years later, I know what he meant, but for a twelve-year-old, work was a dirty word.

Finally, Grandpa told us to stop for a moment. Leaning over, he reached out and pointed with his broad, rugged finger to the growth rings on the wood and said, "You have to read the piece of wood. Look at the grain and find the weakest part of the chunk and take aim at it. You'll wear yourselves out by just hitting anywhere."

And so we did, and you know, it worked. We still had our share of troubles on some of the larger pieces or on those with crazy, swirling grain where a limb had once grown from the tree, but eventually we managed to whittle down the pile. We were proud and tired after the job was done, and I'm sure that the ax handle was a little worse for wear as well.

Years later, I learned that by reading the grain, I could also glimpse into the tree's past. I count the rings to see just how long the tree had been a part of the landscape. Or I could note how close the rings grew to one another and venture a guess as to what years had been good for the tree. Usually, the vigorous, younger years and seasons of ample rainfall provided the broadest space between the annual rings.

I have also learned that summer is no time to split wood. On a cold day, when the snow creaks underfoot, the pieces of wood will leap apart with far less effort put into my swings. Summer's moisture, trapped in the piece of oak, is frozen, making it easier for the wood fibers to pull apart from one another.

Though the air may be frigid, I usually shed layers of clothes as the pile grows, and I am reminded of how cutting firewood heats twice.

Different woods, I have learned, are like different books. Some of them are easy to get through and others are nearly impossible to finish. Elm is a wood that is difficult to read. With its long, intertwined fibers, splitting becomes a grueling job. I'm willing to bet that there are more hydraulic wood splitters in those parts of the county where elm has flourished. After gnashing one's teeth over a piece of elm, it is a boost to the ego to lay the maul to a piece of ash or birch. Their long, straight fibers make splitting seem like child's play.

I have learned that what may be a source of fuel for me might be a home for others. I admit to a sense of guilt when several white-footed mice come bouncing out of the cavernous piece of oak as it splits apart. Perhaps their next refuge will not be claimed by my saw. The black ants that sometimes spill out of a split piece are motionless and appear dead as they lie sprinkled on the snow. Perhaps the ants are the reason for the chickadee's appearance when the maul starts making its music on the woodpile. Their need for fuel is no different than the wood stove that heats my house.

Once I scooped up some of the fallen ants and dropped them into a jar before bringing them indoors. As the insects warmed up, they slowly snapped out of their state of suspended animation. Carpenter ants and a number of other winter-dormant insects have the ability to produce glycerol in their bodies as the temperatures drop in the fall. The chemical recipe of glycerol is similar to that of the antifreeze we use to winterize our cars. The ant slowly becomes hardened to winter by the gradual cooling of its body in the fall. As the days shorten and cool, a hormonal signal initiates the antifreeze production. The miracle solution prevents the insect's tissues from freezing.

Out next to my not-quite-so-full woodshed is a mammoth chunk of antique red oak. I've looked it over and attempted a few swings that only resulted in a tingling felt all the way down to the tips of my toes. For a couple of days, I've taken a few minutes to inspect the hulking piece for a hint of a fracture, but the wood is solid as well as stubborn. As of this writing, it is still whole. I have not tried a wedge to prod it open because I fear that this ominous piece would absorb and claim my three wedges. As it gets colder, reading the grain will become easier, and I am confident that the oak block will be reduced to a two-day supply of firewood.

In fact it's time for a few swings at the sleeping giant. If nothing else, I'll attract a couple of chickadees.

**UPDATE:** Four years have passed since I first put the maul to the stubborn piece of red oak. The top of the piece is scarred with ax and maul bites, but the rest of the chunk is still sound. Admittedly, I have not been as persistent with my roundhouse swings since I noted that the woodshed chipmunk regularly uses the broad surface for a dining table.

# NOVEMBER

# In Pursuit of Suffering

There are many folks who are convinced that to receive something worthwhile, you have got to pay your dues. Perhaps the late outdoor writer Gordon MacQuarrie said it best, "You've got to suffer!"

Like MacQuarrie, author Robert Ruark spoke fondly of the pleasure of suffering in his popular book *The Old Man's Boy Grows Older.* The book is a collection of stories about growing up under the tutelage of his old salty grandfather.

The old man would reminisce about past suffering while sitting in his rocker, drawn up close to the hot stove. "The Old Man had a lot of favorite topics, and one was that a hunting-fishing fellow hated comfort, that he welcomed pain, that he was never so happy as when he was miserable. He was like the gent in the old joke who kept hitting himself over the head with a hammer, because it felt so good when he quit."

Whether it's swatting at hordes of mosquitoes over a shady pool in hopes of tempting a fat trout, pulling weeds in the garden under a July sun, or sitting and shivering on a frozen stump waiting for dawn and a deer, one has to suffer a bit to obtain the desired goal.

The Apostle Paul writes in the Epistle to the Romans that "We rejoice in our sufferings, knowing that suffering produces endurance and endurance produces character and character produces hope."

It was with those thoughts in mind that friend Charlie and I were driving north in pursuit of suffering and bluebill—though not necessarily in that order. It's no secret that bluebills and discomfort often go hand in hand. "Bills," as they are labeled by their most ardent followers, linger on autumnal journeys until they can be accompanied by flocks of snowflakes.

# LEARNING NATURE BY A COUNTRY ROAD

To hunt these birds, you must prepare yourself as if you were going ice fishing on a mid-January day when the snow squeaks crisply and loudly underfoot. Planning what to pack is frustrating. You could need arctic wear, rain gear, and perhaps even skates. November is like that. Maybe that's why it seems that bluebill hunters are practically an endangered species.

Under sunny skies and warm temperatures, we pulled away from my house. The amount of gear we carried seemed ridiculous. Decoys were spread throughout the car, and more sacks of them were tied into the rooftop canoe. A fair herd of sheep had supplied the wool we carried in the form of sox, shirts, sweaters, and pants. Our Duluth packs bulged with boots, clothes, and down sleeping bags.

Charlie has a bad hip, thanks to a runaway boulder that passed over him while on a dinosaur dig somewhere in the Missouri Breaks of Montana. If he is to sleep on the ground, he must keep the bum leg warm. Taking up much of the back seat was a tanned buffalo robe that would easily blanket Charlie, me, and, if need be, four more chilled duck hunters.

We had traveled a mere four miles down the road when the car skipped a beat, faltered, and died. Out of gas. It had been over two years since the fuel gauge worked, but I'm convinced that this car purposely consumes its remaining fuel only at the start of canoe trips or duck hunts. Never has it sputtered dry on the way to work.

We coasted to a stop in front of a farm. I trotted up to the yard and asked a barefoot girl of about seven if her folks were around. Watching her run shoeless into the house really had me questioning the need for packs stuffed with winter gear. Had I not noticed the golden tamaracks in the low land behind the barn or the flock of robins gorging on the frost-touched fruits from the crab apple near the house, I might have mistaken the month for early September.

In short order we managed to pour the most of three gallons into the car. It would be enough fuel to get us the nine miles into Cambridge, where we could find a station. Soon we turned north. We both noted what looked like a dark, ugly front to the northwest. Charlie's hip was starting to ache, so he knew we were in for a change of weather.

In an hour or so we heard the creaks of the taut ropes holding the canoe down as the wind picked up and jostled the car. The tamaracks we passed now were no longer golden. Instead, their naked limbs dueled in the wind with neighboring alder thickets.

One gas station later, it began to get dark. Now there was the telling bite of some slanting snowflakes racing across the car's beams of light. As we continued north, towards the source of the snow, we encountered more flakes and gustier blasts of Canadian-borne winds.

With our destination being about seventy miles between us and the pole star, we decided we had better stop for the last of our supplies. The town we stopped at claims to have a population of ninety-six. That night, I believe that most of them were at the liquor store or at the Cenex station across the street. By the looks of it, these two establishments made up half the businesses in town.

While Charlie sat wedged in the car, I went in for a pint of blackberry brandy to ease our suffering during the coming days of hunting. Blackberry was chosen because it would be a touch of July's sun at the edge of a November marsh.

The town sat perched on a ridge that was at one time an ancient beachline to the greatest of all glacial lakes—Agassiz. Until Agassiz drained away, some nine thousand years ago, it covered an area larger than all of the Great Lakes combined as one. Think of the bluebills that massive lake may have played host to, and not a duck boat on the lake.

Besides the black sediments that are among the richest on the continent, a few remnant splashes of the mighty lake are still evident. One of these is next to our campsite, where we hoped to find some bluebills lingering before the coming ice urged them to the Gulf Coast.

Well into the evening, as we neared the lake of our destination, we passed a small Lutheran church surrounded by stubbled wheat fields. Out front, along the road, was a hand-lettered sign on poster board that read "Lutefisk Supper." From late October until Christmas Eve, scores of such churches in the Scandinavian-rich Upper Midwest will host lutefisk suppers. Some call it fish-jello and consider it a suffering just to sit down at a table where it glistens on a platter.

The evening was late, and a glance through the windows as we passed by revealed men and women busy washing dishes in the kitchen and doing other clean-up jobs. I had enjoyed this annual church feast some ten years before and wished aloud that we could have partaken in it again.

Charlie claims he has never liked Swedes, since they remained neutral in the "big war," and he was not about to try any of their slippery fish. He couldn't figure out why those folks in the church even bothered to wash the dishes. "Could just as well throw those dishes away," he muttered. In his opinion, we had already suffered enough with the white-knuckle driving and the wind doing its best to tear the canoe off the car and put us in the ditch. With the nasty weather upon us, we were not as worried about finding a point on the lake to set our decoys off of. Now we were concerned about reaching the lake and our campsite.

It seemed we had traveled out of October, bypassed November, and halted the car in December. In the darkness, we both wondered if every bluebill around hadn't jumped on that northwest gale and sailed south for an overnight passage all the way to the coastal waters of Louisiana or Texas.

On a positive note, the blustery wind was putting the lake into motion, making it less apt to freeze over. We also knew that if the wind continued, the bluebills would be more apt to break away from their rafts to search for a quiet piece of water. With the passing of each day, the temperatures had dropped, and the lake had become smaller as ice formed from the shoreline and started creeping toward the lake's center.

Sleep was brief that night, and in no time it was dawn. We dawdled some in loading the canoe. There was no need to be on the water at first light, since bluebills don't feel the urge as strongly as mallards to get an early start on the day. Besides, it was easier to battle the ice under grayed skies rather than move in the darkness.

It was slow work breaking a channel out to the open water. Since I was the younger by nearly a score of years, it was my job to lean over the bow of the canoe to jab and thrust my paddle blade through the ice. Charlie kept edging us forward. Sometimes we backpaddled, stopped, and charged forward into the ice in icebreaker fashion.

It wasn't long before I had stripped off a couple layers of clothes; now I wore only three. My nose was dripping, and since there was no time to waste in searching pockets for a hankie, the thumb of my leather chopper mitt soon grew shiny with nose ice.

Earlier, the car's radio had informed us that the wind chill was just below zero. Even our many layers of clothing would have trouble keeping out the penetrating cold. Enduring numb fingers and then warming them, only to bear the agonizing sting of thawing flesh, were part of the price we had to pay.

But it was worth it. Besides the flocks of bluebills milling out over the open water, there were other visitors to the lake. Swans the color of white ice flew low in ragged formations. But rather than their stark whiteness, it was their haunting yodels that will always be with me.

We were not alone in hunting the marsh. Overhead, an occasional eagle or marsh hawk gracefully soared by in search of a duck meal. These birds, along with foxes, coyotes, and crows, do not consider those bluebills lost by hunters to be a waste. The unretrieved ducks will help squelch the predator's hunger.

We were fortunate in that we did not loose any of our ducks. In fact, Charlie, who sometimes likes to come across as an ornery red squirrel, showed his sensitive side when he spotted a bluebill that had been crippled by an earlier hunter. There was no hesitation in his chasing the duck to collect it for his limit. The suffering of a crippled duck produces no hope unless you are an eagle or marsh hawk, who hunt for different reasons.

The birds flew well throughout the day. We realized that it wouldn't take long to get our birds, so to prolong the day, we put our guns down for awhile and uncased our cameras from their ammo box holdings. Banking turns, cupped wings, lowered feet, and birds skimming just over the decoys were all viewed through the lens. We let several bunches of ducks tumble into our spread of decoys and swim amongst the phony callers. After a few pictures, we would stand up and watch them all run pitter-patter across the water to get airborne. Our laughs and smiles warmed our faces and insides.

Occasional small flocks of yellowlegs and other shorebirds, passing too fast to be recognized, seemed out of place flying over ice. Most of their shorebird brethren had left these parts before summer's leaves felt the blush of autumn.

More fitting to the cold scene were the tight groups of snow buntings twittering and wheeling over the patches of new ice. With their white wings flashing, they seemed more flake than feather.

There were also muskrats to watch. They seemed oblivious to the cold as they sat Buddhalike on the ice grooming themselves. Three moose stood back away from the shoreline and scrutinized us.

As for us, we sat out in the canoe taking it all in as we suffered.

At sunset, after our second day on the lake, we watched flock after flock of bluebills lift off the lake and climb high into the sky before flying directly and rapidly for the sliver of a moon on the southern horizon. These birds were leaving the lake, beginning an all-night flight to some body of water south of here. It was an omen of things to come, as it is the bluebill's habit to pull out before a cold weather front.

The next morning, the car radio told us it was ten above zero forty miles to the south of us. Getting out on the lake was out of the question. The ice was too thick to open with a paddle and too thin to stand on. So like the bluebills, we put the wind at our backs and headed home to the south.

When we stopped for gas on the way home, a man dressed sharply in suit and tie came out of the station after paying for his share of gas. As he walked by us, he paused, noting the loaded car and the dead-grass-colored canoe atop the car. He asked, "How did you do?" and "What kind?" He smiled at our answers and said, "Yeh, we just got into a swarm of bills on Saturday—the day of the snow. Nothing beats hunting bills—something special about them." "Man," he added as if hanging onto a memory, "it can be nasty and bitter, but it only seems to make the hunt all the better."

Though he stood neat in his suit next to me, with my stubbled chin and cheeks, soiled pants, and layers of wool, there was a bond—a bond of knowing a satisfying suffering.

(NOTE: To prevent anyone from undue suffering, out of the goodness of my heart, I have deliberately omitted the name of this bluebill haunt.)

# Drumming an Old Tune

When I was a boy, there was a "cannon" in the pastured woods behind my grandpa's barn. The volleys fired were many but were heard only by those of us who armed and fired the cannon.

The armament was positioned back in the woods, a good distance from the barn and outbuildings. The closest building, or at least what was left of a structure, was the rotting framework of the old dynamite shed. My great-grandfather had kept his supply of dynamite far from the barn and outbuildings. Only when there was land to clear and stumps to dislodge would he visit the shed. Knowing that dynamite had once been stored there made the cannon's location more exciting.

This particular piece of artillery was fixed in position, always aimed south, and it could not be raised or lowered to adjust the trajectory of the next discharge. Years prior to my discovery of the fieldpiece, Grandpa had unknowingly created the fantasy cannon.

A stout red oak had had a feeble anchor of roots, and one day, with perhaps a stiff north wind blowing, the tree slowly leaned into the its trunk about four feet from the ground. My guess is that two men pulled he oak stopped its downward, gravity-poweredin musical rhythm on each end of a long crosscut saw. As a team, they sweated and some of its outreaching limbs broke the fall. stared in concentratat the growing cut and spilling sawdust as the saw steadily worked tthe oak.

A chain saw might have been used on the tree, but the height of the ard.

When there is a nearby winter-hungry wood furnace to feed, such cut, an oak is short-lived. The bowing oak was severed from a comfortable one for a pair of sawyers, would indicate the work of a crosscut. A chain saw operator would have made the cut closer to the ground to get all the wood possible.

After the tree was cut, split, and dragged to the house, only the angled butt of the oak remained sticking out of the ground, aimed at the low December sun in the south.

Several years later, on a Sunday afternoon, while the grown-ups visited or played an innocent game of rook up at the house, we kids discovered the pastured cannon out behind the barn. To us, there was no mistaking what the find was. It wasn't viewed as firewood or a once proud oak—this was a massive cannon.

Now, more years than I care to count have passed. The cows are long gone, and my grandparents live only as memories. The barn, I fear, is standing only because it is lashed together by the cobwebs from within. The cannon has fallen in the battle of time to the always-victorious foe of decay. If a youngster came upon the softening log today, it might be used as a bench, a car, or perhaps a racehorse, but never a cannon.

Not only has the oak stump dropped to mingle with the grasses, but the long-cowless pasture has gradually become a woods as the hazel brush, popples, and red oaks, kin to the "cannon" oak, no doubt, have surrounded our old battleground. The woods has lessened in size only because we moved the house built by my great-great-grandfather into it several years ago.

I had all but forgotten about the pasture wars of earlier years until this fall, when the sound of thunder pounded from the thicket where the cannon remains lay. I stopped what I was doing and listened. It was a sound I hadn't heard in recent years from this piece of woods. Not only has this patch of township been cowless but grouseless as well.

The sound I heard was the building crescendo of a drumming grouse. It sounded close, so I walked quietly to the edge of our yard, and as I entered the underbrush, I got down on my hands and knees. Slowly, like a stalking predator, placing each "knee-foot" where my hand had been to avoid the snap of a hidden twig, I moved like a lioness bellying up to a grazing zebra.

The territorial drumming of the male grouse is a familiar roll from the woodlands at that time of the year when the creek bottoms and swamps are aglow with the sunburst of cowslips. During early spring, the male, perched on a favorite log or boulder, will beat his wings, starting slowly, then building, increasing the tempo to a thundering staccato. His intent is to let all nearby mate-seeking hens know of his whereabouts and availability.

On the other hand, nearby males should pay heed to the drumming for another reason. To the competition, other nearby males, the message is a declaration of territorial boundaries and that any trespassing by them would be scorned.

Spring drumming is a welcome sound, no less thrilling than the first returning bluebird, the first tentative chirps of a spring peeper, or the music of northbound geese. But here it was October, when bluebirds and geese have reversed their direction, and peepers have retreated undercover for the winter. Yet it was the unmistakable sound of a drumming grouse and not the firing up of an old John Deere tractor.

Though the annual ritual of mating is half a year forthcoming, the older male grouse often drum in the fall to reinforce their boundaries to other male grouse, particularly those young males who are trying to find their own piece of woods to settle in.

By early September, those grouse hatched last spring are fully grown, and it is time for them to leave the security of mother and the brooding grounds. This period of dispersal is often referred to as the fall shuffle.

Grouse researchers have found that young females tend to roam the region he grew up in, if he can find a vacant territory. In order to let ir male siblings before settling down. these wandering males know sal practices help prevent siblings from mating with each other, assuring a healthier, more mixed gene pool.

The young male is more likely to finally settle down near that a particular piece of woods is already claimed, adult male grouse will drum—not to attract a female but to express their dominance.

After the young birds have spread over the countryside, the young males may likewise drum on their newly claimed log to broadcast their territorial message.

As I have not heard a grouse drumming from this pasture-turned-woods for the past few years, I'm suspecting that this drummer is a young bird staking a claim.

I enjoy following my dog, gun in hand, through tangles, briars, and popples in search of an autumn grouse. However, more often than not, I end up doing a lot of following. There is no disguising the fact that I am less than a fair grouse shot. I'll lay my money on bringing home a passing bluebill or rising woodcock before I'd wager on bagging a flushed grouse.

They say practice makes perfect. If I want to improve my grouse shooting skills, I need to spend more time tramping the thickets. But such efforts aren't easy when in recent years grouse have been nearly as scarce as two dollar bills.

When I heard the grouse drumming near the house I had no desire to fetch up the dog and shotgun; this is one grouse I want to protect. I want to listen to him and tell my daughters about him. He is seed for a future crop.

Slowly, I crawled toward the spot where I last heard the drumming. I had been close enough so that I could not only hear the bird's defiance but feel the reverberating from within. Finally, through the grillwork of hazel stems, I could see the moss-covered log that had once been our cannon. I studied the top of the log for a grouse form—nothing.

I moved forward another foot or so, and then when I looked up there was the bird, head stretched high and nervously flicking its tail. In the next instant it hopped off the log, opposite the side I was approaching.

I moved a little faster now, like my dog does when she closes in on a hot grouse track. Finally, I reached the log, where I cautiously peered over the top. I was half expecting a heart wrenching blast of leaves and thundering wings, but all was quiet. More silently than I had stalked, the grouse had vanished.

On the log were the telltale piles of grouse droppings, proving that this bird spent a good deal of time here. I got to my feet, still expecting a noisy flush, but the only sounds were dry oak leaves tumbling on November's breezes.

That evening, after I had fed the dog, I closed the garage door. Immediately, as if answering the challenge set forth by the bang of the door, the grouse thumped his challenge in the dark from back on the old log. I couldn't help but smile. It's good to see the old "cannon" still appeals to a youngster.

# Swan Days

Eleven months ago, a new year was born. It started as crisp and clean as a wind-dried bed sheet. The whitened landscape was one of sameness. With the passing of moons, the snow blanket disappeared, and born from under winter's cover were tender blades of green and petals of color. Spring's products grew rich and lush during the long warm days of summer. Then, in a final, colorful celebration of accomplishment, autumn made its all too brief appearance.

Now, with the waning of the year, tones are more somber in shades of ash. November's tree lines and often its skies seem well worn and, as is to be expected, a bit soiled.

This second to the last month is also a quiet month. Chickadees and nuthatches are silently busy as they hurry about foraging for calories to purchase another day. In our latitude, November is not a month to learn bird songs. Most trees are quiet, but some oaks, reluctant to drop their parchment leaves, rattle and rustle as cold winds sift through their branches.

But there is one tune November carries that speaks of finality, of autumn's passing. On first hearing it, you pause in midsentence to better hear the call. And only when the haunting music becomes more clear and distinct do you utter "Swans."

All etiquette is forgotten when swans are overhead, and no one seems to mind if a conversation or deed is disrupted.

I recall a late autumn farm auction a few miles from our place, when the day was chilly and colored strictly November. The auctioneer was moving right along from box to item at a good pace. In one hand, he held his cane and in the other was a hot cup of coffee to lubricate his chatter and fuel his innards. He had to be especially observant because most bids were made by the nod of a head rather than a raised hand. On that day, most hands were buried deeply in pockets.

Then, while the auctioneer was coaxing bids in his rapid-fire voice, I heard them—a flock of swans. They came closer, and finally they were right over us. For a few minutes, the chill was forgotten, the bidding halted, kids were lifted up for a better view, and all eyes followed the path of the swans.

Everyone watched the swans with a sense of wonder and childlike awe. For those few moments, I suspect no one thought of anything but the grace of the swans' flight and where the birds were going. After they passed, the spell was broken, and all eyes were once again on the cane-waving man perched on the hay wagon loaded with household treasures.

The swans I speak of, according to updated decrees of the American Ornithological Union, are tundra swans. Formerly, they were labeled as whistling swans, and only in recent years has their name been changed. I'm afraid these great white birds have been whistlers too many years for me to now call them tundra swans. Besides, I'm stubborn and resistant to change, especially when referring to a beast that so gracefully concludes the spectacular fall passage of waterfowl.

It seems you never see the swans before you hear them coming. Day or night, their mellow chorus of high-pitched yodels and hoots will lure folks outdoors to look skyward in search of a drawn out echelon or unsure V of whistlers.

Swans are the largest of the waterfowl. On the North American continent, only the trumpeter swan is larger than the whistling swan.

On that chilly auction day, most folks mistakenly thought the passing birds were geese, but these birds are far larger, have longer necks, and, as adults, are all white. Juvenile swans are November gray in their first year.

Even the snow goose, whose very name implies the essence of whiteness, has wing tips that seem as if they have been dipped in tar. And the calls of snow geese are far different, as they are higher pitched chuckles and barks, not unlike the noises of a sky-bound pack of terriers.

About mid-November every year, I keep my ears tuned to the skies and listen for the swans. They are fairly predictable in their journey, which carries them more east than south. These are hardy birds, and they refuse to be uprooted until their feeding lakes and marshes stiffen with the coming of winter.

As I see it, winter begins not with the first snowfall or with the first frozen lake. Nor does it start when we check off the day on our calendar with the title under the date that reads "First Day of Winter." For me, fall ends and winter is born with the passing of the swans.

On this continent it has been estimated that there are slightly better than 100,000 whistlers. Roughly half of these birds will winter on the West Coast, while the other half, including those that pass over the Midwest, will wait out spring on the East Coast.

Their fall flight began from the sparse forests of the subarctic or the treeless plains of the arctic prairies. As the swans leave in their family groups, they assemble with other family flocks and journey southward. In Saskatchewan lakes and North Dakota marshes, these birds may pause, rest, and feed for several days or even weeks. Then it usually takes the first winter storm to move them along. After the storm, clear skies follow, and, if there are healthy northwest winds fed by cold arctic air, the swans will climb high, usually three thousand to five thousand feet to catch a ride on the wind that carries them perhaps over my house.

The birds I watched last week would travel on a course taking them over the St. Croix Valley and into Wisconsin airspace. Perhaps some would settle down on Lake Winnebago to feed and rest. Others would fly over Michigan and land in the Lake Erie marshes of Ohio. From this traditional resting spot, the birds will push on to the saline waters of Chesapeake Bay and other East Coast estuaries—some two thousand miles from their nesting grounds.

There are days in November that belong only to the swans. On those days—some call them swan days—flocks of these northern birds will pass overhead throughout the day and night.

Last week, a former professor of mine was perched in a deer stand in Pine County. During the course of one day, he counted fifteen flocks of swans moving steadily to the southeast.

Usually, this surge of swan flight will take place in a matter of one to three days. The very briefness of their appearance makes it all the more special.

With the twelfth month before us, there is expectation and joy in the air, and we forget the aging year. But for now, we will live with the grays and be thankful that we are not fattened turkeys. And, with luck, we will hear the musical yodels that comes fom high overhead. Trace the sound to the source, and you will find a twinkling of white wings that seem to shine even whiter than the clouds they pass under.

I don't believe one could expect a more fitting fanfare for the year.

# The Test of a Deer Stand

Under the illumination of the yard light, I checked the thermometer on the woodshed. It read a couple of degrees below zero. Fifteen minutes later, I was eight feet off the ground in a wind-split red oak, settling down to wait for a deer. All was quiet except for one great horned owl just to the north of me and another to the south. Their duet finished as dawn's ashen colors paled toward the break of a new day.

I sat feeling comfortable, warmed by the brisk hike I had taken across a couple of bean fields and a piece of woods before climbing into the tree. However, the glow of warmth was short-lived, and a slight shiver rippled across my shoulders. I knew it would take tremendous patience and fortitude to remain motionless in my perch on this morning, so I tried to combat the chill by concentrating on warm thoughts.

My mind traveled back a mere thirty minutes to when I sleepily crawled out from under a warm down comforter and slowly dressed while standing on the floor grate, which spewed out a rising flow of hot air. My warm thoughts were shattered when I heard the ominous noises of new lake ice, nearly a quarter-mile away, booming and groaning. The ice-sounds clearly remind me that the hot floor grate was a quarter-mile in the opposite direction.

Daylight was slow in coming, and the spasms of shudders became more frequent. I am convinced that there is nothing colder than waiting in a November or December deer stand for the passing of a buck.

Some might argue that ice fishing is a colder endeavor, and sometimes it is, but at least when I ice fish, I don't have to keep still. The law says I can fish from two holes, and if I put them a little ways from each other, I can trot from hole to hole. I can walk circles, do jumping jacks, or bore more holes with my ice auger.

Put simply, when the muscles work, the by-product is the creation

218

of heat. But on a deer stand, much of my success as a deer hunter will stem from my ability to sit motionless.

I could see the makings of a glow in the east, and I wished that the glowing orb of swirling gases that we call our sun, some ninety-three million miles away, would hurry and send some of its heat my way. It has been estimated that the sun's surface is a toasty six thousand degrees Celsius. I only wished for a fraction of that to wash over my frigid form.

Before the sun was even up, my hands, hidden in my chopper mitts, were balled in fists to slow the heat loss from my fingers. Likewise, my toes were numbing, so I concentrated on wriggling them—first the left foot, then the right one, and so on. I played host to dreams of performing a hard driving tap dance shoed in Sorel boots—something that Fred Astaire or Gene Kelly have never done.

I tried convincing myself that it really wasn't that cold by entertaining thoughts of boyhood days scampering as fast as I could across a blacktopped street that had absorbed July's sizzling heat. The summery dream was disturbed by the sharp, riflelike report of a popping tree. All around me, the dawn's stillness was occasionally shattered by trees as their sapwood froze, expanded, and cracked.

I've never considered a deer stand to be known for its comfort—it's the view that counts. I want to see what is going on and yet remain relatively hidden up in the limbs off the ground. Usually, I find a climbable tree and make my way carefully up into the branches. Climbing or shinnying up a tree is not easy when one resembles a fat, orange sausage.

My deer stands are usually just a perch in the limbs of a tree. On a rare occasion I may nail up a step or two or a single board to stand on. The simpler the better. In fact, if I get too comfortable, I run the risk of dozing off and dreaming of deer instead of hunting them. But on the other hand, if I can get comfortable I can stay in my deer stand longer and better maintain my vigil over this corner of the woods. If I am a little uncomfortable, sleep is less likely, and I can remain more alert, though my stay among the branches might not be so long.

A neighbor has a crudely assembled platform complete with an old sofa to luxuriate in. I'm afraid I couldn't stay awake for very long in such a stand.

Tales used to float around about the local cobbler who, with others in his gang, hunted the northwoods near Superior's shores for a span of twenty years. He believed in being comfortable if he was going to subject himself to November's unpredictable weather. His deer stand had four walls, complete with a sliding glass window and a roof. Warmed by a gas heater, listening to a portable radio, he could just as well have been back in his shoe shop. You might think he could spend a day or two in such a stand, but he was by nature a restless man. Others in his party claimed that on opening morning, they could hear the cobbler hammering on his stand back in the woods as he revamped or added on to his cabin in the trees.

I also heard that he never shot a deer—but he was comfortable, while others in his party shivered and got him his venison.

There is a local farmer who hunted his woods in comfort. He liked to stay closer to the ground, so he would annually pull his ice fishing house out in the woods, fire up the stove and sit peering through the window.

Even with the awakening of the sun, I was still cold. It was apparent that I could not retain my heat, so I tried producing some. From under my seven layers of clothes that covered my upper body and the three that protected my lower trunk, I tensed my muscles as if I were pushing a car out of a snow-filled ditch. Then I relaxed briefly before repeating the isometrics.

Every year it seems that I must be painfully reminded of the suffering involved if I'm to take to a November deer stand. It's the price you have to pay. When I got to work the next day and was reliving the cold morning of the day before with a co-worker, she replied, "It must be like having a baby, you forget from one baby to the next just how awful the experience can be."

Finally, I had all I could take. Any more suffering would be masochistic. It seemed an effort to make my legs work as I climbed down. Since I had not seen a single deer, the cold ordeal had seemingly been worse than it was.

I figure if I'm not going to see any deer I might just as well go talk to the cobbler and see if he would share his deer stand blueprints with me.

# Hard to Leave a Good Thing

Along the lake's edge, the long slender spikes of bulrush wore transparent skirts of ice. These encircling platters of ice formed when the small lake was more restless and cresting waves reached high on the stems. In the cold air, some of the water froze on the stem before it could run back down the stem into the lake. With the passing of each wave, the skirt was made more full.

For several days the small lake had shrunk, as a wreath of ice slowly tightened its white noose on the steel gray waters.

Every day, as I passed this lake, my eyes quickly scanned the open water for signs of any stubborn mallards, bluebills, or goldeneyes that lingered on. These birds are slow in leaving autumn behind them, and they seem content riding the cold waves.

There were no ducks. However, I was surprised and a bit concerned when I passed and spotted a lone great blue heron wading in the water. As it slowly lifted its foot and slowly put it back down, its gaze was locked downward into the water.

Herons do not usually find November's waters to their liking and are usually well underway for more comfortable marshes in the southern states. My concern for the dallying heron was that it may have been hurt or sick and unable to get along with its journey.

Late in the afternoon of the same day, I passed the lake again and the heron was nowhere in sight. The following morning, the lake was half covered with a skim of ice. There were no birds to be seen. The winds that day were gusty, penetrating winds that carried a chill but kept the lake water lively and open.

That same afternoon, however, there was a heron again—this time wading among the ice-skirted rushes in the shallows. Perhaps it was the same bird I had seen the day before. Or could there be two herons of the same tardy nature staying on this late?

Herons, unlike swallows, warblers, geese, and blackbirds, do not migrate in large flocks. Occasionally, a small flock might move together, but most of the time these birds are loners. Only in their nesting colonies do we find good numbers of herons gathered together.

In the early spring, it is not uncommon to see these long-legged

221

waders return to their summer haunts when lakes and ponds are still frozen. To survive, they must find food, and to find food they need open water. Fortunately, it is the creeks and streams that burst from winter's bondage first, and it is these waters that early herons hunt. But I don't recall seeing these birds within a week of Thanksgiving.

I still wasn't sure why the heron I had seen was so late in making its move toward southern skies. If it wasn't hurt or sick, why should it remain to share the waters with an increasingly growing ice sheet?

On the third day of sighting the heron, it provided the answer I was looking for. Just as I slowly passed the late wader, it thrust its daggerlike beak into the water and pulled up a frog. The frog didn't struggle, as it was well into its state of winter sluggishness. Within seconds after the frog disappeared into the heron's gullet, a second frog was successfully targeted. Apparently, the intrepid heron had stumbled on a larder of overwintering frogs. I couldn't tell what kind of frogs the bird was catching, as they were visible only for a moment. But I knew leopard frogs frequented these shores in the warmer months, so I assume they were leopard frogs.

Leopard frogs, like most other amphibians and reptiles, are unable to tolerate the freezing months of winter without hibernating. Unlike our constant body temperatures, the amphibians have body temperatures that are more like roller coasters. Depending on the temperature that surrounds them, these animals have warmer body temperatures when it is warm and colder when the mercury drops.

As the days cool in the year's last few months, the frog's metabolic processes slow down and its body temperature falls. A summer frog leaps and swims like frogs are supposed to. But when temperatures fall, the actions of the frog become more slowed. Then youngsters and herons alike will snatch up more frogs with greater consistency.

To survive, frogs must avoid winter by retreating to an area that will insulate them from frigid air temperatures. In the fall of the year, leopard frogs often congregate in favorite, sometime traditional, wintering sites. They settle to the bottom of a pond or lake and spend the winter there. Instead of burying themselves in the mud, they often lie exposed on the mud and waterlogged leaves. With their internal furnace running at a mere idle, there is little demand for oxygen. Though these animals are without gills as adults, they are able to absorb small amounts of dissolved oxygen through their skins.

The water that surrounds the wintering frogs may be cold, but it is a lifesaving layer of insulation that is slightly warmer than freezing. Even the snow and ice will help to some degree in insulating the frog and ensuring us of May tadpoles.

Sometimes, hundreds of frogs will lie torpid on the lake bottom, all in a concentrated area. Some predators, like northern pike and walleyes, cruise the shallows in late fall and gorge upon these "hookless" frogs.

Perhaps the heron I watched had learned that it was worthwhile to stick around until late in the season for a feast of frogs. It may be reluctant to leave "the good times" even if the weather is nasty.

On a rare occasion, I have experienced fishing like that. At such times, I may be heard saying something like, "Oh, let's just catch one more before we go." The only difference is that I do it for my pleasure and greed, and the heron does it for need.

Herons, like frogs, avoid winter. But rather than burying themselves under water or dirt, they leave the season of ice and snow behind them and fly to more tolerable climates, which is where I hope the frog-eating heron is heading now.

Within a couple of days after I had last watched the heron feed, the lake was quiet. There were no more waves, no more ice skirts, and no more herons. Down at one end of the desolate lake, a homemade hockey goal awaits a returning school bus.

# DECEMBER

# The First Snow

I rose from bed the other morning, and in the predawn darkness, I was drawn to the bedroom window. Though the world seemed more gray than white, a transformation had taken place overnight. It had snowed.

I don't believe any of us can ignore that first-snow-of-the-year pull to the window. One such morning stands out when I was a kid and had awakened to find the world cloaked in white. Snowflakes, looking more like fluffy down feathers, were floating in slow motion to the ground.

My brother and I shared an upstairs bedroom, and I was drawn to press my face against the cold pane of the window by his bed. On especially cold days, there was no view other than images of frosted ferns, spruce forests, or castles. The frosted windows gave us a view of a magical world that was as deep as our imaginations. To look beyond the frosted artwork, we had to put our mouths close to the glass and blow a stream of warmed air. Even then, the small portholes didn't offer much of a view.

But on this particular day, the temperature outside was not bitter enough to mask the window in frosty images. From my elevated vantage point, I had a good view over the yard and beyond, out to the field. On that particular morning, there was an added gift besides the snow.

Moving fluidly along the edge of the field, not twenty yards from the yard, was the reddest fox I had ever seen. Its nose was to the ground, and its white-tipped bush of a tail was carried straight out as an extension of its back. After a few moments, it was gone. It had disappeared among the swirling snowflakes. That image will never leave me, and to this day, many foxes later, I have yet to see a fox so fiery orange-red.

There is an excitement in the first covering snowfall of the year. Even if it falls in mid-October, when autumn's colorful curtain has yet to drop and there are storm windows yet to hang, there is an overwhelming newness to everything. Unlike the other seasons of the year, the transition of fall to winter is most dramatic. There is no easing into winter, it usually comes quickly.

The first snowfall gives rise to an eagerness among many folks— an eagerness that is similar to that felt on Christmas morn, when there are filled socks or gifts waiting to be plundered. The snow also is a gift, for it wipes the gray-brown canvas of November and leaves a clean landscape entitled winter.

The snow is a blanket that covers and insulates my mulched strawberries. Without the snow, the strawberries might not be able to withstand the freeze of winter, and I would miss the sweetness of a June strawberry shortcake.

As the days lengthen under the March sun, the snow will melt and refill the sloughs and potholes that will give rise to a spring chorus of peepers and chorus frogs. Slowly, the snowmelt will percolate through the millions of sand grains under my house to recharge the supply of groundwater and assure me of the drink of water I take so for granted.

I'm convinced that we are not alone in our fascination with the first snowfall. Left behind on the covering of snow are the telltale tracks of animals that share the woods and fields with us. Perhaps it is the falling barometric pressure or the urgency of searching out food while it can still be easily found that prompts the activity in foot travel.

Whatever the reason, it seems that the zigzagging deer tracks, the hops and pauses of the squirrel, and the dainty lacework of deer mice tracks are especially numerous. Did the falling snow work its magic on them, or do these creatures always move about so much and we don't realize it until their movements are betrayed by a fresh snow?

I know of a corner in a field that has not felt the bite of the plow for several years and has now grown to grasses and milkweed. The swirling cowlicks of dried grasses are now covered with snow, but underneath this matted canopy, at my feet, are mazes of runways created by meadow voles. No rodent in these parts is more prolific than the meadow vole. A female can breed at the tender age of twenty-one days. Later, she might give birth to five or six young. Not long after the litter is born, the new mother breeds again. It is no great feat to have several litters every year.

After the recent snowfall, I followed the tracks of a fox. Not surprisingly, it is also familiar with the grassy corner of the field. The fox tracks moved directly across the corner, without so much as a pause at one of the many vole burrow openings in the snow. Perhaps the fox's belly was full. I suspect that when winter loses its freshness, the fox will come to better appreciate the "vole corner" and the rodent's ability to procreate.

With the advent of winter finally here, there is a slight sense of sadness, for I know that unless this snow should happen to melt and bring a temporary return of the grays and browns, I must wait another year to feel the pull of winter's first snow.

# The White Mousetrap

More than once this past fall, I have cornered a white-footed mouse in our pantry cupboards. During every encounter, the mouse deftly avoided my misdirected, flailing blows by dashing behind the soup cans, the baking soda, and other pantry necessities. My array of weapons included a phone book, a soup ladle, and a newspaper. Once, I tumbled the invading rodent, but in an instant it was back on all fours and moving rapidly through the canned goods.

The war became more heated when we found that the bewhiskered intruders were sculpting the front edges of the pine shelves with their tiny but effective front chisel teeth. Then one day we found the corner of our *Joy of Cooking* raggedly removed. It was then that my upset wife started to talk entirely too seriously about getting a cat.

I have no qualms about confessing my lack of interest in cats. For one thing, I much prefer an animal that will run up the driveway to meet me with its tail excitedly sweeping the air behind it as it dashes alongside the car. Upon stopping, I am always assured of a wet muzzle shoved into my hand. A dog has an easier time making me smile, while a cat just makes me sneeze.

Even though I had a banner fall in trapping mice, a few always avoided the snap traps. Reluctantly, I resorted to a poison that resembled a large granola bar. Since I have one crawling daughter and one who is a daredevil climber, I had to take great care in hiding the poison baits. The finishing touch was a swatch of steel wool stuffed into a mouse-sized hole that I found neatly hidden in the top corner of the pantry cupboards.

Outside, around the garage, the woodshed, and the house were telltale dainty tracks of other mice that I'm sure were looking for a way in. It seems as if our place has been a real mouse magnet.

Last Saturday I hurried out to the woodshed for an armload of wood to feed the kitchen stove. As I was piling the oak pieces in the canvas firewood carrier, I heard a shrill, barklike cry to my left. I looked down, and staring up at me from within the jumble of firewood was the long, slender, almost serpentine torso, neck, and head of a weasel. It watched me with dark eyes set against a background of snow white fur. We both froze and appraised each other. Suddenly, in the span of a blink, it was gone. In another instant, it popped up again, but this time from another opening in the maze of poorly piled firewood.

My guess is that it was a short-tailed weasel rather than the slightly larger long-tailed weasel, since the short-tailed variety is far more common in our locale. Because male members of the weasel tribe are larger than the female, one can easily confuse a female long-tailed with a male short-tailed, but if you get a good look at the head, the male's is slightly broader. The female's head seems merely an extension of the neck.

Quietly, I put down my armload of wood, ran back to the house, rudely uprooted my pajama-clad cartoon buff, wrapped her in a knit afghan, and carried her outside to the woodshed.

To pacify her for her momentary lack of Smurfs, I excitedly told her that we were going to see a white mousetrap. After standing still for a moment, I pursed my lips and made a series of high-pitched squeaks. Like a jack-in-the-box, the weasel erupted from the pile again. Sitting upright, like a white tent peg, it attentively peered out, searching for the squeak maker.

For a couple of minutes, Britta and I watched the curious little fellow until it became bored with our company and disappeared. On the way back into the house, I told Britta that this little weasel was the best "mouser" in the neighborhood. I explained to her that its snakey body can easily search and hunt for mice in the jumble of firewood and that this little hunter can even enter the burrow of some small rodents. We talked about the weasel's summer outfit of brown and how it sheds its brown hairs in the fall to take on the thicker, white coat of winter. For most of the year, this small carnivore is well camouflaged.

Many folks refer to the winter weasel as an ermine. It was the ermine that was often used to trim the royal robes of kings and queens. Some fifty thousand ermine pelts were said to have been used in making the royal robe of George VI when he was crowned king of England.

Those weasels that live south of the Upper Midwest do not take on the winter color of snow. Instead, their fall coat remains brown. The color change is not triggered by a snowfall but by the lessening of daylight hours in the fall. In a sense, weasels and many other animals have a biological clock that times their activities and bodily changes. In other words, if we had no snow on the ground for much of the winter, the woodshed weasel and others of its kind would nonetheless still be white and hardly considered camouflaged.

When their prey is abundant, weasels will sometimes horde dead mice, shrews, or voles down in their winter dens. To use the autumn tactic of the raccoon and put on great stores of fat would be poor strategy for the weasel. By carrying very little fat, it maintains its sleek, quick form. On the other hand, it needs to eat more than many other predators because of its hyper ways. If the weasel's food cache dwindles or if its hunting grounds become scarce of prey, it will move on no matter how nice a tumble of roofed-over firewood is left for it to explore. In fact, I have just declared the "weasel-pile" of wood off-limits for the rest of the winter. I'm wagering that we have enought wood to let this mouse harvester remain undisturbed.

Not surprising is the fact that mice have been scarce recently. Even the top of my workbench in the garage, which is usually littered with mouse leavings, has been pretty clean. With luck, the weasel will stay on for the next few months. In fact, I wouldn't mind if the energetic little fellow discovered, in its constant ramblings, the chipmunk's wintering burrow underneath the woodshed. The chipmunk's holes are far too plentiful in the yard, and they have now invaded the house-bordering fern bed. I know the dog would be grateful, because a fair portion of her dried dog food was slyly toted by these striped little rodents from the kennel to their underground cache.

There is also a neighborhood cottontail hanging around that I suspect is dreaming of rows of summer vegetables. I wouldn't feel bad if the weasel had a go at rabbit hunting. Even though cottontails may be two or three times their size, the weasel is a fierce little warrior. On occasion, weasels will kill rabbits or confront something much larger than themselves, such as a disturber of wood piles.

For the time being, the pantry cupboards are barren of mice, and only the scarred shelves and a wounded cookbook remind us of the autumn assault. Just the other day, I pulled down the defaced book and looked up the recipe for Brunswick stew. The recipe has been a favorite of mine in fixing up a mess of squirrels.

After a hearty meal of stew there was plenty of leftovers, which now sit waiting in the fridge. Maybe I should leave a sample of the rodent stew out in the woodshed as a token of thanks. It may act as an enticement to encourage the little white mousetrap to stick around and keep us mouseless and catless.

# Caught in the Act

The wind was picking up and seemed to come spilling directly off the arctic ice pack. According to the weatherman, the coming weekend was going to be the coldest so far this winter, with the mercury dropping well below zero and the winds even making it dangerous to be out. So while I was thinking of it, I went out to fill the bird feeders. The seed fuel would be sorely needed by our frequent feathered visitors.

I went out to the garage, lifted off the cover of the garbage can that holds my stores of sunflower seed, and was surprised to find a furred visitor. From deep within the can, on a bed of sunflower seeds, was a white-footed mouse. It was apparent that the mouse's appetite for seeds was far larger than its bulging, black eyes. At the moment of discovery, the gray mouse froze. But in the next instant, it hopelessly tried to leap and scurry up the vertical sides of the can.

Apparently, I had not pushed the garbage can lid on tight enough. The mouse in its search for calories had been tempted to explore the dark, inner depths of the can and ventured over the edge. Now I had to do something with the gluttonous rodent. Should I free it? Or do I kill this uninvited guest to my garage?

All fall, I had waged a crusade against the mice that had mysteriously found their way into our house. These overly productive creatures sometimes number twelve animals to the acre in the fall of the year. A certain number of this rodent crop are destined to provide the inner heat for the resident great horned owl or the short-tailed weasel. But far too many live to play hide-and-seek in our closets and cupboards. I admit, I feel little compassion for these pantry pests.

Snap traps baited with peanut butter were strategically placed. Just to be sure, I still keep a couple of set traps in the pantry and one next to the back corner of the stove. The efficient traps were not invented by a mystery person named Victor, as my traps are labeled. Instead, they were designed in the late 1800s by Pennsylvanian John Mast, who called the instruments of death "snap-shot" mouse traps. The brandname Victor is one letter short of "victory" and easier to print in its bold letters across the width of the trap.

Snap traps are different than contemplating what to do with a captive mouse. When the trap kills the mouse, I feel removed, as if I really didn't have to perform the deed of death. Though I may have baited and set the traps, the mouse's life ends while I sleep. When I awaken, the trap is either untouched or contains a mouse that lies stilled. I tell myself that the mouse hasn't suffered, and then I reverently remove it before my Susan finds it and asks me to remove the carcass. With one more mouse removed, I am hopeful that this will be an end to what some folks politely call "mouse dirt." Whatever it is, it has been found in the silverware drawer, and that justifies a call to arms.

But now I stand over an imprisoned mouse that stares at me with oversized, unblinking black eyes. Gauging its two-legged nemesis, the head nods up and down, with its long, stiff whiskers sprouting out from an inquisitive, sniffing nose. The mouse doesn't run about in a panic. Instead, it waits for my next move.

Somehow I cannot find it within myself to play the role of executioner, even if the mouse has just enjoyed a favorite last meal. This mouse hasn't violated our drawer of forks, knives, and spoons, nor has it roamed the shelves of pots and pans. This mouse is innocent until proven guilty.

But there is no doublt that it has gorged itself during an orgy of feeding in a delightful sea of sunflower seeds—sunflower seeds that I bought for watching the antics of chickadees and bullish blue jays, not mice. Perhaps this was the little fellow that had tucked seeds into the feet of my chest waders. Or was this the mouse whose cache of seeds I discovered in my tool drawer in the garage?

How is it that I can pluck a mosquito out of the air as it whines by my ear, crush it between fingers, and feel no compassion whatsoever? I suspect part of the answer lies in the fact that the pesky insect is guilty of assault and battery, while the mouse is usually guilty of lesser crimes, such as thievery and littering. And it doesn't help matters when the mouse is soft furred and almost cuddly looking. Besides, I grew up wishing I was a Mouseketeer. Where would Disneyland be without a mouse? But the most difficult aspect to deal with are those hypnotic, shining eyes that stare right into one's heart.

No, I couldn't kill this nocturnal marauder. After scooping the mouse out of the seeds with a bucket, I carried the white-foot away from the building and dumped it into the snow. I guess you could say I was passing judgement on to Lord Winter.

I felt good about my decision. At least I was giving the mouse a chance, even if its home wasn't outdoors. After all, these small rodents have roamed the lands since the Oligocene epoch and have had thousands of years to adapt to the rigors of life on earth.

It was too cold to stay out and watch the mouse's next move, so I went inside and watched from the window. Though I couldn't see the mouse, its actions were betrayed by the erratic, molelike ridge it left in the soft snow as it burrowed underneath.

I knew then that this mouse was a survivor. It wasn't about to expose itself to the eyes of a predator or to the frigid cold if it wasn't necessary. Slowly, the tunnel zigzagged. Like a cautious snake, it moved towards the security of a stacked pile of split oak. Secretly, I hoped that the mouse would find a habitable niche to spend the winter, with an ample seed supply.

Come March, with the surge of spring, the freed white-footed mouse will be unconsciously intent on creating more of its kind. Then next fall, four litters later, I will probably curse my sympathy for the mouse as I contend again with silverware prowlers.

# Yule Trees and Memories

"Out in the forest stood a pretty little Fir tree."

So begins Hans Christian Andersen's classic story, *The Fir Tree*. The tale tells of a small tree that yearned for greater things in life. Finally, the fir reaches the highlight of its life when it finds itself in a home on Christmas with colorful adornments and flickering candles gracing its boughs.

It was such a fir that we sought last weekend in a woods not far from our home. According to those in the know of Christmas tradition, there is only one tree that is fitting for the holidays, and that is the balsam fir. I agree. The fir speaks of the yule through both the beholder's eyes and nose. No other conifer, and certainly no synthetic tree, carries the aromatic fragrance that a fir has. The odorous resin is so nostalgic and powerful that I have considered squeezing some resin blisters from a live fir and bottling the fragrant oils. This "essence of Christmas" could be used for those Decembers when we resort to a lesser tree to stand in our living room.

At our latitude, the fir is a transplant, brought south from its more typical northern haunts. So, like hundreds of other folks, my wife, Susan, and I found ourselves walking along packed, sinuous trails that meandered through a commercial tree farm. Here, we could pick out the tree of our choice and perform the ritual of cutting it.

As a youngster, the tree cutting was not my chore, though I did help once or twice. The annual job belonged to my father and sister. In fact, it became such a tradition for the two of them that even after my sister got married, she would still make a pilgrimage back home every year to cut not one tree but two. This was always a two-person job, between father and daughter. Traditions seem strongest when cemented with the glue of Christmas.

Susan and I walked in among the scattered fir and spruce that grew interspersed in an oak woods. Unfortunately, the conifers were tall, lanky and poorly filled out, hardly befitting of the title of tannenbaum.

These trees has probably been planted in April or May's sunshine when there was no canopy of oak leaves overhead. But during the summer months, the shade of the oaks covered the young trees, making it difficult to fill out in typical Christmas tree lushness. It was also obvious that these trees had not been pruned in recent years to encourage the classic taper of a yuletide tree.

Reluctantly, we left the neglected woods and walked among the neat, far-reaching ranks of trimmed Scotch pine. Scotch pine is not one of my favorite trees, but considering the hour, and since I was deprived of a respectable fir, it would do.

In another five months, as soon as the thawed earth can be worked, I'm going to carefully dig up a couple dozen tiny fir trees from an overcrowded piece of northern forest near my in-laws in Grand Marais. The collection of small firs will make the trip south to our place and then be carefully tended, pruned, and groomed towards an eventual December berth in our household.

The saw was sharp, and in less than a minute I had felled nearly ten years of growth. Some cutters feel remorse in dropping the tree, yet many of those same folks will struggle and curse to uproot a bold dandelion from their yard. Yet I wonder if a child were presented two bouquets, one of butter yellow dandelions and one of miniscule, unflowerlike pine blossoms, which would draw more compliments and smiles?

236

The glory hours of a Christmas tree arrive when it stands all lit up and covered with ornaments in a place of honor where all can see, indoors and out.

Not only is the search for and cutting of a tree a traditional event, but more so is the hanging of ornaments on the tree's limbs. Some decorations and objects of jewellike beauty, and some are unbelievably gaudy. But on a Christmas tree there is no need for harmony. Here is where all adornments of mixed race and creed come together in a wonderfully mixed-up, colorful collage of memories and stories.

On our tree are the standard figures of reindeer, angels, bells, hearts, snowflakes, and at least a half dozen Santas. But some decorations bring remembering smiles to our faces as we carefully hang them.

Ten years ago, before I married, I helped my wife-to-be cut a tiny tabletop spruce tree for her equally tiny apartment. In that tree, we found a dainty bird nest of woven grasses, with a lining of soft, pale thistle down. The goldfinch that had built the nest would not use it again. Even had we not selected the little spruce, the nest is an annual chore that must be dealt with every summer. We were careful not to jostle the tree too much as we cut it down, because the nest was a decoration already in place. Every year, that same nest is given special care as we gently place it on a bough.

There are small, red knit hearts, straw ornaments, and small, wood-splint baskets that Susan has crafted. Like the nest, these too seem more special than the store-bought ornaments. Many of the ornaments were gifts, and I rely on Susan to refresh my memory as to who gave them to us.

To honor our Scandinavian heritage, we have strings of tiny flags draped over the tree. Susan is of untainted Norwegian stock, while my blood runs thicker of Swede. Perhaps that is why she has two strands of Norsk banners and only one of the far more colorful Svensk pennant.

The closest thing we have to a "partridge in a pear tree" is a scruffy bobwhite quail that holds its head skyward with beak open, captured in a moment of song. If we tuck it into the branches just right, you can't even see that the bird is without a tail. The quail was once a fine specimen perched on an old piece of weathered fence post. It remains my only attempt at taxidermy, and I might add that in its day, it was a right decent effort. But several years ago, when my dog was a feisty pup, she discovered the mounted quail in our living room while I was busying myself in the basement. Since that little accident, the fence post has become fuel, with its ashes spread over the garden, the bird has become an ornament, and the dog has become a dyed-in-the-wool bird dog.

A Christmas tree's usefulness doesn't have to end after the holidays. Sometime after the new year, we will carefully wrap and place all the decorations in a box marked "Christmas," which we will put above the back porch until we take them out and discover them once again next year. With the ornaments removed, I will carefully get the tree out of the house without leaving too many dried needles behind. Rather than burn the tree or cart it off to a landfill, I will enjoy it from my breakfast table as it sits upright in the snow next to my bird feeder. Lively chickadees, hungry grosbeaks, and the now-drab goldfinches will find its branches most welcome as a waiting perch before flitting in for their seed.

Eventually the tree stand of snow will settle with the advance of spring, and finally the pine will topple on a bed of cast-off sunflower seed hulls. Then I will take the dry, brittle Scotch pine to the woods adjacent to our yard, drag it into the brush, and leave it.

Even in death, the tree will give of itself. Perhaps the brown thrasher that sings over my garden every spring will attract a mate who will find a nook under the discarded tree for building its ground nest. Or maybe the cottontail that now resides in the woodshed and teases the dog will make its nest of soft belly fur under the cast-off yule tree. Eventually, like all objects built of organic compounds, the tree will crumble, giving its last to nourish the earth.

Perhaps someday I will have the joy of finding a pretty little fir tree standing out in the forest. Or I suppose it could be a Scotch pine or some other lesser tree.

# The Christmas Catch

Fishing a new lake is kind of like opening a Christmas present. Under the winter wrapping of ice is a secret gift, and since we cannot see it, we have to rely on our optimism and tales told by others who live by the hook and line.

Lask weekend I tried a new lake that instilled more optimism than usual because it can be found in the "Index of Minnesota Lakes" as Christmas Lake. I had gotten a reliable tip from a very trustworthy friend, and he had ferreted out the information from his neighbor's cousin's brother-in-law. I was a little suspicious with the source and the network that the tip had traveled, but I was intrigued with the lake's name.

The fish I intended to hunt were northern pike, or as the learned Swede Carolus Linnaeus classified them, the *Esox lucius*. Linnaeus took on the monumental task some two hundred years ago of assigning Latin names to some twelve thousand plants and animals.

He gave these organisms two Latin names—the genus, which placed it in a group of similar things, and the species, which described an obvious characteristic that made it unique from other members of the same genus.

For example, a northern and a muskie are similar, hence found in the same genus, *Esox,* which is Latin for pike. Yet these two fishes are distinct species. The muskie's species name is *masquinongy,* which translates to an Indian name for this fierce fish. The northern's species name is *lucius,* which is the Latin name for the pike.

By assigning a Latin, or scientific, name to an animal, a northern for example, the fish would universally be known as *Esox lucius*. On the other hand, confusion sets in when someone is talking about going fishing and catching a "snake," a "hammer handle" or an "ick fish" (because of the northern's slimy nature). In this case, we are not talking of slithering reptiles, carpenters, or carp, but a northern pike.

Linnaeus was eventually knighted by the Swedish royal family for his tireless attempt to inventory all living things—though most of us have enough trouble with the English names, let alone the Latin counterparts.

Laden down with my auger and ice fishing accoutrements, I

239

walked over the frozen lake towards a cove that looked like a reasonable place to find a hungry pike. When I bored through the five inches of ice and the water came surging up, there was a release of an odor that hung in the air. It was peculiar in that the aroma was both offensive yet somehow pleasant and strangely nostalgic—kind of like smelling a February or March skunk that signals spring's charge.

As I fished, the smell lingered, and I found myself putting it aside by daydreaming of past Christmas Eves at my grandma and grandpa's house.

It didn't take long before I had something softly hit my baited offering. I set the hook but missed. Several times in the next half hour, I hooked the fish again, but each time the struggle was brief because I could not hook the fish well enough. The mystery fish appeared to have a very soft mouth, as it was difficult to set the hook without pulling it free.

I changed lures and baits several times, but the results were the same. Not only was I becoming frustrated, but the unkown smell seemed to get less nostalgic and more annoying.

I took a break to eat a *sylte* sandwich (a Norwegian headcheese) and then got an idea. There has been, in the past few years, a real trend, or marketing coup, in promoting the use of various commercial scents applied to fishing lures and baits to attract and entice all the fish you could possibly desire. Since I had no such product in my tackle, I remembered a piece of *sylte* from the sandwich, rolled it into a hard ball, and impaled it on the single treble hook of my lure.

I was jigging, using a slender, silver jigging lure that wears the title of Swedish Pimple, yet it is manufactured somewhere in Michigan. The lure's name is definitely not a Linnaeus christening.

I have had reasonable luck with a Swedish Pimple in the past, but now I had created the perfect alliance between two antagonists—a Swedish-named lure and a Norwegian food. Such efforts should not go unnoticed when it comes time for Noble Peace Prize nominations.

I didn't have to wait long before my baited Pimple was grabbed. The fish appeared well hooked this time, but it was fighting very differently from any other fish that I have ever caught. There were no line-peeling runs or bulldogging surges, instead the fish was sluggish. I could just as well have been reeling in a sack of potatoes. If there was any action, it was almost a slow vibrating or quivering.

Finally, I could see that victory would be mine, and with a last pull, the catch flopped out on the ice. I stood, shocked and for a moment horrified, until I recognized the stilled form as a member of the genus *Lutes*. My apprehension changed to excitement when I looked closer and recognized the faceless species of *fiskus*.

There are infinite common names that describe *Lutes fiskus,* but most are unprintable and only belittle this trophy fish.

As I stood over the pulsating mass of fish, it became clear to me why the aroma of Christmas Lake had spawned daydreams of past Christmas Eves at my grandparent's farm.

The fish slid easily into my five-gallon bucket, and I sauntered off the lake with a skip in my step, carrying a fish that even Linnaeus could not adequately describe.

I'm hoping my best catch has been you, the reader, and that you took the story hook, line, and sinker.

To all of you, I wish peace, health and happiness. God Jul!